£14·99

Donald Macleod is the people's theologian – or at least he would be in a sane world. He combines a profound grasp of the language of Scripture and the history of Christian doctrine with a penetrating understanding of the dilemmas of life at the end of the second millennium. Through it all shines his adoration of Jesus Christ and his deep sympathy with people. He never loses sight for a moment that he is addressing people – people who are hurting or confused or ill-informed or tempted. This is theology straight from the heart of a great preacher of the gospel.

Alex J MacDonald
Buccleuch and Greyfriars Free Church of Scotland, Edinburgh

Donald Macleod is one of the finest theologians Scotland has produced in a long time. He has the gift of being able to explain complex theological doctrines in a way which can be understood by everyone who truly wants to know more about the Christian faith. Those who have read his previous books will find here the same mixture of solid Calvinistic theology, deep pastoral concern and evangelistic zeal. Professor Macleod also displays an originality of thought and sharp clarity of expression which will enable a new generation of readers to enter sympathetically into an understanding of the Reformed Faith.

Dr. A.T.B. McGowan,
Director, Highland Theological Institute

What A A Hodge's *Popular Lectures on Evangelical Theology* did in the 1880s, bringing theology out of the seminary and into the daily lives of intelligent lay people, this book does today. It reflects the environment, not of the classroom or the minister's conference, but of a city-centre church and a diverse public audience. Macleod writes with lucid and sparkling clarity, without sacrifice of detail and definition. Here is excellent theology made both relevant and exciting. Doctrine is forcefully related to ethics, popular assumption carefully weighed by Scripture, and Christ brought very near. I can think of no better book for equipping Christians to present their faith intelligently and attractively to real people.

Dr John Nicholls
Candidates' Secretary, London City Mission

Donald Macleod's *A Faith to Live By* is an accessible but profound introduction to some of the fundamental truths of the Christian faith. It will prove to be useful to intelligent Christians who are just beginning in their more serious study of Christian truth (because Professor Macleod is a master of making difficult things seem simple, without compromising their profundity or detracting from the proper mystery which should characterize our study of God), and to teachers, ministers, and academics (because behind Macleod's crystal-clear prose lies an imposing grasp of historical and systematic theology, evident exegetical prowess, and an almost unnerving ability to put his finger right on the most important issues on any particular subject).This survey of Bible teaching is vintage Macleod: biblical, thoughtful, clear, and practical. Indeed, it is an important study of biblical truth by an astute evangelical theologian in the great Reformed tradition.

Macleod's statement of our doctrine of Scripture is superb and reflects the special attention which he has devoted to this subject in his own labors as a minister and theologian. His treatment of creation, still a controversial issue in our time, offers important contributions to Christian discourse: especially in his observations on the tensions between Genesis and evolution. His observations on total depravity and hermeneutics are vital in the current evangelical context, and his five marks of the church are sure to spark debate! Macleod's chapter on the covenants reflects the mature observation of a theologian who has done more, perhaps, than any other in our generation to defend and advance the classic federal theology. More could be said: in his treatment of the atonement Macleod is at his best, and one leaves his treatment of hell wondering how even the most hardened cynic could be unmoved by such a forceful presentation.

Macleod is simultaneously an able apologist (I'm glad he's on our side!), a true systematic theologian (a rare breed today: our divinity halls are mostly populated by so-called 'biblical theologians', that is, merely thematic theologians with little time or capacity for synthesis); and a world-class exegete (one does not hesitate to mention his name alongside Warfield and Murray in exegetical competence). Read the book. Learn from Macleod. Argue with Macleod. And then bow the knee to your Savior, the Lord Jesus Christ, and worship!

J. Ligon Duncan, PhD
Minister, First Presbyterian Church
Adjunct Professor, Reformed Theological Seminary
Jackson, Mississippi, USA

A Faith to Live By

Studies in Christian Doctrine

Donald Macleod

Mentor

© Donald Macleod

ISBN 1 85792 428 2

Published in 1998
in the Mentor imprint
by Christian Focus Publications
Geanies House, Fearn, Ross-shire,
IV20 1TW, Great Britain

Cover design by Donna Macleod

Contents

PREFACE

This book had its origin in two series of lectures delivered on Friday evenings in St Vincent Street Free Church of Scotland, Glasgow, during the winters of 1988-89 and 1990-91. I am grateful to the Reverend Ronald Mackay (now of the Free North Church, Inverness) and the Kirk Session of St Vincent Street for organising the lectures and for their encouragement to publish.

Special thanks are due to those who had the unenviable task of transcribing the tapes: to Mr Evan MacDonald, who took the initiative; to Mrs Alison Macdonald, Mrs Flora MacKinnon (nee Pegg), Mrs Lorna Muller (nee MacIver), Mrs Joan Murray, Mrs Janice Robertson and the late Miss Margery Silvey, who together transcribed the first series; and to Mrs Mary Ferguson who transcribed the second series.

The final chapters are taken from a later series of lectures given in Smithton-Culloden Free Church, Inverness, in 1991-92. Thanks are again due to Mrs Mary Ferguson for transcribing the tapes (and for checking references throughout the book). I would also like to thank the Reverend David Meredith and the Kirk Session of Smithon-Culloden for inviting me to give the lectures and for making the necessary arrangements.

All three series were well attended and I would like to record my appreciation of all who braved the winter nights and whose regular presence was such a tremendous encouragement.

Further thanks are due to Miss Christine Maciver, Secretary of the Free Church College, Edinburgh, who came to my rescue in innumerable emergencies; to Dr. Andrew McGowan, who prepared the typescript for publication; and finally to Mr Malcolm Maclean, Managing Editor of Christian Focus, who kept on insisting that this project was worthwhile.

Alert readers will immediately notice one glaring omission: there is no chapter on Justification. I realise now that this was a mistake, but I hope that the chapters on *The Atonement* and *What is faith?* will go some way towards making good the deficiency.

My main hope is that these chapters will lead, in Anselm's words, to ordinary Christians coming to a better understanding of what they already believe. But I also hope that they will contribute in some small way towards rekindling throughout the churches a passion for the rigorous and reverent study of Christian truth.

Donald Macleod
Edinburgh, July 1998

1

The Inspiration of Scripture

We must begin this study in Christian doctrine by saying a word or two about the use of the mind in religion and by emphasising the importance of applying rigorous Christian thought to every area of our Christian lives. We aren't called simply to enjoy some particular experience. We are called upon to think through all the implications of our faith, girding up the loins of our minds (1 Peter 1:13) and presenting our bodies to God in what Paul calls 'reasonable', or even 'logical', service (Romans 12:1). This means that we have to apply Christian thought to evangelism, to worship, to church government and even, of course, to our own personal witness. But it surely implies above all that we apply Christian thought to the question of what it is we believe, and why it is we believe it.

There are three main reasons why it is important to apply our minds to Christian doctrine.

First, because of the demands of personal witness. We can testify to our faith only if we know first of all what we believe. Supposing we were challenged, can we tell what our view of God is, or our view of the world in which we live? Can we tell men what we mean when we say, 'You must be born again'? Can we answer the question, 'How do I become a Christian?' We can never bear effective personal witness unless we know what the gospel actually is.

Secondly, we need to know why we believe what we believe. Can we, as Peter urges us, give a reason for the hope that is in us (1 Peter 3:15)? It isn't enough to know what we believe. We must know the grounds for our beliefs. That is especially important today when our fellow-men are so sceptical and so cynical. They want to know the logic of our particular position. If we are to answer them we must know the Biblical reasons for believing in the deity of Christ, life after death and so on. We must also, of course, know how to answer common objections to those doctrines.

The third reason for studying Christian doctrine is its importance for our personal religion. For the sake of our own souls we must know the full content of the Word of God. I say that because it seems to me that many of our most pressing problems in areas of personal faith are due simply to ignorance. Problems of assurance, problems with depression and problems in coping with such traumas as bereavement often stem either from ignorance of Christian doctrine, or from a failure to apply it. The same is true of the church itself. Many of its problems are really problems in relationships, and these are often the result of a defective Christology. We simply fail to live our lives in the light of the fact that in Christ God shows Himself as the One whose nature it is to put the interests of others before His own.

The importance of knowing Christian doctrine being clear, we must now embark on the study of the first of the topics before us, the inspiration of scripture. There are two chapters on the Bible both because of its fundamental importance, and because there are two distinct emphases to make. There is, first, the emphasis on God's own activity in relation to His Word. But there is also a second side: the human side, or the input of the character and personality of the men through whom the Bible came.

First, the divine side, the inspiration of the Bible. I want to begin by looking briefly at the Bible's own claims, and in particular at three New Testament passages which speak of Holy Scripture in the most exalted terms.

2 Timothy 3:16

Verse 16 is particularly important, but I want to look at the whole context from verse 15 downwards. It reminds us of the function performed by the Bible. It is able, we are told, to make us wise unto salvation (2 Timothy 3:15); and it makes the man of God perfect (2 Timothy 3:17). Taken together, these statements mean that scripture gives us a saving knowledge of God and fully equips us for the life of discipleship.

But how is it able to do so? Because it is inspired by God. In the Greek there is simply one word, *theopneustos*, made up of the word *theos* for God and the word *pneuma* for breath. The literal meaning is that all scripture is breathed out by God, or God-breathed. There are three points worth noting with regard to this proposition.

First of all, the word *theopneustos* points not so much to *inspiration* as to *expiration*. The meaning is not that God breathed into the Bible. It is that God breathes out the Bible. It is the breath of God. The word *inspiration* is a Latin word, borrowed from the Vulgate, not from the Greek New Testament. It has its own value, but the idea here is certainly not one of God breathing into the Bible but of God breathing out the Bible. According to this, the subject of inspiration is not the human author, but the book itself: the *scripture* is breathed out by God. We are familiar today with the idea of inspired men: for example, poets, composers of music and great orators. These men are said to be inspired and to give inspired performances. But the Bible doesn't speak in this way. It speaks of the quality of *theopneustos*, of God-breathedness, as a quality of the actual book itself.

Secondly, the Bible has this quality invariably and inalienably. Inspiration is completely independent of our feelings with regard to the Book. The Bible won't allow the idea that somehow when you enjoy this book, or when this book moves you, or when this book comes at you, then it is inspired. The Bible's position is that even when this book is, so far as our experience goes, as dead as dead can be and as dry as dry can be (and that can sometimes happen) it is still *theopneustos*. It is still the breath of God. That does not depend on our human emotions at all, and it does not vary with our human emotions. The Bible does not *become* God's word when it encounters us 'existentially'. The Bible is always God's Word.

Thirdly, according to this statement *theopneustos* belongs to the whole of scripture: to the Bible in its entirety. *Every* scripture, we are told, is breathed out by God. *Pasa graphe*: every single scripture! Whatever is scripture has the quality of *theopneustos*. Now that does not mean that every part of God's Word is equally interesting, or that every part of God's Word is equally stimulating, or equally elevated, or equally moving. The Gospel of John, for example, is far more elevated than the book of Esther. But the Gospel of John is not more inspired than the book of Esther. The book of Esther, the Epistle to the Romans and the Gospel of John all share equally in this quality of divine expiration. God has breathed them all out. If you can say of something, 'It is written', then you mean, 'It is God-breathed'. The inspiration defined here – the expiration – belongs to every single entity that qualifies for the designation 'scripture': to Old Testament and New Testament, to doctrine and history, to theology and precept, to experience and ethics. Every chapter and every verse have the quality of *theopneustos*.

2 Peter 1:20-21

The second passage I want to look at is 2 Peter, chapter one, from verse 20 downwards. Here the Apostle is discussing prophecy. He begins with a negative point: prophecy is not a matter of 'private interpretation' (2 Peter 1:20). These men were not simply giving their own opinions: not even their own *expert* opinions. Nor did prophecy come 'by the will of man' (2 Peter 1:21). It wasn't a case of a man saying, 'I'm going to prophesy.' The initiative did not lie with man at all. You see that so often with regard to such figures as Moses and Jeremiah and Jonah. We can almost say of them that they were dragged kicking into this particular ministry. It wasn't their own choice. And when they spoke, the message they proclaimed wasn't from themselves at all.

But then there follows the great positive statement: men spoke as they were carried by the Holy Spirit. The emphasis in this sentence falls firmly on the word *men*: 'carried by the Holy Spirit spoke from God *men*.' We'll come back to this emphasis on the human side of scripture in the next chapter. But for the moment the concern is this: these men spoke from God, and they spoke as men carried by the Spirit of God.

Both points are important. They spoke from God. The prophet was the spokesman of God. He had had an audience with God. The very word *prophet* means to *speak forth*. These men were taken into God's audience chamber, they were told God's secrets and they came forth as God's spokesmen. There is an interesting illustration of that in the story of Moses and Aaron, when Moses protests, 'Lord, I'm not eloquent.' Among other things God says to him, 'In that case, Aaron can be your *prophet*' (Exodus 4:16). In other words, 'Aaron can be your spokesman. You just tell him what to say.' That was the prophet's function. He spoke from God and he spoke for God: 'I will put my words in his mouth' (Deuteronomy 18:18).

But then there's also this marvellous picture: they spoke as men *carried* by the Spirit. We could almost say they were *ferried* by the Spirit. Now when you're carried, you aren't led and you aren't prompted. There's a degree of passivity here: an emphasis on the controlling influence of the agent doing the carrying. In the production of scripture God superintended and supervised the whole process, so that as the human agents thought and spoke and wrote, and as they used their sources, He was in control, setting them down at His own chosen destination and ensuring that they spoke exactly what He intended them to speak.

John 10:35

We have, then, two pictures so far. We have *theopneustos*, the word of God *ex-pired*; and we have these great prophets literally carried by God himself.

We turn now to the Gospel of John and the tenth chapter, from verse 34 downwards. Here we find the Lord's own view of scripture. He has been challenged because He's been making astonishing claims on His own behalf, claiming in effect to be God (*theos*). Not surprisingly, the Jews accuse Him of blasphemy. Jesus, in reply, uses a very interesting argument. 'Look,' He says, 'it cannot always be wrong to apply the word *god* to a man, because in your own scriptures, in the book of Psalms, the word *god* is applied to your own rulers.' That's the Lord's argument: 'Is it not written in your law, "I said, Ye are gods?"' (Psalm 82:6). Now, He says, 'You can't accuse me of saying something that is always blasphemous when in your own scriptures your rulers are addressed as gods by God himself.' What I'm interested in for the moment is this: the Lord adds, 'Scripture cannot be broken' (John 10:35). This is a great statement about the Bible itself: scripture cannot be violated. The word which occurs here is the word used for breaking a commandment. The Bible, in the judgment of Jesus, has the authority of law: absolute and infallible authority. It can't be wrong. It can't be false. It can't mislead. It can't deceive. It can't be violated. That is the Lord's own testimony.

There is nothing I can say which is more important than this. Let me put it to you this way. We evangelicals are often accused of what's called 'bibliolatry', that is, the worship of a book. 'Ah, you worship the book, this dead book,' they say. 'You have a paper Pope. You are bibliolaters.' Well, I say, It's not bibliolatry. It's Christolatry! It's the worship of Christ. Christ has said this Book is infallible. He has attested it as the unbreakable Word of God, and it is because of His testimony, given through the apostles and given in His own words before us here, that I personally believe in the full, final, infallible authority of scripture. I cannot see how one can be loyal to Christ and yet defy him on something as fundamental as His view of the status of the Bible.

It isn't only here that the Lord makes this kind of claim. He reminds us in the Sermon on the Mount that He came to fulfil the law and then adds, 'One jot or one tittle shall in no wise pass from the law, till all be fulfilled' (Matthew 5:18). Similarly, He rebukes the multitude by saying, 'You do err, not knowing the scriptures' (Matthew 22:29). And He fights the devil with the same weapon, 'It is written' (Matthew 4:4). Equally significantly, there is no record of His ever finding fault with the Bible.

Now the point, surely, is this. We're told often that in the Old

Testament in particular there are deficiencies of theology and even deficiencies of morality. We're told that it contains sub-Christian teaching. Well, I can only say, If that's the case, Jesus Christ didn't see it. In fact, He said, 'Scripture cannot be broken.' For me, belief in the God-givenness of the Bible is simply an aspect of devotion to Christ. I believe in inspiration not because I can prove the Bible to be inerrant, but because the Lord and His apostles attest it as being inspired, as coming to us through men carried by God, and as having an infallible authority. It is on this self-attestation of God's Word that we rest our doctrine of scripture.

Alternative views of scripture
Our view of the Bible is not the only one on offer, as all of you know. I don't want to waste your time by going into other views in detail, but there are at least three which are widely current and deserve a brief notice.

First, there is what may be called the *liberal* view. The better term, I suppose, is *modernist*. This view minimises the divine element in scripture and sees the Bible as an essentially human document. It would say that at best the biblical authors were only experts in their own fields, and their authority only the authority of genius. In its extreme form (in the teaching of, for example, Rudolf Bultmann) the gospels are regarded as in their entirety works of the free creative imagination, with not even a historical core. All is mythology unless proved otherwise. Such an approach may seem very alien to us, but it is the assumption behind much of the RE taught in Scottish schools today. Our children are told from a very early age that the Bible is 'just a human book'.

Then there is the Barthian view, now going out of fashion, but still prevalent in some quarters. The essence of this view is that the Bible *becomes* the Word of God. This idea reflects the existential philosophy which lay behind Barth's theology. Sometimes you had a living, transformational encounter with scripture and in that moment it became the Word of God. This is why Barth's early theology was known as the theology of paradox. The Bible was deemed to be full of errors and contradictions, full of bad theology and even full of bad ethics and bad morality. The paradox was that God could take this very human thing, with all its errors, and work wonders. This meant that Barth had a vested interest in maximising the defects of the Bible; and that's why, although in Barth there are many evangelical notes, his whole view of scripture was so destructive. He accepted the most extreme critical views, because the more defective the Bible was, the more glorious the paradox. It's just as if we were to argue that the greater a sinner a preacher is, the more glorious it is that God should use him. To me, this is a fundamentally unbiblical approach to the Word of God and so, although I can follow Barth in some things, I can't follow him at all in his doctrine of scripture.

Thirdly, there is the neo-evangelical view, which is becoming increasingly popular and influential even in high academic circles. It is called *neo-evangelical* because it no longer stands four-square on the idea of plenary or full inspiration, preferring instead a theory of partial inspiration. Those who hold this position say, 'We have a high view of scripture, but we don't regard it as infallible and we don't think it is inerrant. It is inspired only in certain areas.' Unfortunately, it isn't always easy to know in what areas! The general position is that it's inspired in its doctrine, but not in its historical statements; or inspired in what the authors intended to say, but not in the assumptions which they made.

The evangelical doctrine
Over against these views, I'm driven (not by obscurantism, I hope, but by Christolatry) to the historic evangelical doctrine which was assumed by the church for centuries, and crystallised in the magnificent work of B. B. Warfield of Princeton in the late nineteenth century. That doctrine is encapsulated in three particular words. You can take them all, or you can choose the one that you think best.

First, it may be said that the Bible is marked by *infallible* inspiration. This means either that the Bible is never deceived, or that the Bible never deceives. The trouble with it is that it is negative. Even a railway timetable may be said to be infallible in the negative sense that it contains no errors. But that does not make it inspired. The word *infallible*, then, has its uses, but it reminds us only that the Bible does not deceive. It doesn't take us much further than that.

Secondly, there is the word *verbal*, stressing the totality of inspiration. It literally means that every word in scripture is inspired and I'm quite happy to endorse it. The difficulty with it is that the *word* is not the unit of meaning. You don't get the meaning of the Bible by taking a word and looking at it till you've taken all the blood out of it. The unit of meaning is usually the sentence. But if we want to emphasise the totality of inspiration, meaning that every unit of meaning is given by expiration of God and by the supervision of God, then the word *verbal* can be useful.

My own preference is for the third word, *plenary*, which means simply *full*. What this highlights is that the Bible in its entirety is inspired by God. Whatever the authors intended to say, and whatever they taught – their history, their ethics, their chronology – is all covered by inspiration.

There are, then, three words: *infallible, verbal* and *plenary*. I haven't used the word *inerrant*, because inerrancy is a consequence of inspiration, not a quality of it. But it is indeed a consequence of it. There is, of course, much that is inerrant that is not inspired. But what is inspired – what has God for its author – must be inerrant.

There is yet another word which I want to sow in your minds: the word *organic*. Inspiration is infallible, verbal, plenary and organic. I use the word *organic* because it encapsulates the idea that the scriptures are given through the organism, the human personality. I'll come back to that in the next chapter. But if we want a complete picture of inspiration, we must keep this word *organic*, to safeguard the idea that in inspiration God uses human character and human gifts and personality.

The attestation of scripture

Well, what have I done so far? We've seen the Bible's claims for itself and we've seen the doctrine which we build upon those claims. We come now to this question: Can we substantiate these claims? It's all very well to say the Bible makes these claims, but can we substantiate them and if so, how?

In the Westminster Confession of Faith there is a superb chapter on scripture. I want to pause here for a moment, just to make this point: this chapter is the greatest single statement on scripture to be found anywhere in the English language, and I commend it to you most warmly. It's a piece of superb prose, it's a piece of superb theology, it's a piece of superb pastoral counselling. It isn't long, so read it and digest it.

In the fifth section of this chapter there is a great statement as to the way we come to be persuaded of the infallible inspiration of the Word of God. The proof, says the Confession, takes the following course: first of all, the testimony of the church; secondly, the internal excellencies of the Bible itself; and thirdly, the witness of the Holy Spirit. Note carefully that not one of these points taken in isolation, but all three of them taken together, form the process by which we come to be persuaded that the Bible is the Word of God. Let me just touch upon each of them briefly.

First of all, the testimony of the church. We could reword that and say quite simply 'tradition'. I don't want to be sidetracked on this, but if we go back into Puritan theology we find that men like John Owen, for example, tended to minimise the importance of the church's role. It's quite fascinating to see how the Free Church fathers in the nineteenth century, William Cunningham in particular, sought to redress the balance, and really re-introduced this emphasis on the role of the church. If you can obtain Cunningham's *Theological Lectures*, you will find there a superb, though sadly neglected, discussion of the whole doctrine of scripture.

Well, what does the church do? Fundamentally, it tells us what the Bible is. What is scripture? How do you know what constitutes the Old Testament? How do you know what constitutes the New Testament? The church tells you. It tells you, for example, that the list of books in the Old Testament as we have it today is exactly the same as the list of Old Testament books in the days of our Lord himself. We know that because of tradition: because of the church's testimony.

But what of the 'longer canon' and the Apocrypha? It is alleged that at Alexandria there was a longer list than the list at Jerusalem and that this Alexandrian list contained the books called the Apocrypha, which the Roman Catholic and Greek Orthodox churches accept as canonical but the Protestant churches do not. I don't want to go too far into this, but the basic Protestant position is that there is no evidence whatever that that longer list was ever deemed canonical. It was a list, in fact, which came into being only when the Emperor Ptolemy asked for a translation of Hebrew literature. He seems to have said, 'Give me everything you've got', and the translators did just that. They gave him the whole lot – all the Jewish literature they had, scripture plus other things: a whole library. But there is no evidence that those other things were ever regarded as canonical in Judaism, and certainly not in the Christian church until quite late in its history.

What about the New Testament? The position is this. The church always had a canon: it had the Old Testament. But from the resurrection of Christ onwards – indeed, from the commencement of the Lord's ministry – that canon was being constantly augmented. It was being augmented by the Lord's own oral teaching, by the apostles' oral teaching, and by the apostles' written teaching in their epistles, gospels, and so on. That written teaching quickly came to be recognised as scripture in its own right. In 2 Peter 3:16, for example, Peter refers to Paul's writings as *scripture*: 'which they that are unlearned and unstable wrest, as they do also the other *scriptures*, unto their own destruction'. What happened was that the church put those other elements – the Lord's oral teaching, the apostles' oral teaching and the apostles' written teaching – on a par with scripture.

The question then becomes, how do we know which are the

apostolic writings? The answer is, the church tells us. Tradition tells us. We can go right back into the age of the apostles and the age immediately succeeding them and see which church-writings of the period were deemed canonical. We can also see that there were other writings, such as the *Shepherd of Hermas* and the *Epistle to Diognetus* and some others, which were Christian and which were in fairly wide circulation but were not deemed of apostolic provenance, and therefore weren't regarded as canonical.

What tradition does, then, is to tell us which books formed the Old Testament canon and which books are apostolic. It also tells us that the church has found these books "profitable", making believers wise unto salvation and fully equipping them for every good work (2 Timothy 3:15-18). The Westminster Confession puts it this way: 'We may be moved and induced by the testimony of the Church to a high and reverent esteem of Holy Scripture' (1:5). As a matter of personal history, all of us first met the Bible through the church, and all of us first came to love it through the church's recommendation (or maybe through parental recommendation: it's the same thing).

The second line of proof consists of what the Confession calls the 'incomparable excellencies' of scripture: the internal qualities of the Bible itself. In other words, this book bears upon itself the marks of divine authorship. All you would expect in a book which comes from God is found here. It has a marvellous unity. It has an unsurpassable elevatedness of concept and grandeur of thought. It has a majestic ethic which our consciences fully endorse. There is nothing in its view of God, or of ourselves, which is repugnant to what we know of ourselves or of our environment. Above all (at least for me) there is this: Christ Himself. That is the supreme 'incomparable excellence' of the Bible – the picture of the way of salvation, with Christ at its centre.

Modern scholars tell us that the Christ of historic Christian belief is a creation of the faith of the early Christian community. Now, I think I've read a fair sample of the world's greatest literature and it seems to me that there is something here that belongs to a different order altogether. Indeed – and I think I've said this often enough – if I couldn't worship the Christ of the Bible, I'd worship those who invented him. There is no record in the whole of literary history of a community creating a figure comparable to Christ: such grandeur, such compassion, such magnificent teaching, such magnificent *ways* of teaching, such marvellous relationships with men, with women, with children! So good, and yet so credible; so divine, and yet so human; so real that the narrative totally convinces us that if we came to Him we'd find rest for our souls. As far as I am concerned, I am a Christian because of what the Christ of the Bible does to me, and I come at the Book through Him. I accept it as God's Word, because it has this incomparable excellence, Christ Himself. Even as a concept, He is unsurpassable. There is no way in which I would want Him improved or want Him altered. When I find Him, I find the Absolute and I find the Ultimate. My spiritual quest is over.

Notice carefully what our Confession says about these excellencies: that they 'abundantly evidence' scripture to be the Word of God. These evidences are fully cogent. The reasonable or spiritual mind has no doubt, when confronted with this Bible, that it is the Word of God. You do not need some further evidence. You have the church's witness and you have the Bible's own characteristics, and these carry total logical and probative force. There are, of course, men and women who say that they aren't convinced. But the defect is not in the evidence. The defect is in ourselves. This is the essence of the Reformed and Confessional position. We have every right to present our neighbours with the evidence, but the evidence, substantially, is this: Read the Bible for yourselves! Let it make its own impact upon you. Come into contact with its Christ, with its concepts, with its morality, with its knowledge of your own soul. Come into contact with these and you will find that the Bible attests itself as the Word of God. It bears the impress of the divine personality. This is why John Owen could say that there are more marks of divine authorship in the Bible than there are in the creation itself.[1]

The third line of testimony to the divine authority of scripture is the witness of the Holy Spirit. This witness is not to be separated from the others. Nor is it to be regarded as an additional revelation. It isn't the Spirit saying in a revelatory flash, 'This is the word of God!' Nor is the Spirit's witness an additional *evidence*. The position is this: Imagine a court of law – you have an advocate, and you have evidence. In this instance, the evidence is 'the incomparable excellencies' and the advocate is the Holy Spirit. He is not Himself part of the evidence. He uses the evidence there is, but He gives that evidence cogency. He gives it force and power.

But what does that mean? That He changes us! He conditions my mind to respond to the evidence. You can link this with two similar phenomena at different ends of the intellectual spectrum. There are those, for instance, who don't enjoy watching cricket. That is a serious problem. But the problem is in themselves, and the change must take place in themselves. And there are those who don't like Mozart or Bach. Again, the problem is in themselves. It is they who have to be changed.

Similarly, there are those who can't stand the Bible. It doesn't impress them at all. When the Spirit comes, He doesn't change the Bible, although there are many folk who will testify that when they were converted the Bible became a new Book to them. The truth is that they became new people. They were blind, but now they see. It may happen in a flash or it may happen gradually, but the important thing is that the Spirit changes the mind so that it is now sensitive to, and responsive to, the divineness of scripture. George Gillespie once said, in a different connection, 'All thy marks will leave thee in the dark.'[2] In other words, you can have all the evidence in the world, but without inward illumination you still remain in the dark.

Three final points:

First, the *sufficiency* of scripture. The Bible contains everything we need to know for salvation and everything we have a right to lay down as a condition of church membership.

Secondly, the *finality* of scripture. It is the supreme judge in all matters of controversy. We sometimes speak of 'subordinate' standards, but this is a misnomer. As the Shorter Catechism itself points out (Answer 2), 'The word of God ... is the *only* rule to direct us.' You cannot have a subordinate standard. You have one rule, and everything else is under the control of that rule. The Bible is the only touchstone. It judges the preaching. It judges the decrees of councils. It judges the creeds of the church. It judges even our interpretation of the Bible itself.

Lastly, the *perspicuity* of scripture. The Bible has clarity. This is of enormous importance. Indeed, it was one of the great achievements of the Reformation to give the Bible back to the people, stressing that 'not only the learned, but the unlearned, in a due use of the ordinary means' could attain to a sufficient understanding of the scriptures (Westminster Confession I:VII). Today, we need to get back to this. The Bible is not targeted at experts, yielding its meaning only to priests or scholars. You don't need rows of commentaries to understand it. You don't need to go to a theological college. If you are a Christian, it is for you. Hunger, it has been said, is the best *hors d' oeuvre;* and spiritual hunger is the best hermeneutic. If we come to the Bible as needy sinners ('poor in spirit', as Jesus Himself put it) then we'll understand it because we'll find it speaks to our condition.

The Bible, then, is our authority; and it is a sufficient authority, a final authority and a perspicuous authority.

References
1. John Owen, *Works*, vol. IV, p. 91
2. George Gillespie, *A Treatise of Miscellany Questions*, chapter XXI

2

The Humanness of Scripture

In 2 Peter 1:21 we are told that the prophets spoke as they were 'moved' or 'carried' by the Holy Spirit. That brings before us two great facts. First, scripture is divinely inspired; and, secondly, it is the product of men. We saw in the previous chapter that inspiration covers the whole of scripture. There is nothing in the Bible that is not 'breathed out' by God Himself. In that sense He is the author of the entire Bible. Yet we are told equally clearly that it was men who spoke. In fact, the emphasis falls on this fact: 'carried by God spoke *men*'. They were God's spokesmen, but they spoke very much as men. They weren't automata, used by God as shorthand writers or mere typewriters. Their whole personalities were involved in the work God gave them to do. Their hearts, their minds, their memories, their emotions, their whole experience and all their gifts went into creating the Bible for us. Far from suppressing their personalities, God used them. Indeed, their personalities had been moulded for this very purpose. They were chosen for their work from eternity, and all that ever happened to them happened within God's determination to use them as authors of His infallible Word.

There is something here of enormous importance for our own Christian service. When God uses us He doesn't suppress our personalities. He doesn't flatten us off and make us just units in some kind of assembly line. He uses us as we are. We are all different in our temperaments and aptitudes and sometimes, just because we're different, we feel useless. And yet what God wants of us is exactly our personal kind of service. That's why Peter says, 'This is Peter speaking', and why Paul says, 'This is Paul speaking', and John says, 'This is John speaking'. What they were was part of what they offered to God. They were engaged, with their own temperaments and their own gifts, in doing the will of God.

That is the position, then. At one level the Bible came to us from God and at this other level it came through men; and all that these men were went into producing these holy scriptures.

What is the evidence of this?

Individual styles
First of all, the books of the Bible all have their own individual styles. If the Bible had come simply from God and from God alone, there would be one uniform style from one end of scripture to the other. There would be a monotonous sameness about all the books. Since they came through different men however, all the books have their own distinctive style. There is narrative style. There is poetic style. There is gnomic or proverbial style. There is prophetic style. There is allegory. Every author, too, has his own personal style. There is Isaiah, for example, a literary genius, a superb orator and poet. Then there is Jeremiah, a much more subjective and introspective personality. Then again, Ezekiel, using vivid and sometimes almost grotesque imagery.

When we turn to the New Testament we find the same phenomenon. Each gospel has its own individual style. There is Mark's, with its simple syntax. Mark doesn't subordinate clauses. Instead he co-ordinates them endlessly, often linking them by the phrase, 'and immediately'. Matthew, by contrast, has a very Jewish and very formalised style, dividing his gospel into five great sections on the pattern of the five books of Moses. He never speaks of the *Kingdom of God* but of the *Kingdom of Heaven*, because he is writing for Jews who never used the divine name if they could avoid it. Luke's Gospel, again, is completely different. It is very difficult to translate because of its intricate, elegant style. In his own way the Apostle John, too, is a consummate artist, using simple, almost monosyllabic, words to express profound and monumentally important ideas. Take, for example, the opening words of his Gospel: 'In the beginning was the Word, and the Word was with God, and the Word was God.'

There are no big words there. There are only simple, everyday vocables such as *beginning*, and *in* and *was* and *with*. Yet John uses them to make distinctions and convey profound ideas.

Paul, again, has his own style and yet he tells us very plainly that he didn't study style. He spoke the words which the Holy Spirit taught him and he seems to have held style in some contempt (1 Corinthians 2:1 ff.). Maybe that's why many of his sentences don't have verbs and why many of them were never completed. In Hebrews, by contrast, we see a very self-conscious stylist. Is it not indeed rather remarkable that Paul should say style doesn't matter and Hebrews should say, at least by implication, that it does? In the Bible, then, we have great stylists and we have non-stylists. What we don't have is uniformity and flatness.

Affinities with surrounding culture

Secondly, because the Bible is a human book it has close affinities with its own cultural and spiritual environment. The writers borrow the vocabulary, concepts and literary forms of their own day. Take, for example, the biblical covenants. These covenants are exactly the same in form and structure as other covenants known to us from the ancient Near East. In fact they are very similar to ancient international treaties, particularly treaties between a victorious king and his conquered vassal. In the same way we find that the apostles modelled their epistles on the epistles of the period. The salutations and the conclusions are exactly identical to those of their own particular culture. They didn't invent a distinctively Christian epistolary style. They simply adapted the current style to their own purposes. Similarly, they expressed the fundamental concepts of the gospel in language borrowed from their own day and even from contemporary religion. This is particularly interesting in view of the fact that the New Testament has some very distinctive concepts such as atonement and incarnation and justification. Yet all of these have at least linguistic parallels in the world of the first century. When the New Testament spoke, for example, of atonement by a blood-sacrifice which effected propitiation and reconciliation and redemption, it was using a whole body of concepts which had long been familiar to the Hebrews, to the Greeks and to the Romans. They all knew from their own everyday lives what propitiation was. They knew what ransom was. They knew what the redemption or manumission of slaves was. The New Testament writers borrowed these words and concepts and used them to express distinctive Christian ideas.

We find this, too, with regard to the person of Christ. The most common New Testament designation of Jesus is quite simply *Lord*. This was a word in common use among Hebrews, Greeks and Romans. Jehovah was Lord, the Greek gods were lords and the Roman gods and emperors were lords. It is remarkable that the apostles did not feel they should use some special word for such a sacred concept. They chose, instead, to express the concept in language familiar to those to whom they wrote and to whom they preached, and so they called Him *Kurios* (Lord) and the Jews, the Greeks and the Romans knew exactly what they meant because the designation was a familiar one. It was the same with *justification*, a forensic concept taken from the Roman law courts; and with *adoption*, a very common practice among the Romans, although alien to the Jews.

What the apostles were doing was to take the concepts available in their own culture and baptise them into Christ. We ourselves do the same thing today. We use such concepts as computers, transplants and so on to express certain facets of the gospel. When we do so we are using an apostolic methodology.

Use of ordinary sources
Thirdly, the humanness of the Bible appears in the fact that when the New Testament and Old Testament writers wrote history they used ordinary documentary sources. I don't mean that they never had insight or knowledge above the ordinary. They obviously had. After all, they had had an audience with God, they knew the Lord's secret (Psalm 25:14, AV) and they knew the mystery of the gospel. But when it came to dealing with such things as times and places and dates and names, it's very clear that these men,

inspired though they were, used ordinary historiographical processes and consulted the obvious authorities. For example, the Books of 1 and 2 Kings and 1 and 2 Chronicles allude very often to various other books which they had used, such as the book of Gad the Seer and the book of Nathan the Seer. The writers say, 'We used these. You'll find the information in these books.' They were inspired men, but they still used these books. They weren't hyper-spiritual. They didn't say, 'We can't use books'. On the contrary, they were happy to use ordinary sources of information.

We find this, too, with the Gospels. Luke explicitly tells us that he consulted three kinds of authorities: eye-witnesses, oral tradition and earlier documentary accounts (Luke 1:1-4). Now Luke, of course, wrote by inspiration. Yet he wasn't above consulting ordinary historical sources.

Where did inspiration come in then? It came in in the use these men made of those sources. They were kept from error and inaccuracy, controlled and guided by the Spirit of God as they made use of their respective sources.

Distinctive contributions

Fourthly, because the books are human each of the writers makes his own distinctive contribution to Christian theology. In other words, every one of them has his own unique phraseology, his own unique standpoint and his own unique emphasis. We can think, for example, of the prophet Isaiah and the way he speaks of Christ as the Servant of the Lord. That is unique to Isaiah. Again, there is his remarkable designation of God as 'the Holy One *of Israel*', emphasising both the augustness of God as the Holy One and also His involvement and commitment as the Holy One of Israel. Other prophets, too, have their distinctives. Hosea, for example, is the prophet of God's loving-kindness; and it is he who first compares the relationship between God and the church to that between a husband and wife.

The same theological distinctiveness appears in the New Testament. It is Paul, for example, who uses the concepts of justification and adoption, and portrays Christ as the form of God and the image of God and the glory of God. The apostle John, too, has his own unique Christology. He alone calls Christ 'the Word of God'. John also has a very distinctive doctrine of sin, defining it as lawlessness and then portraying it as simultaneously impossible and inevitable for a believer.

All these men, just because they are men, have their own unique theology; just as Augustine and Martin Luther and John Calvin and John Owen, although sharing the same basic message, have each his own standpoint and phraseology, and even his own particular obsession. Every book of the Bible makes a unique contribution to the theology of revelation.

Cumulative revelation

Finally, because the Bible is given through men the revelation it brings is progressive or cumulative. It isn't all given to us in Genesis chapter one. God built up the message, line upon line, precept upon precept, as the church was able to bear. In the Old Testament, for example, there is very little information with regard to the Trinity; there is little on life after death, or the resurrection, or hell or heaven; and there is little on the incarnation of Christ. All the blocks of the later doctrine are there, but there is no evidence that the men of the Old Testament put the blocks together and grasped the fact that one day God would become man. Only in the final phase of God's self-disclosure do we come to that mystery.

Even in the New Testament there is onward movement. The Lord had enormous difficulty getting His message across to the disciples because they were slow to learn, and when He died they had no comprehension of what His death was going to mean. Only after the resurrection and Pentecost did they come to understand the incarnation and the atonement and the full glory of Christ Himself. But the early church, too, had to move on, progressing in insight from the early preaching in Acts to the profundities of John's Prologue (John 1:1-18). Between these two poles there lay some forty years of reflection, preaching and divine illumination as God built up the understanding possessed by His church.

The principle is clear, then. Revelation is progressive or, perhaps better, accumulative. This means that Old Testament religion lacked some of the comforts available to us. A man like Job, for example, did not have our understanding of the glories of the world to come. He didn't know with our certainty that immediately after death the believer is present with the Lord. We should feel a real sense of privilege that our light is so much greater and so much clearer than the light these men enjoyed. We live in the age of the fullness of divine self-disclosure.

Biblical Criticism

Why do I devote so much time to the humanness of the Bible in a book as this? Mainly because this is what mandates Biblical Criticism, and all who are involved at any level in religious education, whether as teachers or students, must face the challenge of this particular discipline. I know that the word *criticism* as used here is open to misunderstanding because it suggests that we are finding fault with the Word of God. But I use it in a different sense. A Biblical critic is not someone finding fault with the Bible, but someone trying to find answers to various literary and historical questions. In that sense he is a judge, a discerner, trying to come to a conclusion in respect of various questions arising from the human aspect of the Bible. Because the Bible has been produced from within history and because it is a human document, it inevitably has some of the characteristics of ordinary human literature. That is why it is legitimate to engage in biblical studies and biblical criticism.

What, then, is involved in Biblical Criticism?

(1) Textual Criticism

First, the question of the Biblical text. What did the writers actually say? The Westminster Confession draws a sharp distinction between the inspiration of and the transmission of the Bible (Chapter I. VIII). At the point of origin the Bible is fully and infallibly inspired: those who wrote the original autographs were controlled entirely by the Spirit of God. By contrast, however, those who copied and transmitted the text were not inspired. Instead, the Confession says, their activity was covered by the 'singular care and providence' of God and although this secured a high degree of accuracy, it did not secure that the copies were faultless copies of the original.

We have one outstanding advantage with regard to the text of the Bible: the possession of a huge number of manuscripts. There are some books from classical antiquity for which there is only one extant manuscript. For the New Testament, by contrast, we possess around 5,000 manuscripts in varying degrees of completeness. In addition, we also possess a large number of ancient versions, as well as a substantial body of quotations of the Greek text in the writings of the ancient Fathers. These manuscripts are the raw materials of what is called Textual Criticism. The discipline is often misunderstood. It is true that no two of these scripts agree in every detail. But it is also true that the number of disputed or doubtful words in the New Testament is infinitesimal and the disagreements are almost always insignificant (such as, for example, whether we should read 'our' or 'your', only one letter's difference in Greek as in English). Let no one tell you that the text is in confusion. The text is not in confusion. There are so many manuscripts that we know the exact text with a very high degree of certainty; and where we don't know with certainty, the doubt is seldom of any theological importance. In fact, you could take the 'worst' manuscript and what you would have would still be the Word of God. You could take the least critical edition of the New Testament and it would be the Word of God. And if you take a competent scholarly edition of the New Testament you can know with almost absolute certainty that you hold in your hand the exact words written by apostles and evangelists.

It is often put to me that modern editions have taken large bits out of the Bible. Many people find this unsettling, particularly because Revelation 22:19 warns against taking away from 'the words of the prophecy of this book'. On the other hand, the preceding verse in Revelation contains an equally solemn warning against *adding* to the Word of God. It is as sinful to add to the text as it is to subtract from it. Now there are one or two places where we know that the text of the Authorised Version contains more words than the original, and scholars have taken these words out. But we also know how these extra words came in. An ancient scribe, faced with two variant readings, thought the best course of action was to put them both in. Rather than choose, he simply put them together. The process is called *conflation*, and is quite easy to detect. This all arises from the humanness of the Bible. The transmission of the text was left to copyists controlled by 'God's singular care and providence' rather than by inspiration. These men, for all their meticulousness, made mistakes here and there. The task of the textual critic is to identify these minor blemishes and eliminate them.

(2) Higher Criticism

Secondly, Biblical Criticism involves the study of the literary and historical origins of the various books. This is what scholars call Higher Criticism. Let me put it to you this way: simply because Jesus Christ came into the world we can ask, When was He born? Where was He born? Who were His parents? Where did He die? When did He die? These are historical questions and, although Christ was the eternal Son of God, by becoming incarnate He opens Himself to that kind of question. In the same way, the Bible, because it is part of history, is open to these questions.

For example, there are questions of authorship: Who wrote a particular book? Sometimes the answer is plain enough. The book says, for example, that it was written by the apostle Paul. Sometimes we have a very early tradition which tells us that this Gospel was by Mark, or by John, or by Matthew and we are confident that the tradition is correct. But sometimes there is no claim as to authorship, and tradition is uncertain. Who, for example, wrote the Epistle to the Hebrews? John Owen was confident that the apostle Paul wrote it and said so at great length[1], but few scholars have shared Owen's confidence. Origen said in the fourth century, 'As to who wrote Hebrews only God knows,' and that's the way it is still. Luther didn't know. Calvin didn't know. B. B. Warfield didn't know. In fact, the authors of our own Westminster Confession of Faith didn't know. The list of canonical books in Chapter One refers simply to 'The Epistle to the Hebrews' and attributes it to no author.

Here, then, is an area of legitimate discussion. The same is true of questions of date. When was a certain epistle or document written? Some modern scholars are at pains to date the entire New Testament as late as the second century in order to break the connection between it and the apostles.[2] But such men are mavericks. There is cogent evidence that the whole of the New Testament was completed before the end of the first century. In the case of such epistles as Galatians and 1 Thessalonians the dating is particularly important, because if we can establish, as I think we can, that these come from the early 40s AD. then we can show that already, only ten years after Christ, we have a very sophisticated theology and a very firm grasp of the deity of the Saviour. In other words, as early as AD 44 the church is already in full and confident possession of the message that the pre-existent Son of God became man to bear our sins and to die for our salvation. This makes it impossible to argue that such a gospel is a corruption of the primitive message, because it is found in our earliest documents.

We can enquire, too, into the author's aim and purpose. Why did he write this book? We know, for example, that Paul wrote Galatians because of a problem in the churches of that province and that he wrote 1 Corinthians because of a problem in the church at Corinth. In other words, these are what we might call *occasional* compositions, and if we know why they were written that helps us to interpret them and to apply them to our own particular situation.

So we ask, *Who* wrote? We ask, When? And we ask, Why? We can also ask, To whom? We know that Mark, for example, wrote his Gospel for Roman Christians; that Matthew wrote for Jews; and that Luke wrote for Greek-speaking Gentiles. Such information is often helpful in trying to understand what these men are saying. On the other hand, the interpretation of Hebrews and 1 Peter is often difficult precisely because we do not know the original readers the authors were aiming at.

(3) Source Criticism

Thirdly, Biblical Studies involves what is called Source Criticism. Evangelicals often find this a difficult concept, probably because they usually meet it in some unfavourable environment. For example, the view is widely held that the Pentateuch is made up of four documents J, E, D and P, all of them much later than Moses. This requires a re-writing of Jewish history which is totally at variance with the story related by the Old Testament. On the other hand, there is nothing in documentary theories as such which is inconsistent with the idea of plenary inspiration. We know that the biblical writers did on occasion use sources and it is, in principle, possible to identify what these sources were. I believe, for example, that behind our fourfold Gospel there are four sources: the Gospel of Mark; another source which scholars designate as Q; a body of material peculiar to Matthew known as M; a body of material peculiar to Luke known as L. I don't have all that much confidence in the fine tuning of this particular analysis, but in principle it is possible to identify which parts of the gospels come from which sources. What I really want to stress, however, is this: if you come across these theories at school or college, don't feel that they threaten your faith. There are sources behind our gospels, there are sources behind the Pentateuch, there are sources behind 1 Kings and Esther and Nehemiah; and the study of these sources is perfectly legitimate simply because the Bible came through men.

Now you may ask, 'Of what value is that?' Not of outstanding value, in my view. But with regard to the gospels such study has established several important facts. In particular it has established this: analyse the Gospels how you will, and go behind them as you will to what you may call a more primitive layer than the Gospel itself, you will find only a divine, incarnate Christ. In other words, there is no stratum of the Gospels that is not supernatural. The Christ of Mark and the Christ of Q and the Christ of L and the Christ of M have been shown to be as utterly other-worldly and heavenly as the Christ of St John. From the very beginning, not only in our earliest gospels themselves but in the most primitive sources behind these gospels, you find this Colossus of a Christ.[3]

Minute analysis of the gospels and their sources has also established this: the gospels are only passion narratives with an introduction. All the authors give disproportionate emphasis to the story of the cross. That's true of Mark and equally true of Q. Everything builds up towards the cross. The passion-story begins at Caesarea Philippi with Peter's confession. In Mark's Gospel that occurs in the eighth of sixteen chapters. In Matthew it is in the sixteenth out of twenty-eight. In other words, it is at the halfway-point in both Gospels. Now, it is a very strange biography that devotes half its attention to the last few days of its subject's life. Yet that's what our Gospels do, and nothing could underline more dramatically their sense of the importance of the cross. Not only, then, is Source Criticism perfectly lawful in itself, but it can sometimes provide useful data for the theologian.

(4) Redaction Criticism

Let me take another example, in some ways even more controversial: the procedure known as Redaction Criticism. This is a more recent, although by no means the most recent, arrival on the Biblical Studies scene. In essence it means that the gospel writers edited their material. They inherited certain material, but they didn't simply reproduce it, they re-worked it. Put it this way: if you are a reporter and you receive a press-release, there are three things you can do with it. If you are really lazy, you can reproduce it simply as it stands. If you are a little lazy, you can edit it. If you are not lazy, you will re-write it. The Gospel writers did all these things. Take, for example, the way they use Mark. If we look at any story in Mark we can see what Matthew did with it and what Luke did with it. Sometimes they omit it altogether.

Sometimes they reproduce it almost word for word. But sometimes they modify it either by improving the grammar and style or by removing harsh expressions or by taking away phrases which might be found offensive or be misunderstood. We have an example of this in Mark 6, were the evangelist says (verse 5): 'He could do no mighty work there'. It's easy to imagine somebody saying, 'That's limiting the Saviour: Christ *could* not.' Matthew puts it differently: 'He *did* not do many mighty works there' (Matthew 13:58). It isn't a big change but it is significant that Matthew felt *could* was the wrong word for his readership. For Mark's readership, *could* was perfectly alright, but not for Matthew's. Hence the alteration. And time and again we find this same kind of editorial process going on, because Matthew and Luke didn't simply copy Mark. They re-worked his material because they were real authors and not mere copyists.

What I have been trying to say is this: we must not be afraid of Biblical Studies. We must remind ourselves that the Bible is a human book. It isn't only a human book. In fact it isn't even chiefly a human book. But it is a human book and as such it has a history of transmission and it has its own literary characteristics. With respect to any of its documents, we can ask who wrote it, when he wrote it, where he wrote it, why he wrote it, and to whom he wrote it. We can ask what sources he used. We can ask what editorial processes were engaged in. And we can do all this because the answer to bad criticism is not no criticism but better criticism. In fact we have no alternative because God chose to give us the Bible in such a way as makes it an inevitable object of academic enquiry.

Parameters and qualifications

But we engage in this study subject to certain parameters and qualifications, and I want to mention these briefly.

First of all, if the New Testament or the Lord Himself tells us that somebody wrote a particular Old Testament book then that closes the question of authorship. Take, for example, the authorship of the Pentateuch. Christ often ascribes these books to Moses. Therefore, I do not believe that Christians can then regard the authorship as an open question. Nor can I see how Christian denial of the Mosaic authorship of the Pentateuch can be anything other than an affront to the Lord Himself.

Secondly, if a canonical book claims to be written by a particular author, that closes the question. Take, for example, the Pastoral Epistles: 1 and 2 Timothy and Titus. All of these claim to be of Pauline authorship. They bear Paul's name and claim to have Paul's authority. Now that closes the question. We couldn't accept this book as God's Word if it engaged in pretence and falsification as to its own authorship. On the other hand, Hebrews is anonymous, and so its authorship is an open question.

The third parameter is that if the Bible in its entirety is of divine authorship we cannot come to any critical conclusion which is incompatible with divine authorship. You can, for example, say, 'Yes, Matthew was a redactor. He did re-work the Marcan material.' But you can't say, 'Matthew invented that story!' or, 'Matthew falsified this account!' because that would be incompatible with divine authorship.

I am, then, saying Yes! to Biblical Criticism. But I am also saying that such criticism, so far as Christians are concerned, must operate under certain controls: respect for the New Testament's attestation of the books of the Old Testament; respect for a book's own claims as to its authorship; and respect for the fact that the Bible in its entirety is the very Word of God.

Conclusion

Let me make two points in conclusion.

First of all, let us never forget the purpose for which God gave us the Bible. It was given as a means of grace, to feed our souls. I say that because it is all too easy to become engrossed in the academic disciplines of Biblical Studies and to spend our lives pondering who wrote what, where and when. These are interesting questions, but they are subordinate questions. In fact, their contribution to our understanding of God's Word is not all that significant. It is the content of scripture that should fascinate us, not the history of its transmission, because it is the content that makes the man of God perfect. Let us remember, too, that what God ordained as a means of grace is not the original source behind the Gospels or behind the Pentateuch, but the Bible in its current form. It is quite fallacious to imagine that what lies behind the tradition is more authoritative than scripture itself.

My second point is this: it is surely a large part of the Bible's ministry to us that it allows us to encounter its own humanness and to observe the experiences and torments and tortures of its authors. Is it not a great thing to find a man like Jeremiah wrestling with his own commission and protesting angrily to God? Or to hear the apostle Paul telling us that he was cast down beyond measure, tormented by his thorn in the flesh and praying passionately that the Lord would remove it? Don't we then say, 'I can understand that man and that man understands me. He's been where I've been.' God didn't give this commission to angels, but to men like ourselves.

That's why, even at the purely human level, as literature, as autobiography, as affording a window into a man's soul, this Book is unsurpassable.

References
1. John Owen, *Commentary on the Epistle to the Hebrews*, vol. I, pp. 65 ff.
2. See, for example, *The Churches the Apostles Left Behind*, by the Roman Catholic scholar, Raymond E. Brown.
3. See further Hoskyns and Davey, *The Riddle of the New Testament*, London, 1958.

3

Divine Pre-ordination

In Ephesians 1:11 we are told that God is working throughout created reality, and that He is doing so in accordance with the counsel of His own will. It was upon this passage that the Shorter Catechism built its affirmation that God has 'fore-ordained whatsoever comes to pass'. To this fore-ordination there is no exception whatsoever. There is nothing which is merely permitted without being fore-ordained. Every occurrence and every entity in the universe lies under the control of God's fore-ordination. The fall of the sparrow, for example, is controlled by God's eternal purpose. So, too, are contingent, accidental events such as the throw of the dice. And so, equally, are the free actions of men. In Philippians 2:13 Paul tells us that God works in us the willing and the doing according to His own purpose. Not only is the *doing* under God's fore-ordination but also the very *willing* itself. Every free human decision lies under the working of the will and purpose of God. In fact, even the sinful actions of men lie under God's fore-ordination. The most spectacular sin in the whole history of mankind, the betrayal of Jesus Christ, lay under God's 'determinate counsel and foreknowledge' (Acts 2:23). 'YOU, with the help of wicked men, put him to death,' says Peter to the Jews; but this was done under God's determinate counsel and foreknowledge. Even the minutiae of our own individual lives lie under this purpose of God: the very hairs of our heads are numbered (Matthew 10:30; Luke 12:7).

And so we have this great principal statement that God's purpose over-arches everything (*ta panta*). Every occurrence in the physical universe, every contingent event, every free action of men, every sinful action, even the minutiae of our individual existences: all lie under this principle of God's all-embracing fore-ordination.

This principle is of enormous comfort and importance to the Christian because it reminds him that history is purposive. It is teleological. It is moving in a certain deliberate direction. It is not meaningless, directionless and cyclical. It is being worked out according to the plan of God. That is true of the macrocosm: the universe in its magnitude and its infinitude has this great over-arching purpose. But it is also true of the microcosm. The smallest details are embraced within this great comprehensive principle of purpose and intelligibility.

The principle is also important for man's scientific quest because science is based on the assumption that every event has meaning and that every event has a cause. Science assumes intelligibility, and the only foundation for such an assumption is that the universe finds coherence in the will and purpose of God Himself. Only because God Almighty has established bonds between the various events, occurrences and facts can we hope to discover purpose and elucidate meaning. Before God spoke the universe into being, God thought it. It was in His reason (*Logos*) before it was spoken; and because it was in the reason of God, it is logical with the logic of God.

We live today in an age which is dominated by despair and by an overwhelming sense of meaninglessness and pessimism. Over against that is one of the great gospel affirmations: there is a King, there is a Sovereign, there is control, there is purpose, there is Someone who knows where it is all going and who is determined to bring it to the destination of His own personal choosing.

Caveats

In Reformed theology, however, the statement of this principle has been surrounded by three great words of caution.

The first of these is that God is not the author of sin. God has fore-ordained sin. He has fore-ordained whatsoever comes to pass, and sin has come to pass, and God's purpose controls, limits, preserves and governs the universe even in the presence of this fact of sin. So sin does not lie adrift from the purpose or beyond the divine control. And yet the Westminster Confession stresses that God is not the author of sin (III:I). He does not Himself sin. He does not condone sin. He does not constrain to sin. He does not induce to sin. He does not tempt to sin.

How then does sin come in and how does it relate to the purpose of God? Sin, according to 1 John 3:4, is *lawlessness*. Sin has no meaning, no logic, no purpose, no fruit. Sin is the end of law. When we ask, Why sin? How sin? we are really forgetting that. We are assuming that there is some logic to sin. But at the point of sin logic collapses because sin is the Black Hole whence there is no light and for which there is no logic. There is no way of knowing how or why sin entered heaven. There is no answer to the query, How could Satan tempt Adam and Eve when they were perfect and holy and so close to God? There is no answer to the question, Why did God permit it? Because it is a Black Hole. This is equally true of Hell: the Black Hole into which at last all the lawlessness is thrown. We know this principle at the personal level, too. We know the absurdity of sin. We know its utter indefensibility, its inexplicableness in our own lives. How can a person who is a new creation, indwelt by the Spirit of God, united to Christ, sin? How can we sin *en Christo*? We cannot suspend the union and the indwelling while we go and sin. We sin *in Christ*; and that surely is the ultimate in lawlessness and anomalousness.

The second caveat is this: God's fore-ordination does not eliminate contingency. It does not rule out what we call chance or accident. Very often we hear good and pious people saying there is no such thing as chance or accident. Our Confessions do not agree with that. The Westminster Confession tells us that fore-ordination does not take away the liberty or contingency of second causes (III:I). When we say that some things are contingent, that they occur by chance, that they are accidents, we do not mean that they are not foreseen by God or not covered by His fore-ordination. What we mean is that they are, in principle, unpredictable so far as we humans are concerned. In other words, supposing we knew all the facts and could gather them all into our own statistical calculations, there are still certain events which are contingent and accidental and inherently unpredictable. This is not simply a matter of the limitations of our human powers of observation. Physicists tell us there is a principle of uncertainty at the very heart of the physical universe. It is in principle impossible for us to predict simultaneously both where the primary particles of mass and energy are and where they are going. We can predict the behaviour of large masses (*quanta*) of particles but not the behaviour of individual particles. The same is true, at a more mundane level, of the fall of the dice. Such an event is in principle contingent so far as our human observation is concerned, and divine fore-ordination does not eliminate that fact. It is a very interesting question how the behaviour of atomic particles relates to God's fore-ordination, but the position that there are in our physical universe particles which behave contingently and unpredictably seems clearly established. God has fore-ordained that they behave randomly.

Thirdly, God's fore-ordination does not eliminate human freedom. It does not take away our liberty or absolve us of responsibility for our personal actions. Judas Iscariot betrayed the Lord Jesus Christ; and he betrayed Him by God's determinate counsel and foreknowledge. In other words, God fore-ordained that Judas would betray Jesus. But God also fore-ordained that Judas would betray Him freely, that he would choose to do it and that he would desire to do it. God's fore-ordination does not mean that His whole purpose moved in and forced Judas to this particular act, rather God fore-ordained that, without compulsion or coercion, Judas would freely, volitionally, and with all the moral force of his own personality, express himself in betraying the Lord Jesus Christ.

This is something the Confession insists on with a remarkable explicitness when it says that God ordains whatsoever comes to pass, yet so as the liberty of second causes is not taken away, 'but rather established' (III:I). Fore-ordination is not destructive of freedom; God has fore-ordained freedom and the Confession, with great courage, says that in fact fore-ordination is what *establishes* freedom. In other words, nothing can take away from the human being the liberty essential to moral responsibility, because God has fore-ordained the freedom of men at the point of moral decision-making. God fore-ordains their actions, but He fore-ordains them as free actions: as things they do by their own personal volition.

We can put it another way. It is very often assumed that Calvinism, if it is not the same as determinism, will at least support and identify with it. But there is a radical confusion in such an assumption: a confusion between a philosophical theory and a theological doctrine. Determinism is a philosophical theory to the effect that every event has a cause which makes the event itself inevitable and infallibly certain. In accordance with this, many philosophers have argued that even our human moral choices are determined by our history, our heredity, our genetic composition, our environment and so on. Calvinism is not a philosophical theory. It is a theological statement to the effect that God has fore-ordained whatsoever comes to pass – not that all events in history have a cause within history. Some Calvinists have been determinists; some have even confused Calvinism with determinism. Jonathan Edwards and Thomas Chalmers, for example, were determinists. But there is no reason why a Calvinist should not, at the level of his philosophy, be a libertarian and believe in human freedom of choice. In fact, the Confession seems to be pointing very firmly in the direction of libertarianism.

Over a century ago, the great Princeton Calvinist, Archibald Alexander Hodge, pointed out 'that the need of the hour is not to emphasize a fore-ordination, which no clear, comprehensive thinker doubts, but to unite with our Arminian brethren in putting all emphasis and concentrating all attention on the vital fact of human freedom'.[1] That was very perceptive in the late nineteenth century because at that time the practice of imposing the methodology of the physical sciences upon the behavioural sciences was just beginning. Hodge was quick to see that the concept of freedom, and with it the more important concept of responsibility, was under threat because these sciences, under the impulse of Darwinian determinism, were beginning to say that human beings could not help the way they behaved. Their behaviour was the result of various glands and other biological factors. How much more do we need Hodge's word of caution today when one of the great problems of society is precisely this elimination of freedom, the elimination of the whole idea of responsibility! This is clearly recognised by such writers as the historian Paul Johnson: 'Marxist and Freudian analysis,' he says, 'combined to undermine, in their different ways, the highly developed sense of personal responsibility, and of duty towards a settled and objectively true moral code, which was at the centre of nineteenth-century European civilisation'.[2]

Sociology, criminology, penology and pyschology are largely based on the assumption that environment, education and genetic inheritance not only influence but determine human behaviour and that individuals are therefore only minimally answerable for their own conduct. In the light of this, it is of paramount importance for us to grasp this synthesis that we find in A. A. Hodge (and in William Cunningham and 'Rabbi' Duncan) between fore-ordination on the one hand and freedom and responsibility on the other. Fore-ordination, says our Confession, does not destroy liberty. In fact it establishes it; and it is well worth our glorying in it. I am free because God fore-ordained my freedom. I am not the plaything of pressure and circumstance, or even of internal and endocrinological factors. I am free. I make my own decisions. I am the cause, the ultimate, answering cause, the responsible cause, of my own decisions.

Election
Our second area of concern is the doctrine of election. 1 Peter 1:2 gives us a great statement of this doctrine: 'Elect according to the foreknowledge of God the Father, through sanctification of the Spirit, unto obedience and sprinkling of the blood of Jesus Christ.' The word 'elect' means simply 'to select'. When David went to meet Goliath, for example, he chose five smooth stones out of the brook. There was a selection of five, there was a non-selection of others and when the Bible uses the word 'election' it does so conscious of this particular background.

The doctrine means, first of all, that God has set His special affection and love on particular men and women from all eternity. Peter speaks of election according to God's foreknowledge. In the Bible the idea of foreknowledge is generally held to mean God's prior love: knowledge and love overlapping very significantly. 'In love, He fore-ordained us to the adoption of children by Jesus Christ to Himself' (Ephesians 1:5). There is a love on God's part for the whole of mankind. God loves all men. But there is also a love which is special, which secures for the elect not simply the blessings of common grace but something more. There are individuals who are precious to God, whose names are in the Lamb's book of life (Revelation 21:27) and engraven on the palms of Jehovah's hand (Isaiah 49:16). It is selective love. It is particular. It is personal. He loved *me, He gave Himself for me* (Galatians 2:20). I am poor and needy but the Lord thinks on me (Psalm 40:17). This really is the basic idea of election, that beyond the general love of God for the whole of mankind there is a special love for those who are His own choice people. Indeed, there are people with whom God is in love, and futhermore there has never been a time when He has not loved them. The love of God the Father for God the Son is essential to the very nature of God Himself. It is part of the shape of God, part of His being. But God's love for His people is optional and discretionary and gracious. It is contingent. How amazing, then, that it is eternal: there has never been a time when God has not loved his people! He has never been without knowing them, without caring for them. That has always been a factor in the consciousness of God. There was no point at which God fell in love with them or began to love them. The love was always there with an intense personalness and particularism.

Secondly, God has destined these choice ones to salvation. God's general love for the human race confers upon mankind a vast array of precious blessings: the sun shines, the rain falls and we enjoy all the benefits of art, science and technology, of affluence, of global fecundity, of human friendship and love and all the preciousness of human relationships. But for the choice ones there is more. For them God wants something greater and something stupendous. They are elect unto the 'sprinkling of the blood of Jesus Christ'. They are chosen to be beneficiaries under Christ of everything that His obedience and sacrifice deserve. They are chosen to be in Christ: to be covered by the righteousness, by the intercession, by the pleading, by the status of Christ in Heaven. It is not merely that they are elect to hearing the gospel or to church membership. It is much more. It means being elect into the very experience of salvation in the fullest possible degree. They are elect 'unto the adoption of children by Jesus Christ to himself' (Ephesians 1:5). They are elect to participating in everlasting life. They are elect to having all their needs met according to all the glory that God possesses and according to all that Jesus deserves (Philippians 4:19). Being elect means having fellowship with Christ, sharing in the things of Christ. It means sharing everything Jesus has: sharing His righteousness, His Spirit, His Sonship, His inheritance, His Father's love. It is a great question whether God loves His own Son more than He loves His people. God gave His own Son for them (John 3:16). They are chosen in Christ to be partakers of the divine nature (2 Peter 1:4). 'Father, I will that they also, whom thou hast given me, be with me where I am' (John 17:24). We know that 'we shall be like him; for we shall see him as he is' (1 John 3:2). We are elect to salvation on this scale of hyperbole. We are more than conquerors (Romans 8:37). We are hyper-exalted (Philippians 2:9). We are filled with all the fullness of God (Ephesians 3:19).

Being elect means that God has always loved us. Being elect means that God cannot do enough for us. He wants to lavish upon us every spiritual blessing in the heavenlies in Christ Jesus (Ephesians 1:3).

Thirdly, election means that it is God Himself who originates spiritual life in us. We participate, of course, in salvation through faith and repentance, but how can we believe and how can we repent? In ourselves we have no capacity for either of these graces. We have no desire for Christ, no appreciation of Him, no patience with Him. By ourselves we cannot want Him. We cannot stand Him. We cannot not resist Him. We cannot prepare for Him. We cannot even not be averse to Him until God Himself comes and gives us that faith which is not of ourselves but is the gift of God (Ephesians 2:8). The risen Christ pours upon us the grace of repentance. Or, as 1 Peter 1:2 puts it, 'elect ... through sanctification [consecration] of the Spirit'. God's chosen ones, when God chooses them, are spiritually dead. They have to be born again. They have to be quickened into life by the impulse of grace. It is *this* intervention that makes the difference between this man and that man. Some are spiritually alive – why? Because God quickened them; and He quickened those whom He chose to quicken and there is no other reason for the difference.

Fourthly, election means that God is committed to our sanctification. He is Himself assuming the responsibility for making us holy. We see this clearly in Peter's statement about election: 'through sanctification of the Spirit'. Paul puts it even more explicitly: 'elect unto holiness' (Ephesians 1:4). One common argument against this doctrine of election is that it encourages Antinomianism: careless living, ungodliness, impiety, immorality. After all, if we are elect we are going to be saved anyway. If we are not elect we won't be saved, so let's live as we please. The elect are saved, do what they will; the non-elect are damned, do what they will.

It is easy to argue thus, in terms of mere logic. But the argument is an absurdity at the level of experience because we are elect unto holiness. We are elect to not being able to live as we please. We are caught up in God's determination to save. The primary commitment of God's love is to conform us to the image of His Son (Romans 8:29). God has fore-ordained that we shall be Christ-like. We cannot, in the face of all this, say, 'Oh, I'm elect, I'm going to live like a devil.' God has fore-ordained good works for us to walk in (Ephesians 2:10). Christ loved the church and gave himself for it that he might sanctify and cleanse it with the washing of water by the word (Ephesians 5:25-26) – that is what God's love means. He is able to keep us from falling and to present us faultless before the face of his glory with exceeding joy (Jude 24), and that joy will be due to the fact that every single member of God's ransomed church will bear the exact image of His beloved, only-begotten Son. That is what God's electing love means: God is invincibly determined to make us Christ-like. Augustine spoke of irresistible grace – *irresistibilis*, meaning invincible. As we struggle with ourselves, our temperaments, our personalities and so on, it is a great thing to be able to grasp this fact that God is invincibly and irreversibly committed to making us like the Lord Jesus Christ.

Reprobation

Having considered something of cosmic predestination and election we must see something also of reprobation. It is very solemn and very difficult teaching. Calvin is supposed to have spoken of the 'horrible decree' of reprobation. What he actually spoke of was the *decretum horribile*, which in Latin means terrible and awe-inspiring, and it is certainly that. It reminds us so vividly of the holiness of God and of our total dependence on Him to be told that even our unbelief and our being offended by Christ do not lie adrift from the divine purpose.

The Westminster Confession speaks of the elect being predestined to salvation and then goes on to say: 'The rest of mankind, God was pleased ... to pass by, and to ordain them to dishonour and wrath for their sin' (III:7). There are two elements in this doctrine: one sovereign and one judicial.

The first element is *preterition*, which is simply the Latin way of saying 'passed by'. God sovereignly passes by with His grace the non-elect. He finds them sinners: He passes them by. The Lord Jesus referred to this fact in these terms: 'I thank thee, O Father, Lord of heaven and earth, because thou hast hid these things from the wise and prudent, and hast revealed them unto babes' (Matthew 11:25). There is a not-revealing. There is a not-enlightening. There is a not-illuminating. There is a not-effectually calling. There is a passing by. This sovereign element in reprobation is not effective or effectuating. It does not change people at all. It leaves them. That is how Calvinism has put it.

Secondly, there is *condemnation*. Preterition is sovereign; condemnation is judicial. Men are ordained to dishonour and wrath for their sins: not because they are non-elect, but because they are sinners. God will not, does not, condemn any non-sinner. Not a single non-sinner will go to Hell. God is a just Judge. He is a most compassionate and fair-minded Judge and if any individual has a good case, has excuses, explanations, extenuations, mitigations, He will listen to all of them. Why? Because He will do right and will ordain someone to dishonour and wrath only if he or she is a sinner. There is a passing-by, then, which is sovereign; but the condemnation is not sovereign. God does not condemn people just for the whim of it. As Robert Burns suggested in *Holy Willie's Prayer*:

O Thou that in the Heavens does dwell,
Wha, as it pleases best Thysel,
Sends ane to Heaven an' ten to Hell
A' for thy glory!

Apart from the proportions being all wrong – the Bible speaks of the salvation of a vast multitude which no man can number (Revelation 7:9) – God sends men to Hell only most reluctantly. He has no pleasure in the death of the wicked. He does it only because it is right.

Are the two decrees, election and reprobation, symmetrical? Or, as it is sometimes put, are they equally ultimate? Is the one of the same status and of the same importance and of the same revelatory impact as the other? I do not believe so; and that is why I am reluctant to speak of double predestination. It distorts the biblical perspective.

There are two differences.

The first is that the decree of election is effectuating; the decree of preterition or reprobation is not. There is an effectual calling to holiness and faith in Christ. There is no effectual calling to unbelief and impiety. God's grace works along the channel of election, invincibly, creatively, redemptively, transformationally. It renews. It sanctifies. It transforms. The decree of preterition does not make men unbelievers: it finds them unbelievers. God is not the author of the unbelief of the impenitent as He is the author of the faith of His children. The two decrees are asymmetrical at that point.

The second element of asymmetry is that the two decrees do not equally express God's nature. They do each express it; but they do not express it equally. The God of the Old Testament is reluctant to condemn: judgment is His strange work (Isaiah 28:21). In Hosea 11:8 He says, 'How shall I give thee up, Ephraim?'; Ezekiel 33:11 tells us that God has no pleasure in the death of the wicked. In other words, God loves saving people. He feels fulfilled in saving people. He delights in pardon. But God is not sentimental the way we are. He will condemn if need be. But He will do it reluctantly; He has no pleasure in it. There is in God a shrinking from condemnation. Thus the two decrees do not contribute symmetrically and equally to the picture of God. We see God really throwing Himself with all the fullness of His being into consummating His purpose of election.

Objections

There are many objections to this doctrine and most of them are philosophical rather than theological. Almost all are of this form: How do you reconcile election with this or that? How do you reconcile divine fore-ordination with human responsibility? How do you reconcile election and reprobation with the free offer of the gospel? Any answer would also be philosophical. There is no theological (that is, revealed, biblical) solution to that dilemma. It is a problem of reconciling two equally important truths, but there is no biblical revelation of the solution to the problem.

What then do we do? Well, we believe the doctrines – fore-ordination, responsibility, human freedom – and we do not try to reconcile them. We take each of them on its own independent evidence. We do not know how to reconcile them. God knows. We offer Christ to every creature because that is what the Sovereign commands us to do.

'I believe in the sovereignty of God,' the Calvinist says and the Sovereign says, 'Go to every creature'; and the theologian says with such boldness, 'Ah, but God on the throne, you haven't chosen them all' – and God on the throne says, 'You GO; who are you, man, to reply against God?'

Emphasis?

How much emphasis should this doctrine be given? It is biblical; and so it must be preached. But it must be preached in biblical proportion and balance. It would be a sad thing if it came to be the foremost element in our preaching and witness. Charles Hodge put it this way. This doctrine of the divine sovereignty bears the same relation to other doctrines as the granite does to the other strata of the earth's rocks. Undergirding all the strata, all the deposits on the surface of the earth, there is granite. That granite is everywhere. But it does not out-crop everywhere. It out-crops only here and there. In the same way, Hodge said, the sovereignty of God underlies all our theology and all our preaching. But woe betide us if it crops out in every sermon, because then we've got the balance wrong. It is a great doctrine. But it can all too easily become the war-cry of sects. It must never do that: it is too precious. It must live and function in biblical proportion and balance.[3]

Lastly, and most important of all, at the heart of the sovereignty of God there lies Jesus Christ. All authority in heaven and earth is His. The decree is Christ-shaped. Cosmic fore-ordination is fore-ordination by Christ. Election is election by Christ. Even at the point of reprobation, Christ is there, so that in the dread realities of preterition and condemnation there is no unChrist-likeness at all. Everything in the decree is consistent with the definition God has given of Himself in Christ. It is the one thing we must never forget: the Lamb is in the very centre of the Throne.

References
1. A. A. Hodge, *Evangelical Theology*, Banner of Truth edition, 1976, p. 134.
2. Paul Johnson, *A History of the Modern World*, London, 1991, p. 11.
3. Charles Hodge *Princeton Sermons*, 1879, r.i. 1958, p. 6.

4

Creation

The essence of the doctrine of creation is encapsulated in the various words the Bible uses to express this idea. Four of these words are of special importance.

First, the Bible often speaks simply of God *making* (*'asah*) His own creation. This word is used even with regard to man: 'Let us make man in our image' (Genesis 1:26). It is a very general word, yet it is often used to express this very distinctive idea. It carries, too, a very clear implication: that as bearers of the image of God we bear the image of the great Maker, which means that it is part of our human dignity also to be makers. Every human being ought to be a maker and it is incumbent upon educators and politicians to create environments within which people can express this divinely implanted impulse. It is a large part of our current human tragedy that many of our fellow men and women are experiencing frustration at this point: they cannot *make* because of the context in which they are forced to live their lives.

Secondly, the Bible uses the word *formed* (*yatsar*): God formed man of the dust of the ground (Genesis 2:7). The word highlights the artistry of creation. It is used, for example, of the potter moulding and fashioning the clay and speaks of the intimacy and dedication and even of the imaginativeness of the divine operator. The idea of what He wants to make is present to begin with in God's own mind, or *logos*, and is brought into being by the processes of the divine artistry. In the case of man, *yatsar* is also allied with the fact that God breathed into man's nostrils the breath of life, expressing the closeness of the divine involvement.

I commend this word to you in particular in the context of our own human artistry. There is a whole area still to be explored here with regard to the relation between God and beauty; the fact that beauty is what conforms to the absolute norms of beauty in God's own mind. Those whose talent is artistic, whether in words or pigment or whatever, should rejoice in the fact that they have God Himself as their Model. He is the Supreme Artist.

A third, very interesting, word occurs in the context of the creation of woman. The verb *banah* means primarily *to build*: God *built* the woman (Genesis 2:22). It suggests that particular care went into this specific act of creation. It also suggests that the woman, if not the man, is built on architectonic principles. I shall leave it to yourselves to work out what this should mean for the self-esteem of both sexes!

Fourthly, and most importantly, there is the word *bara*. This word has some remarkable peculiarities. For example, it is used only with God as its subject. Creation in the strict and final sense is the prerogative of God. This does not mean that we cannot also speak by extension of human creativity: that is a very important concept within historic Reformed theology. But we have to face the fact that there is a specific form of creativity which is peculiar to God.

We notice, however, that God engages in this activity comparatively infrequently. In the first chapter of Genesis the word *bara* is used very economically. It is used with reference to the primary creation of the particles of mass and energy (1:1), of the creation of the great sea creatures (1:21) and of the creation of man (1:27). It is remarkable that even in the story of creation itself this majestic verb should be used so sparingly and such economy of usage surely points to the dignity and majesty of this particular mode of God's operation.

We find, too, that this verb is never used with an accusative of materials. That is not because God did not sometimes use materials. It is, rather, that the materials are irrelevant because they cannot frustrate the purpose of the Creator or limit His ability to give perfect expression to the idea in His own mind. The Bible never speaks of God creating *with* something. In the case of a human artist, the medium in which he works is always very important, whether it is wood or stone or pigment or words, because he can use its inner qualities to express his own creativity. It is important, too, because the material always imposes constraints upon the artist. But when God creates, His sovereignty over the material is so complete and so absolute that the materials are irrelevant to the artistry and to the ultimate creative achievement. He is not limited by the substances with which he has to work. There is no constraint upon the Great Creator. God is able to impose His will so unconditionally upon the medium in which He works that in and through it He can give perfect expression to the concept in His own mind. He can take the dust and create beauty with it. He can take the bodies of our humiliation and create out of them the bodies of our glory (Philippians 3:21).

But the most fascinating thing is that within Genesis 1 there is a clear distinction between two different kinds of creation, to each of which this verb *bara* is applied. We distinguish them by referring to the one as mediate creation and the other as immediate creation.

Immediate creation is that form of God's creativity in which He literally *makes out of nothing*: *creation ex nihilo*. That is not the intrinsic or necessary meaning of *bara*; but it is sometimes the meaning of it. For example, in Genesis 1:1 we read that 'In the beginning God created the heaven and the earth.' There are no materials used. God *speaks* things into being. In the same way, God created light (Genesis 1:3). God does not create light out of something else. The idea of light is formed in the divine mind, in the reason or *logos* of God, and then it is spoken into being. God speaks the thought into existence; and light *is*. There is no material used. There is no second cause. There is no other agency. There is simply the creative word of God.

But it is made very plain in Genesis 1 that *bara* can also refer to *mediate* creation, in which God does use pre-existing materials and second causes and other agencies. In fact, that is the predominant use of the idea of creation throughout the chapter. We see it in such statements as, 'Let the earth bring forth grass' (1:11). Although the verb *bara* is not actually used here, the activity referred to is distinctly creative. Vegetation emerges as a consequence of God addressing the earth itself so that it brings forth. In verse 20 the same idea is applied to the creation of the sea creatures: 'Let the waters bring forth'; and verse 21 announces that 'God created great whales'. The two ideas stand side by side: the waters bring them forth and God creates them. The use of the verb *bara* does not preclude this other agency. We find the same thing in verses 24 and 25 with regard to the creation of the beasts of the earth: 'Let the earth bring forth the living creature after his kind.' Here again there is creation, but it involves the use of second causes.

But the really fascinating thing is the occurrence of this idea of mediate creation in connection with the origin of man: 'God created man in his own image' (Genesis 1:27). There the verb *bara* is used quite specifically. Yet we know from Genesis 2:7 that God did not create man *ex nihilo*, out of nothing. He 'formed man of the dust of the ground,' and He made or built the woman (Genesis 2:22). We find, therefore, that man is formed out of pre-existing materials – there is mediateness – and yet, man is also said to be created. We have to conclude, therefore, that the verb *bara* does not by itself mean *to make out of nothing*. It does not preclude the use of second causes or the use of pre-existing materials. In actual fact, we may conclude from the total picture in Genesis 1 and 2 that God, in huge areas of His creative work, used this process of mediate creation, involving pre-existent materials, the operation of other agencies and, probably, great periods of time. Creation does not necessarily mean, then, immediate or instantaneous *fiat* creation.

Creation progressive
Another feature of the narrative in Genesis 1 is its clear emphasis on creation as progressive. The word *bara* is used in the context of the calling into being of more and more complex forms of reality and of life itself. The background to this progressiveness is indicated in Genesis 1:2: 'And the earth was without form, and void; and darkness was on the face of the deep.' That means that

at this particular point in the creation sequence, reality, or what Francis Schaeffer calls 'bare being'[1], was characterized by three negatives: it was without form; it was void or empty; and it was dark. In other words, there was no light, no form and no life. The ensuing narrative goes on to indicate the process by which God progressively eliminated these negative factors. He eliminated the darkness by creating light, the foundation of all that follows. He eliminated the formlessness by dividing the waters above the firmament from the waters below, separating the land and the sea and placing the light-bearing bodies in the heavens. And He eliminated the emptiness by creating life in all its forms. The remainder of Genesis 1 goes on to describe the various forms of life that God created.

It is a very economical narrative but it indicates that God created vegetation, then the sea-borne life forms, then land-borne life forms, and finally, as the great climax and Omega-point of creation, man. Hugh Miller, the great nineteenth-century Christian geologist and palaeontologist, suggested that when we speak of certain eras being, for example, the eras of the emergence of vegetation, this does not mean that no other life-forms emerged during that age.[2] What it means, Miller argued, is that there was a period when the predominant life-forms were vegetative, another when the predominant life-forms were sea-borne and yet another when the predominant life-forms were land-borne; and although the argument is extra-biblical it has some plausibility. My main concern is, that according to Genesis, there was progression from vegetation to sea-borne to land-borne forms and at last, to the emergence of man himself. At the risk of over-simplification we can say that the narrative indicates a movement from simple life-forms to more complex life-forms; and certainly the fact that man is the climax is profoundly interesting, especially when one notices that there is no special day set apart for the creation of man, as a work of fiction would almost inevitably have suggested.

Time-scale?

There, then, is a brief overview of the Bible's concept of creation. We can now take this basic biblical pattern and try to apply it to various current questions and debates. It is important to start with the fairly uncomplicated biblical teaching first of all, and use it to lead into the contemporary issues.

First of all, there is the question of time-scale. How long ago did all this occur? How long did this process take?

The consensus currently accepted by science appears to be that the earth is some 4.4 billion years old. Scientists also argue that the most distant object we can see from this earth is 8,000 million light-years away. Now there are enormous problems involved in trying to work out whether this is even a meaningful discussion. What we are really asking is, When was light created? When was time created? It is probably impossible in principle to answer that. But this leaves unaffected the argument that we are looking at objects 8 billion light years away. If that is correct, we see things as they were 8,000 million years ago. This is obviously a far cry from the time-scale envisaged by Archbishop Ussher's famous chronology which argued that the world came into being in 4004 BC. Ussher simply took the various biblical genealogies, added them up and concluded that Adam came into being four millennia before Christ, that is, 6000 years ago.

The result is an enormous apparent discrepancy: 8,000,000,000 years on the one hand *versus* 6,000 years on the other. Is there any way out of this dilemma?

One possible way out is to argue that science is monumentally wrong, and 'monumentally' is a modest description of an arithmetical error of such magnitude. It is, of course, entirely possible in principle that science is wrong. But if we take this position we must take it consistently. It means having to accept that the whole of modern science is fundamentally flawed in its methodology. It means that assumptions made in, for example, quantum mechanics are erroneous and would have to be discarded. We cannot really pick and choose, because these calculations are multi-disciplinary and we can only reject them if we are able to argue that the whole methodology underlying the mathematics is wrong. Now it may be that the calculations are completely flawed. The difficulty is that they work in practice. They enable scientists to create the marvels of micro-electrics and nuclear physics and to plot the precise location of oil fields under the North Sea. This makes it very difficult to be confident that the theoretical framework is wrong. We would certainly need more evidence than the bare fact that it conflicts with Ussher's chronology.

It is possible, however, to escape from this conflict by interpreting the days of Genesis not as 24-hour days but as creation eras. The notion of these days being creation eras seems to have a great deal to be said for it. I am not prepared to endorse theologically the current scientific consensus. But I am prepared to entertain the possibility of harmonising what I know about God's creation from the Bible with what I know of that same creation from scientific evidence and research.

But how can I possibly entertain the notion that these days are creation-eras and not 24 hour periods?

First of all, because that interpretation has a very honourable pedigree. It is completely false to imagine that it was only adopted by the church as a counsel of despair in the light of the challenge from Darwinism. It was the prevalent view of the Fathers even before Augustine and certainly from Augustine onwards. Augustine spoke of 'God-divided days' and W.G.T. Shedd writes, 'The doctrine of an immense time, prior to the six creative days, was a common view among the fathers and schoolmen.'[3]

Secondly, the peculiar use of the word *day* in Genesis 1 inclines one further towards this view. It is peculiar because the first three days existed before the creation of the light-bearers, the sun and the moon (Genesis 1:16). How could there have been 24-hour solar days before God made the sun? No doubt there are plausible solutions of that difficulty within the framework of Ussher's chronology, but it is still a difficulty intrinsic to the narrative itself: a difficulty posed, not by the scientific data, but by the biblical data.

Again, in Genesis 2:4 the word *day* is, in fact, used to describe the whole creation period: 'In the day that the Lord God made the earth and the heavens.' The word is obviously being used figuratively, as it frequently is in Scripture: for example, the day of the Lord; Abraham saw 'my day'; that day; the day of judgment.

There is surely great truth, then, in the cautious position adopted by Charles Hodge, himself the author of an exhaustive refutation of Darwinism: 'It is of course admitted that, taking this account by itself, it would be most natural to understand the word in its ordinary sense; but if that sense brings the Mosaic account into conflict with facts, and another sense avoids such conflict, then it is obligatory on us to adopt that other.'[4]

As I said, I am not prepared to endorse theologically the current scientific consensus or its methodology. It may be monumentally wrong. But it may also be right; and if it is right, *day* in Genesis 1 and 2 cannot mean a 24-hour day or point to a creation-period of 6 literal days, 6,000 years ago.

Since delivering the original lecture upon which this chapter is based, I have become increasingly concerned that we may be asking Genesis the wrong questions. Several factors have contributed to my unease.

One is that the first chapter of Genesis is a highly stylized narrative of immense literary complexity, using a wide range of rhetorical devices to put its message across.[5] It is entirely possible that the days are part of this sophisticated structure rather than of the substance of the message.

Another factor to be borne in mind is that at some points it is impossible to reconcile the natural science of Genesis 1 with what we know today about our world. The outstanding instance of this is the reference to the *firmament* in Genesis 1:6 ff. It is virtually certain that the Hebrew word *raqia* meant not some vaporous canopy or cloud-cover between us and the sun but a rock-solid floor/ceiling separating the ocean above from the ocean beneath.[6] It is impossible to reconcile this with the truth as we know it today. The safer course may be to treat this passage as we do other pseudo-scientific passages in the Bible. For example, scripture often refers to the bowels and the kidneys as the organs through which we experience affection and emotion. But is this part of the *teaching* of Scripture, so that it is heresy to deny that compassion comes from the bowels? Such allusions belong to the framework of revelation rather than to its content. Seely comments: 'Of course, the ancient science employed in giving this revelation cannot be completely harmonised with modern science. This gives a clue, I think, as to why ... neither concordism nor literalism has genuinely been able to harmonise modern science with Genesis.'[7]

A third factor behind my unease is the question of the purpose of the author of Genesis. There can be little doubt that it was largely polemical. The author wished to repudiate the polytheistic cosmology of his day; to insist that the entire universe was the creation of the one, living God of Israel; and to proclaim that every other pretended deity was a creature, and a vassal of this God. This is why there is such explicit stress on the creation of the sun, the moon and the stars, so often objects of worship in the ancient world (and even today). This is also why the narrative describes the Almighty's effortless creation of the great sea-creatures.

To stress the unity and eternity of God; to insist that the whole universe is His work; to emphasise that we live in a world of order, not of chaos; and to put the gods of Egypt and Babylon firmly in their place: these were the intentions of the author of Genesis 1. I suspect that if we had asked him, 'But how long were the days?' he would have looked blank. He was *assuming* a natural science rather than advocating it.

The Parable of the Mustard Seed would soon lose its effect if we became obsessed with the question, 'But is it really the smallest of all seeds?' And our Lord's encounter with Nicodemus would teach us little if we focused only on the question of reconciling John 3:8 with modern meteorology. I am not sure that our treatment of Genesis 1 has been much more intelligent.

Flood Geology

There is also the problem of what is known as *flood-geology*, popularised by Whitcomb and Morris[8] but already sufficiently prevalent in the nineteenth century to attract attention and refutation by Hugh Miller.[9] The essence of this position is that the geo-physical features of the earth's surface are the result of the Flood. It maintains that the Deluge itself, by its hydraulic action, is sufficient to account for the patterns of stratification on the earth's surface and for the immense sedimentary deposits which are found all over the world. In other words, we owe our rock formations to the Flood; and these formations are therefore extremely recent.

This theory has the advantage of adducing an apparently biblical explanation for the way things are and this has won for it widespread popularity in evangelical circles.

I shall say of it, first of all, that, as we have seen, it was already looked at and rejected by our theological forebears in the nineteenth century. I know that this is only an *ad hominem* argument. There is nothing wrong with such arguments. Even the Lord Himself used them. In other words, He took people where they were and He argued in sympathy with their prejudices. For example, we see Him doing this in John 10:33 ff., when He turned on the crowd and said, 'Why do you call me a blasphemer simply because I call myself "God"? Your own Bible, which cannot be broken, calls your elders "gods". It isn't necessarily wrong, then, for a man to be called "God".'

Now I know that you have prejudices. Some of you may be prejudiced, for example, in favour of the Free Church of Scotland and its traditions. One of these traditions is the rejection of Flood Geology by such men as Hugh Miller and William Cunningham and their acceptance of the geological time-scale.

My second response to Flood Geology is that it is a scientific rather than a theological construct. Now it may, as a scientific theory, be perfectly valid. I am not competent to assess it on that level. But I am not prepared to grant it *theological* status. I am not prepared to grant that it has the support of Genesis. The arguments in favour of it are drawn from hydraulics and geology and chemistry and crystallography and so on. They are not arguments which are drawn from the Bible itself (even though the impulse to deploy them does come from a certain interpretation of the Bible). The Bible nowhere suggests that the current features of the earth's surface are the result of the Flood. In fact, it seems to me that all the Genesis evidence is against it and that when Noah came back he came back to a world that was essentially familiar. We meet the great rivers already in Genesis 2. We find the great minerals in Genesis 2. We find the dove coming back with an olive branch from a familiar world. We find the ark grounding on a well-known mountain, Ararat. Such biblical data surely preclude the idea that the Flood itself radically altered the earth's surface.

Evolution

So much for Flood Geology. My third concern is this: how does all this relate to the theory of evolution? If I am not hostile to the notion of a universe thousands of millions of years old and if I am prepared to accept that life-forms emerged according to a progressive pattern, from the simple to the more complex, does this make me a Darwinist? Not for a moment! I draw a very firm distinction between such a position and the position of consistent evolutionism.

Let me identify, briefly, three areas of tension where it is impossible, in my view, to harmonise Genesis with the current consensus among scientists.

First of all, the eternity of matter. Consensus science assumes that matter in some form or other (mass, energy, space) always existed. That is where science starts. It starts with matter. Theology, on the other hand, begins with nothing. Matter came into existence only by God's *fiat*. That conflict is irreconcilable.

Secondly, there is the notion that the organic emerged from the inorganic: life from non-life. There suddenly emerged, so we are told, some protein, the precipitate of inanimate, inorganic chemicals, and this became the primary building-block of subsequent life-forms. It is impossible to fit such a theory into the biblical pattern, because in the Bible we get from non-life to life only by God's direct action. God said, 'Let the earth bring forth!' It was not spontaneous. From this point of view, mediate creation is as supernatural and miraculous as immediate creation. The gulf between organic and inorganic, between life and non-life, is bridged only by the creative word of God.

Thirdly, there is the idea that human existence is simply a continuation of animal existence. Here again the conflict with scripture is irreconcilable. It is an integral element in the theory of evolution that there is a direct line of continuity, some kind of unbroken genetic chain, directly linking what we may guardedly call 'lower' life-forms and the human life-form. Man belongs to the animal kingdom and is a precipitate of that kingdom by the mutation of some gene. In the Bible, by contrast, we get from the lower life-forms to man only by divine intervention: God said, 'Let us make man!' Indeed, this passage describing the origin of man (Genesis 1:26ff.) is one of the greatest pieces of literature in scripture. God places this tremendous gulf between man and all that has gone before. He does not simply allow the universe to precipitate man. There is this great pause. He doesn't even say, 'Let the earth bring forth!' Instead, God deliberates and takes counsel and then says, 'Let us make man in our image'. He takes the dust and lovingly makes it into a man. He kisses the man into being (Genesis 2:7). This creature is not the result of the chance variation of a chimpanzee gene. He is the work, the direct work, of the divine artist; just as in the Virgin Birth the Father and the Holy Spirit create the humanity of Christ, the Omega-point of all creation. You could not get to Jesus Christ from anything that had been done before, and you couldn't get to man from anything that had gone before. Here there is a making which precludes any mere evolution.

I must now bring this to a conclusion. There are two final points to be made.

One is this: please remember that the alternatives to the Christian doctrine of creation are very limited. Take a simple question: What existed before this world? It is widely believed that there is a virtually infinite number of possible answers to that query. In fact there are only three.

: The first is that before this world nothing existed: absolutely nothing. Now just contemplate that! Where did this world come from? From nothing! Where did the brain of Einstein or the brain of Shakespeare or the brain of Mozart or the brain of Augustine or John Calvin or St Paul or (in their thinking) Jesus Christ come from? From nothing! That surely requires an enormous leap of faith.

The second possibility is that before creation an *impersonal* something existed: a great, incredibly dense – shall I say, lump? – of mass or energy, self-existent, eternal and pre-programmed. It had in it the atomic number of every element. It had in it every genetic blue-print. It had in it the score of Beethoven's symphonies. It had in it the plot of *Hamlet*. All was in the lump. Such a postulate is as offensive to the radically sceptical intellect as the existence of Jehovah Himself.

The third possibility is that before creation there was a *personal* something, the living God: an infinite mind, infinite wisdom, infinite power and infinite love that explain all other forms of existence. That is the Christian doctrine; and what we face is a straightforward choice between this on the one hand and Nothing or the Lump on the other.

Finally (and I would want this to be the thing which remains with you), there is the unsurpassable biblical idea of creation in Christ. How often is that note sounded in the New Testament! Remember John 1:3: 'All things were made by him; and without him was not anything made that was made'; and Hebrews 1:2: 'by whom also he made the worlds'. A world made *by* Christ! One that has impressed upon it all His characteristics: His wisdom, His truth and His love. We love it because He made it. But there is something even greater: the world made *in* Christ. Creation is Christ-shaped. The space-time curve is Christ-shaped. It is built on the Lamb of God, expressing the same heart as broke on Calvary. This helps us understand how, in the incarnation, God can come into such intimate union with His creation. He identifies with created spirit in the mind of Christ. He identifies with created matter in the body of Christ. That, surely, is the glory of matter: that God saw fit to take it to Himself, and even to *become* it, in the body of His Son. Beyond that there is only the supreme achievement of the Maker, the Omega-point beyond the Omega-point: the resurrection body of Jesus, where the great Artist takes the dust of the earth and forms out of it the body of His exalted Son, with such triumphant success that in and through that dust we see the glory of God in the face of Jesus Christ.

That is why we can never despise the material and the tangible and why we can never despise or abuse the world in which we live, or be afraid to ask it questions. Christ is the truth of creation as surely as He is the truth of redemption.

References
1. Francis Schaeffer, *Genesis in Space and Time*, London, 1972, p. 34.
2. Hugh Miller, *The Testimony of the Rocks*, Edinburgh, 1857, pp. 134 ff.
3. W.G.T. Shedd, *Dogmatic Theology*, 1888, Vol. 1, p. 474.
4. Charles Hodge, *Systematic Theology*, London and Edinburgh, 1871, Vol. 1, p. 571. Hodge, *Darwinism*, London and Edinburgh, 1874.
5. Gordon Wenham *Genesis 1-15*, Word Biblical Commentary, Waco, Texas, 1987, pp. 5ff.
6. Paul H. Seely, 'The Firmament and the Water Above' in the *Westminster Theological Journal*, Vol. 54, No. 1, pp. 31ff.
7. *op cit*, p. 11.
8. John Whitcomb and Henry Morris, *The Genesis Flood*, London, 1961.
9. Hugh Miller, *The Testimony of the Rocks*, pp. 267ff., 383ff.

5

What is Man?

The doctrine of man is by any standards an important area of Christian teaching because it impinges at so many points upon our responsibilities and our daily behaviour. Many of our current problems stem from defective understanding not simply of God and of Christ but even more obviously of man himself. Only as we see him in biblical perspective can we honour him as we ought and educate and make laws for him in a way that befits his position in God's creation.

The origin of man

The Bible uses two key creation-words to bring out the way that God brought man into being.

As we saw in the last chapter, the word *bara* is a distinctive word referring to God's own activity, a word which in itself reminds us of the momentousness of this new development, the emergence of man. The narrative moves on rapidly through the various days to this great pause in Genesis 1:26: 'And God said, Let us make man....' Here is a new departure, and this word, used so very sparingly in scripture, is used at this point because here God is bringing into existence something completely new. Man was not made by *immediate* creation. He was made using pre-existing material. Yet he is so brilliantly new, so spectacularly different, that the Bible speaks of him in terms of this uniquely divine activity.

Secondly, in Genesis 2:7, God is said to *form* man from the dust of the ground. This reminds us that man is not simply the result of God saying, 'Let there be man', which was how He made light, but that his creation was a process in which God used pre-existing material: material which to us seems so humble and common-place (the dust of the ground). This reminds us that, although man is the result of God's direct creative initiative, he also has close affinities with the rest of the organic creation. In his bio-chemistry man has the closest possible affinities with other organisms. At the same time, the word *formed* speaks of the artistic involvement of God, reminding us of the love and care, even the imagination and dedication, that have gone into this new creature, man. God took enormous trouble over him, forming and fashioning him lovingly. The process culminates in this marvellous idea that God 'breathed into his nostrils the breath of life; and man became a living soul' (Genesis 2:7). There is no room here for a remote, deistic activity, as if God wound up the universe and left that universe to precipitate man. Nor is there room for a self-sustaining and self-monitoring evolutionary process. Man doesn't simply 'happen'. God breathes him into being, so that in the very first breath man draws he is in fellowship with God and the moment he opens his eyes he is looking into the face of his Maker. There is more here than simple propositional truth. There is poetry: God making man with loving artistic care and breathing animation into him. The directness of the divine involvement could hardly be expressed more forcibly.

Clearly, this portrayal of the origin of man differs fund-amentally from that of modern anthropology. The Bible cannot allow that man is simply the result of the mutation of the gene of some other animal. His emergence is due to the activity of God Himself. As I have indicated already, I have no great quarrel with the time-scale demanded by modern science. Neither have I any quarrel with the idea that creation was sometimes a process, using pre-existing materials. But there is no way that a biblical theologian can get over this fact that between man and the nearest other form of creation there is a gap that can be bridged only by the creative activity of God. You cannot get from the so-called higher animals to man by a series of minute genetic adaptations which somehow render this creature fitter for survival. That is not biblical teaching. The Bible argues that God specifically intervenes in the creation process. He creates and forms the man. That does not mean that there are not close affinities between man and other animals. There is, for example, a close anatomical affinity between man and the ape and there are close physiological affinities between man and the pig and between man and the dog. There is also said to be a close genetic affinity between man and the chimpanzee. All of this fits perfectly well into the Bible's own portrayal. The Bible does not allocate to man a separate creation day. Nor does the Bible argue that man is the product of fiat or immediate creation. It describes him as made from pre-existing elements. The Bible does not even put man into a separate zoological category. It describes him as a *living soul*: a classification he shares with the cattle and the beasts (Genesis 1:24). All this would lead us to expect affinities between man and other creatures. It would also lead us to expect that science could conduct experiments on animals and extract from them conclusions relevant to human medicine. None of this is precluded by anything the Bible says. What is precluded is the notion that man is the result of an evolution, itself guided by natural selection and taking place through minute, chance variations over many millions of years. The Bible portrays man as new; and as the specific product of divine activity.

My personal view of the creation week is that within it there were long periods during which the procedures defined in Genesis operated in terms of the Lord's word, 'Let the waters bring forth' (1:20), 'Let the earth bring forth' (1:24). These processes went on over many millions of years. The waters kept bringing forth and the earth kept bringing forth. But there are specific points in the process where God intervened, initiating a new departure. It is true, of course, that God is immanent, operating in the whole process. The whole sequence is under His control. But there are points where God's intervention is cataclysmic: where He intervenes to initiate some great new departure. That is what He does specifically in the creation of man. He pauses, deliberates and then proceeds to form and to build.

This provides us with a foundation for intellectual security when we are told, 'Man is like the chimpanzee', or 'The valve of a human heart is similar to the valve of a pig's heart'. That is no contravention of Biblical teaching. On the contrary, it is what the Bible's teaching would lead us to expect because it places man in such close affinity to the rest of creation. But those affinities do not, by any logical process, require the conclusion that man is simply a development from those other animals. The similarities are due not to evolution but to the fact of a common Creator duplicating His systems in more than one form of His Creation. To use a rather mundane illustration: the Mini is similar in many ways to a double-decker bus, but that does not prove that it has evolved by spontaneous mutation from a double-decker bus, even though the same systems are used and the same basic laws are in operation.

The nature of man
The second area we need to examine is the Bible's teaching on the nature of man.

(1) Psychosomatic unity
Firstly, man is a psychosomatic unity. His soul and his body do not function as independent entities. Instead, they function in the closest possible union. Our physicalness is one of the great facts of our human condition. We are told to present our bodies as living sacrifices to God (Romans 12:1). Those bodies are material and have their own biochemistry. They are subject to the laws of decay and the laws of senescence and they give us access to the physical world with all its beauty and all its dangers. There is nothing evil or contemptible about the body. As far as the Bible is concerned, the body has immense dignity, because God personally formed it. Furthermore, in the incarnation God took a body. In Christ there dwells all the fullness of the Godhead bodily (Colossians 2:9). There is an entity in the universe called the Body of the Son of God.

Prudishness may make it difficult for us to get to grips with this fact of our physicalness, but it is in the body that we are called to serve God, and we are also called to keep that body fit for service. We have no right either to pamper and indulge it, or to abuse and exhaust it. We have to keep it at a pitch of maximum efficiency because in our current condition we have nothing else with which to serve God.

But man also has a soul. His humanness has a psychological dimension according to which he is able to think and decide and feel. Man is an emotional creature: a creature of feelings. We do ourselves great injury by denying or minimising this. To be human is to have feelings of joy, of sorrow, of fear and apprehension, of hope, of elation and of disappointment. To be human is to love and to need to be loved. These things are not weaknesses. They are what God conferred upon us when He made us souls. We are not meant to face bereavement with impassivity or stoicism. We are not meant to face exposure and condemnation and guilt without shame. We are not meant to hear good news and experience success without joy and elation. It is surely a very unfortunate part of our Western inheritance that we often find it so difficult to accept and to express our own emotions.

The most important point, however, is that for all the validity of the distinction between the body and the soul they nevertheless constitute one human being, they affect one another most intimately and they interact with one another most directly. We must come to grips with this fact that we are a *unity* of body and soul, and that the neglect or abuse of either of those components is going to have disastrous effects on the other and on our personhood in its totality. A great many of our emotional problems are caused by physical factors – by overwork, by lack of exercise, by exhaustion. We owe it to God, if we have any proclivity towards emotional lows, to exercise the most prudent management of our bodies, because if we do not we shall reap the emotional consequences, causing suffering not only to ourselves but also to those dependent upon us and even to the church and the kingdom of God.

For the same reason, we have to face the fact that there are certain emotional disorders for which it is our responsibility before God to accept medication because these disorders have, if not an organic base, at least an organic dimension. For example, there are forms of depression which yield very readily to chemical control. It is dishonouring to God and cruel to dependants to refuse to accept such medication on the basis of the arrogant principle, 'I do not take drugs'. If the alternative is misery for those with whom we live and incapacity for the work to which God has called us, then it is our responsibility before God to manage our temperaments through these medications. In the same way, of course, our emotional state will have an impact on our physical condition. If we go through emotional lows and traumas there will be physical consequences. It may be helpful to remember this because it will sometimes save us from worrying that there is something sinister behind our physical symptoms.

Man, according to Genesis, is a living soul (Genesis 2:7). His soul is not an appurtenance or possession or some kind of external adjunct to his personality. It is what he is, rather than what he has. He is an embodied spirit and the combination of the physical and the spiritual, the physical and the psychological, is what makes us human beings. We are all familiar with psychosomatic illnesses and it is a great pity that we tend very often to attach an element of guilt to such a condition. To say that an illness is psychosomatic is not to say that it is a pretence. It is to say that it is a physical condition resulting from an emotional state. That does not mean that there is no physical problem. There obviously is. But it is rooted in a psychological problem. This whole area requires the sympathy and understanding of Christians because those who go through such illnesses face so much trauma, solitude and hostility. If we realise that man is a soul we shall grasp at once that it is often impossible to say where the physical ends and the psychological begins.

(2) Sexuality

In the second place, there is the Bible's emphasis on human sexuality. The differentiation is very clear from Genesis 1:27: 'Male and female created he them'. This may tie up with what will be my third point about the nature of man: that he is made in the image of God. We recall that at the very heart of God Himself there is differentiation between the Father, the Son and the Holy Spirit. Similarly, at the very core of our humanness there is differentiation: the sexual differentiation. This differentiation is God's will for mankind and it is inescapable. Freud, although using the word sex in a very specialised way and although guilty of giving undue prominence to this whole dimension of human existence, was nevertheless substantially correct in saying that there is no area of human activity that is unaffected by this sexual differentiation. It is something of enormous potency for good and ill.

Today, there is a widely prevalent assumption, derived from the more popular magazines (especially the women's magazines), that sexuality is a matter of almost infinite gradation from absolute maleness on the one hand to absolute femaleness on the other, with all kinds of shadings in between. The intention behind such an analysis is, of course, to suggest that what I may guardedly call sexual deviancy is perfectly natural. It is simply a result of this fact that sexuality is a matter of degree. Now I do not profess to be fully conversant with this problem, but it is safe to say that human sexuality is a matter not of hormones but of chromosomes; and that the differentiation is absolute. There is maleness and there is femaleness and that depends simply and absolutely upon the presence of a single Y chromosome in the gene. Part of the difficulty, of course, is the prevalence of sexual stereotypes, according to which, for example, women are gentle and men are leaders. It is not at all difficult to find men who are gentle men and women who are made for leadership. But that has no bearing on the question of sexuality. We are either male or female.

With regard to the ethical problem of homosexuality, it has to be accepted simply on biblical grounds that there are human beings who were born with no interest in the opposite sex. The Lord Himself acknowledged this: some, He said, are born eunuchs (Matthew 19:12). There is no moral judgment or disapproval to be passed upon a human being merely because he has that kind of personality. The ethical problems arise only when a person who is so built seeks illicit outlets in homosexual acts and practices. There appears to be no genetic predisposition to such practices.

This brings us into an area in which guidance is hard to find because of the risks involved even in raising the question. If Jesus Christ became man, as He did, He did not become mankind or the human race. He became a specific human being, with a unique human individuality. He became a Jew of the first century, born in Bethlehem to a particular set of parents. He is specific racially. He is specific in terms of family ties. He is totally specific and unique in His genetic composition. It is also implied in this that He is specific in His sexuality: He is either male or female. In the Bible, of course, the Lord is clearly male. That fact should serve to make us very careful in what we say in response to sensational films that seek to exploit for commercial gain the sexual aspect of the Lord's life. In our concern to defend His purity we must be careful not to deny His sexuality, because we then run the grave risk of portraying Him in homosexual terms. The Lord was not only human, He was male, and we must not overlook this fact. Nor need we suppress the fact that as such He would undoubtedly face temptations in this area as He would in every other area of His humanness. He was without sin, but He was not without temptation.

(3) Image of God

The Bible tells us, thirdly, that man is made in the image of God (Genesis 1:27). At the point of his origin, he was modelled upon his Creator. The same general meaning attaches to this idea as is attached to that of Christ being the image of the invisible God (Colossians 1:15). It means that there are resemblances between God and man. It is crucial to our understanding of this whole issue to remind ourselves that this statement is not made about any other creature, only man. We seem to have inherited the idea that the angels are somehow superior to man, but the angels are never said to be made in the image of God. They are servants of the redeemed. All the biblical indicators point to the conclusion that man is the apex of God's creation, not only in the physical and terrestrial sphere, but also in the spiritual realm. There is nothing higher than man because he alone bears the image of God.

And here we come to a remarkable fact, which sometimes causes evangelicals a great deal of trouble: the Bible never suggests that man lost this image. It never even says that this image is marred in man.

Let me say at once that I would yield to no one in emphasising the enormity of indwelling sin, the reality of total depravity, and the extent and power and pervasiveness of corruption in the heart of a human being. I happen to regard that doctrine as the single most important doctrine in the whole area of practical religion. Indeed, the view we hold with regard to the extent of human sin will determine whether we are evangelicals or non-evangelicals. As Anselm said long ago, the whole reason why people so often have low views of the Person of Christ and low views of the Cross is that they have not pondered the gravity of sin. Similarly, the reason why the Bible is a closed book to the natural man is that it is addressed to sinners, and unless you know yourself to be a sinner it will make no sense whatever to you. I want to stress, then, that I believe in total depravity, that I believe in the pervasiveness of sin, that I believe in the spiritual powerlessness of man and that I believe original sin to be a fundamental doctrine, maybe the fundamental doctrine, of evangelical religion. But I also believe that man still retains the image of God and I maintain that not on any grounds of pure logic, but on grounds of explicit biblical teaching.

In Genesis 9, for example, when God, responding to the violence that prevailed in the world before the Flood, moved in to protect human life and to assert its sanctity, He laid down that very solemn ordinance, 'Whoso sheddeth man's blood, by man shall his blood be shed' (verse 6). Why? Because 'in the image of God made He man'! The whole logic behind the principle of the sanctity of human life and behind the ordinance of capital punishment was that even man in the person of Noah and his descendants, fallen man, was deemed to bear the image of God.

We find the same idea in the Epistle of James: We use our tongues, he says, both to praise God and to 'curse men, who have been made in God's likeness' (3:9, RSV). This clearly assumes that man as he exists today is a bearer of the image of God. That is why slander and defamation are so serious.

The same assumption underlies Paul's argument in 1 Corinthians 11:3ff. A man's head must not be covered because he is the image and glory of God (verse 7). There is, of course, a problem here, because it is to the male of the species that the concept of divine image-bearing is referred and the ladies do not, at least on the face of things, come out of the passage with quite such a halo as the men. But the point is that even after the Fall man is deemed to bear the image and to be the glory of God.

It is of enormous practical importance that we should view our fellow human beings in this light. As bearers of the image of God they are gifted with rationality, creativity and an aesthetic sense. They are gifted with a capacity for fellowship: 'Let us make man in *our* image', not, 'Let me make man in *my* image'. Man is made in the image of the withness, the togetherness, the socialness of God Himself. 'It is not good for man to be alone': there is tremendous teaching there for us. God lives in, and is blessed in, relationships. He is blessed in the togetherness of Father, Son and Holy Spirit. If He made us in His image, then we, too, are made for relationship. And yet how many human beings are frightened of relationships! The great teaching of Genesis 2:18 is that it is not good for man to be alone. The human tragedy is that while we can avoid all the pain in life by avoiding relationships, in following that safe and lonely road, we also avoid all the joy in life. It is at the very point – *withness* – where man ought to have found his fulfilment, that he so often finds frustration and pain. Even in evangelical churches there is a drawing away from relationships. There is a fear of getting hurt. There is much emphasis on individualism and solitude: and a reluctance to commit ourselves to others. That is a violation of our nature as bearers of the image of God.

Men and women can never lose the image of God. It is so important for us to remember this as we teach our children in our homes and schools, as we serve in the various caring professions, as we meet men and women in the courts, as we see them in the gutters, as we legislate for them and as we try to rescue them. At those very points at which we are tempted to despise them, we despise Him in whose image every human being is made. Is it not the very core of the horror of fascism and apartheid and anti-Semitism that they forget this great primal fact that man in all his ethnic, social, economic and moral variety remains a bearer of the image of God?

I have had the privilege of visiting the Holocaust Memorial in Jerusalem and to stand close to the overpowering evidence of the inhumanity of the Gentile to the Jew. Those Jews, slaughtered in circumstances of indescribable barbarity, bore the image of God. The death-squads and the doctors who committed those appalling experiments on Jewish men, women and children, the crematorium-attendants who moved the corpses into the pits and pushed the living humans into the incinerators and shovelled the dust and the ashes into the bins also bore the image of God. They shall answer, and have answered, for what they did, precisely because man never ceases to bear that image, and man never ceases to be responsible for his conduct. The Nazi cannot turn to God and say, 'Ah, Lord, but that day I was an animal.' No! On that day he was a human being. On that day he acted as one made in the image of God.

It is a cause for deep concern that evangelical pronouncements and social judgements so often reflect the security born of self-righteousness. If only we remembered what we ourselves have sunk to, and would have sunk to but for the grace of God, it would temper many of our sweeping condemnations.

The directives given to man
Some brief comments, finally, on the directives that God gave to man.

He told them, first of all, to be fruitful and multiply (Genesis

1:28), that is, to procreate intelligently, responsibly and believingly, trusting in God to provide. Their sexuality was not to be used irresponsibly, but neither was it to be suppressed because of unbelief and unfaith.

Secondly, He told them to fill, or 'replenish', the earth. They were to move over the horizons, over the hills and the rivers, into the unknown. They were to be creative and adventurous, to want to know, unable to be content with not knowing. God put that drive into every human being and into all authentic humanness. The young should never be discouraged from experimenting, innovating and exploring. It is their God-given destiny to move out and to live on the frontier. The church of God, too, must live on the frontier, creatively and imaginatively as God meant her to do. Eden was a great place. But the man and the woman were not meant to stay there. They were meant to move out and fill the whole earth.

They were also told to subdue and dominate their environment. We take this to mean that man was to research and harness the forces and resources of the cosmos through the procedures of pure science and technology. But we remember with gladness that God put the first human pair into a garden, not into an academic institution, and that they were to express their divine image-bearing by digging and delving, by the great conjoint operations of conservation and improvement. This is surely our responsibility too: not only to keep, but to till; not only to conserve, but also to improve whatever has been entrusted to us, whether it be a garden, a landscape or a theological heritage.

Let us remember, in conclusion, that Christ is the true definition of man, just as He is the true definition of God. He is the mirror of what it means to be human. For the moment I recall just one aspect of this, contained in His own words to the disciples: 'The Son of Man did not come to be served, but to serve' (Matthew 20:28). Is that what it means to be a real man: to be willing to be, and to be thought, a slave?

6

Sin

The doctrine of sin is hardly the most attractive or popular of Christian tenets and yet as far as religion goes it is utterly fundamental. Unless we understand sin and its solemnity and the damage it has done to our human existence, we cannot hope to appreciate such evangelical doctrines as the Cross and the Person of Christ. Religion begins with a sense of sin because it is in conviction of sin that all perception of God's Word and of the glory of Christ have their origin.

Terminology

There are four New Testament words which express vividly what sin is.

First, *hamartia*, which means specifically, *a falling short of the target*. The archer draws his bow, aims at the mark but somehow the arrow falls short. In the same way our human lives fall short of God's ordained target. That target is clear enough: that we should so live as to glorify God and enjoy Him for ever. But our lives fall short. They do not measure up to the standards which God has set for us. Indeed, they fall short even of the standards set by our own human consciences, which is why our hearts condemn us (1 John 3:20-21).

Secondly, there is the word *adikia*, which means *iniquity* or *unrighteousness*. The basic idea here is that God has given us a *dike* or a norm, a straight- edge, and our lives do not conform to it. Essentially, they are not straight. They are not on the level. We could move that slightly into this area: we do not give others their rights. God has His rights. Other people have their rights. But the unrighteous life does not give others their rights. We can combine these two ideas by saying that our lives are not straight because they do not give others their due.

Thirdly, there is the word *paraptoma* which means *transgression* (Romans 5:15). The picture here is of a road ordained by God: 'This is the way, walk ye in it' (Isaiah 30:21). But we transgress. We go off God's road. We have sought out our own devices (Jeremiah 18:12). All of us like sheep have gone astray and have turned to our own paths (Isaiah 53:6). We take the path that lies beside (*para*) God's road because we imagine that God's road leads nowhere, whereas this other road seems to promise so much pleasure and so much fulfilment.

The fourth word is *anomia*: 'sin is lawlessness' (1 John 3:4). This is in many ways the most important definition of sin in the New Testament. It reminds us that God has given us His law, His own *nomos*, summarised for us in the Ten Commandments, and man has rebelled against it. Man has not simply transgressed it. He has gone against it with all the force of his being. Sin is not only transgression of the law. It is also want of conformity to the law and at last rejection of the law and of the law-giver Himself. God meant man to live a *heteronomous* existence, that is, an existence under the law of another; or, more narrowly, a *theonomous* existence, under the law of God. But man wants to be autonomous (auto - nomos). He wants to be his own law and so he throws off God's law by not only defying it, but rejecting it in principle. Sin, then, is persistent, constant violation of the law of God in our own personal lives.

This definition reminds us that sin in its very nature is anomalous. The English word 'anomalous' comes from this same Greek word, *anomia*: without law. If something is an anomaly, that means it goes against all law and all reason, and that is a marvellous way of describing sin. Sin is the ultimate anomaly.

We are always reluctant to accept that sin cannot be understood. We want to ask, How? and, Why? How did it come? Why did God permit it? We want to reason through all those questions. But we have to come back to this: Sin is the end of law. Sin is an anomaly, and an anomaly by definition is what is beyond reason and what cannot be understood. How can we understand or explain how sin came into heaven? There was this great, brilliant angel, now known as Satan, but also known as Lucifer, the Light-bearer. He was perfectly blessed, magnificently intelligent, morally upright and totally integrated. Why should he choose to sin? How can I explain the Luciferian decision to rebel against God? How can I explain the lawlessness of the Light-bearer? Why did the Light-bearer choose darkness? I have no answer to that at all.

Nor do I have any answer to the question, Why did Adam choose to sin? There was no need, no defect, no pressure, no threat, no danger, nothing to be gained. The Satanic arguments look so absurd and yet the first man freely chose to sin.

We have an even greater dilemma in the fact that the Christian (newborn, indwelt by the Spirit of God, united to Christ, rooted and built up in Him, in possession of all these spiritual impulses and resources and driven by a dynamic towards holiness) chooses to sin. The Christian sins and (I say this advisedly) sins in union with Christ. He cannot say to God, 'Lord, suspend the union while I sin,' because at this level what God joins together man cannot put asunder. What a monstrous anomaly it is: a redeemed soul united to a risen Saviour committing an act of lawlessness. We are so tolerant of sin in ourselves. Instead, we should be outraged and angry. It was C H Spurgeon, I think, who once said, 'The only heresy to which I have any inclination is perfectionism.' He was trying to express how absurd it is that a believer should sin. The Apostle John says, in fact, that it is impossible (1 John 3:9). John's reason has a very modern ring to it: because the Christian is born of God, because the sperm of God is in him, he cannot sin. John wants us to know that when we sin we are committing the gravest anomaly and perpetrating the most appalling absurdity because, as Paul tells us, we are sinning in union with Christ (1 Corinthian 6:15). Great damage has been done by our attempts to evade the force of this teaching. Daily, we do this absurd, impossible thing and take it in our stride, as if it were the most natural thing in the world that a Christian should sin. Sin is that which absolutely ought not to be, anywhere, and least of all in a Christian.

The origin of sin

Having considered something of the nature of sin, we can now look at the question of its origin. Here we find a very sharp divide between modern theories and biblical theology. According to all the modern theories, man at his point of origin is a sinner. He is only one mutation removed from the brute. He is controlled by his animal nature, by impulse, by appetite and by lust. He is a savage; and in his very first breath he is a sinner, a low-born, depraved sinner.

The great difficulty with this theory, quite apart from it being unbiblical, is that it makes sin a necessity of our human existence. It roots sin in the constitution, even in the metaphysics, of man. It says, 'Man has always been a sinner. He is a sinner by necessity of his nature, by genetic programming, by force of environment.' Here again we catch up with the determinism so prevalent in modern thought: this human being, who has never been anything but a sinner, cannot be anything but a sinner.

The Bible's story of the Fall is, apart from all else, a relief from the problems inherent in such a doctrine. According to modern theology, man, as created by God, was a sinner. According to the Bible, man, as made by God, was upright. He was made in God's image. He was absolutely sinless. Apart from any other argument in its favour, the doctrine of the Fall relieves God of the guilt of creating a sinner. In most modern forms of non-evangelical theology man is a sinner at his origin; and that means that the responsibility for his sinfulness devolves upon his Creator. In the Bible, by contrast, God creates man upright.

I have a horror of anything which reflects adversely on Adam. I do not like to hear him in any way belittled. I even hesitate to contrast him too unfavourably with Christ. There is a contrast, of course. But Adam was glorious. He was holy. He was not neutral, ambivalent between good and evil. He had a positive bias and inclination to the good. He was a magnificent example of the creativity of God. Let us resist, then, any suggestion that belittles him, or detracts from his intelligence, his blessedness and his power. Whatever man is today he is by virtue not of his creation but of his fall.

The Fall is a reminder, first of all, that sin began in Heaven among the angels. It came into our human existence only through this fallen angel, Satan, the great tempter. He got at Adam through Eve, and he got at Eve through deception. The attack on Adam was not frontal. It was devious. So often, temptation comes to us in the same way: through those we respect and love. More solemnly still, we ourselves often become temptations to those we love. Whenever we command affection, we have it in our power to become a spiritual danger to others, as Eve did to Adam.

The second thing is that sin came in through deception. Eve, the woman, was deceived. The narrative emphasises that the serpent was 'more subtle' than any other creature (Genesis 3:1). He sowed in Eve's heart the suspicion that God was being very harsh: "Is it true that God has forbidden all the trees of the garden?" Her response reveals that she had caught the serpent's spirit: 'He said not to eat of the tree in the middle of the garden, or to touch it.' God had said nothing about not touching it. The serpent then eroded her confidence in God's threat, 'You will not die' (verse 4). But above all he said to her, 'Look, God is holding you down. He knows that if you take this fruit you will be like God and you will know good and evil' (verse 5). He has sown the seed of suspicion: all the trees? He has sown the seed of doubt: you will not die. And he has sown the seed of ambition: you will be like God. Poor Eve violated God's law in this great confidence that thereby she was going to be like God. You see the marvellous anti-climax in verse 7. She had Satan's promise, You will know good and evil! After the Fall, what did she know? That she was naked! That, surely, is the greatest anti-climax in history.

The extent of sin
What of the extent of sin? How far does it reach?

The first part of the answer is that sin is universal. It embraces every single member of the human race: 'For all have sinned, and come short of the glory of God' (Romans 3:23). There are, of course, variations in guilt and depravity, but the Bible is adamant that sin is absolutely universal. This does not mean, unfortunately, that *conviction* of sin is universal. Many human beings live lives of perfect complacency. They have no sense whatever of sin. God had to send a prophet to tell David that he was guilty of glaring iniquity (2 Samuel 11 and 12). It is difficult to believe, after all he had done, that he had no sense of his own sin. But it is a great picture of conviction of sin, a reminder that only God can really tell us the truth about ourselves.

Secondly, sin affects all of us totally. *Total depravity* (a notorious phrase that invariably raises people's hackles) means that according to biblical teaching every single aspect of our human personality is affected by sin. This does not mean that all human beings are equally evil. It does not mean that any human being is as bad as he might be. And it certainly does not mean that all human beings are devils or demons. There are real gradations in sin, there is real progress in sin and there is a real distinction between the human and the demonic. What we mean by total depravity is that, having made due allowance for every single variation, for all the restraints of common grace and for all the adornments of personality which we find in our human situation, it still remains that in every human being the totality of his humanness is affected by sin.

His mind is sinful. He cannot think straight. He cannot make proper deductions. He cannot pursue proper arguments. In the gathering of information, in organising it, in reasoning from it, his intellect is sinful. It will function in a way that is anti-God, because 'the carnal mind is enmity against God' (Romans 8:7). Human thought-processes, human presuppositions and assumptions and human logic are all hostile to God. It is completely wrong to imagine that the reasoning faculties remain unimpaired. The distortions of sin, the anti-God bias, has come in even at the level of understanding and intellect. We think crookedly. We think in an ungodly way.

This is equally true of our human emotions. Our feelings are depraved. The wrong things make us happy and the wrong things make us sad. And over and above that, of course, we have all the neuroses: the depression, anxiety and discontent that sin has brought into our human situation. That is why we have so much clinical disorder in the realm of the emotions. It is all rooted in sin. That does not mean that it may not require and yield to clinical treatment. But the disorder itself is rooted in sin.

And there is sin in our affections, too, in the very love that we manifest. This is why *eros* (the most beautiful and noble thing in the world) is also the most destructive and the most horrific, wreaking more havoc than any other force in the moral universe.

There is sin also in the human will. Our wills are in bondage. 'How often I have longed to gather your children together, as a hen gathers her chicks under her wings, but you were not willing,' says the Lord in Matthew 23:37.

There is sin even in the conscience. We cannot assume, as we often do, that the conscience, God's monitor, remains unaffected. Frequently, the light within us is darkness. Many of the fiercest of the church's persecutors have been men of stringent conscience. Saul of Tarsus thought he was doing God's service by trying to strangle the church in its cradle. Throughout history, those who have been most virulent in harassing God's church have often been men of great principle: men like Marcus Aurelius, an outstandingly upright Roman emperor whose conscience nevertheless impelled him to persecute the church of God. And all of us know from our own experience, as we grow and mature in our Christian lives, that we cannot afford to go by our consciences. Our consciences need to be enlightened.

The Bible confronts us, then, with this terrible fact that we are depraved totally. The Christian has no quarrel with this doctrine. It is one thing in our spiritual lives we can test empirically for ourselves and know it to be only too true. When the Bible says that the heart is deceitful above all things and hopelessly wicked, we instantly know that this is absolutely correct.

We can put it another way. Every human life is marred by *original sin*. This is what the Anglican Articles call *birth sin* and what philosophers call *radical evil*. The Bible tells us that this is the way we are born: 'In sin did my mother conceive me' (Psalm

51:5). The Psalmist went to God and said, 'Lord, it's not the things that I've done recently – it's not that alone that bothers me. In fact, it isn't what I've done that bothers me at all. It's the way that I am! It's the shape: it's all wrong. I was shapen in iniquity. I was wrong right from the womb. The whole mould was wrong. The programme was wrong. The trouble is *me*: my shape.' 'I abhor myself,' said Job (Job 42:6).

The Shorter Catechism defines original sin like this: 'the want of original righteousness, and the corruption of [our] whole nature' (Answer 18). In virtually any reference to Calvinism by an academic or a man of letters you will find great scorn poured upon this idea of total depravity. Yet surely it is the teaching of the Bible that our whole nature (humanness as found in every human being and all the humanness found in every human being) is affected by sin and corruption. Some philosophical theologians tell us that sin is a defect, the absence of a quality, the absence of good. But the Bible does not portray sin as a mere defect. It is a corruption, a putrefaction, a cancer in the life of a human being. It is a rampant, productive, energetic, multiplying, self-propagating entity. It is fierce. It is fire. It is living. It is a force, a tremendously powerful force. And our century has experienced its force in a degree beyond precedent in human history. We have seen it in the horrors of the Pogroms and of the Holocaust. We have seen what human beings (not savages, but literate, artistic, creative, intellectual, sensitive human beings; good fathers, devoted husbands, loyal friends) are capable of. We have no right to stand by and say that we do not belong with them, that they are wholly different from us and that we could never have done these things. What God is showing us in these terrible tabloids is what our nature is capable of (the nature of each one of us) given the requisite conditions.

The effects of sin

We have seen something of the nature of sin, its origin and its extent. What about its effects? The short answer is that sin leads to death, in all its forms. But in Genesis 3, the key element is not simply death but the alienation which sin has brought into our human existence. This alienation has various forms.

First, there is alienation within man himself: 'they knew that they were naked' (Genesis 3:7). They were overwhelmed with a sense of shame, with a sense of the vulnerability of their own lives. They had to hide themselves from God. They had to cover up before God. They were divided within themselves. In conviction of sin the Christian experiences the divided-self in a unique way as he endorses God's judgement upon his life. But it is very important to remember that, for believers, this sense of shame and self-abhorrence is taken away, or should be taken away, in Christ. God has accepted us, and we must learn to accept ourselves. We are told that we are precious to Him and that we matter to Him, and every redeemed child of God can begin to build a legitimate and God-given self-esteem on that knowledge. It is important, of course, to experience conviction of sin. But if there is an above-average prevalence of neuroses within some believing communities it is due to the neglecting of this other aspect, this voice from God that says, '*You* are the salt of the earth.' Certainly we are sinners and we know our own spiritual nakedness. But in redemption God has given us back ourselves, put together again and re-integrated. Who among us does not need, along with the motivation of criticism and denunciation, the word of encouragement which says, 'Look, you really matter'? Love, God's love, accepts us as we are.

Secondly, there is alienation between person and person. Adam and his wife fell into instant tension because of their sin: 'The woman whom thou gavest to be with me ...' (verse 12). The whole relationship has fallen apart because sin has divided them. They thought they were going to be like God. They did this thing to make themselves 'Godlike and divine', and at once they showed how un-Godlike and un-divine they were by falling into discord and disharmony. But this is a mirror-image of redemption. God does not simply reconcile us to Himself. He also reconciles us to one another. In Ephesians 2:14 the 'middle wall of partition' speaks of barriers between Jew and Gentile, between man and man, between group and group. God has taken those barriers down in the Lord Jesus Christ. It is of enormous importance that our churches should reflect this. If we want to evangelise the world effectively, we must ensure that our churches are places of reconciliation where people find acceptance and see harmony and accord.

Thirdly, there is alienation between man and his environment. The ground is cursed (verse 17). Man and the created order were made to work together in harmony, man subduing it and tilling it and keeping it and exercising dominion over it. Then with his sin it all went wrong and all the tensions we have today between ourselves and our environment began to appear. Today, we have to earn our bread by the sweat of our faces; and even as we toil our stewardship is often so prodigal and so irresponsible that we pile up insoluble problems for future generations.

Fourthly, and most important of all, sin brought alienation between man and God. Adam hides from God. He was made for God and yet now he is on the run from God. We have already seen that sin affects the intellect. This is brought out so clearly in the narrative in Genesis 3. This man who had been so clear-headed only moments before is now hiding from God under a tree! He thinks God cannot see him under a tree! His mind has gone, because of sin. Man is still in that same position: hiding from God behind fig-leaves and trees.

Conclusion

I close on two notes.

First, sin remains in the regenerate. We have seen that it ought not to. But it does. We are born again, we are Christians and yet sin rages within us. Our lives fall short of their potential. Our lives are not straight. They are transgressive and anomalous. There can be no bigger mistake than to forget this power and force and prevalence of sin in our lives. Indeed, we must build our whole spiritual strategy on this fact. We must remember that because there is sin in us we are spiritually inflammable. One thought from Hell, one suggestion, one opportunity to sin, can set

our whole lives ablaze. That means that, as Christians, we have
to live far from the boundary. We cannot live at the outer limits
of the permitted. So often, we do just that. We ask, How far can
I go? and we forget that the limits of the legal may not be the
limits of our own tolerance of temptation. We must learn to draw
the boundary, not at the point of illegality but at the point of our
own temptability. Indwelling sin is not an abstract thing. It is
intensely personal. The Christian, despite being in Christ, indwelt
by His Spirit, born again and so splendidly resourced, is still so
temptable!

The answer to all this sin is Christ. Evangelical religion, as we
saw, begins with a sense of sin. We will never produce evangelicals
if we eliminate this emphasis. Evangelicalism is not, first and
foremost, belief in an inerrant Bible. It begins with a certain kind
of self-understanding: the knowledge of our own guilt, our own
depravity, our own alienation from God. That is the best, in fact,
the only hermeneutic. The only key to the scriptures is a sense of
sin. The only proper standpoint from which to view Christ is as
a lost sinner. The only proper perspective on the cross is that of
the convicted sinner. Christ came to seek and to save that which
was lost; and what a splendid job the Lord made of it! Christ is
the total answer. Christ puts us right with God, all our sins
forgiven, our reputations vindicated, our names enrolled in the
family-register of God. We have exactly the same relationship to
God as Jesus Christ. He is begotten, we are adopted, and in its
way that is a mighty difference. But there is no difference in our
rights: an adopted son has the same rights as a natural son. We
have fellowship with Christ in His whole standing before God.
God in Christ has put us absolutely right. He has dealt with all the
guilt of our sin.

The sad thing is that we so often leave it there and forget that
Christ is also the answer to sin ontologically and structurally.
The redemptive work of Christ does not terminate in justification,
but in sanctification. That is the Bible's overriding concern: to
conform us to the image of His Son. Christ will so deal with us
that one day our lives will no longer fall short of the mark. They

will no longer be inequitable, transgressive and lawless. Instead, they will conform exactly to God's objective for us. Our lives will meet the target. Our lives will be straight. Our lives will be on God's road. Our lives will gloriously fulfil the law. Christ will end all the alienation. He will put us together within ourselves. He will put us right with each other. He will put us right with our environment, securing in the last Adam the fulfilment of the mandates reneged on by the First.

But above all, Christ will end the alienation between ourselves and God and bring us so close to Him that the New Testament's promises in this connection almost defy belief. His own prayer was 'that where I am, there ye may be also' (John 14:3). We shall be as close to God, psychologically, spiritually, emotionally and effectively, as His only begotten Son, Jesus Christ.

Sin is the disease, Christ is the remedy. The more we reflect on our plight the more we see its gravity; and the more we see its gravity the more we appreciate the glory of God's deliverance through the gospel of His grace.

7

The Covenant

We meet the word covenant frequently in both the Old and New Testaments. It is an ordinary, secular word which does not in itself have any special technical or spiritual meaning. For example, we read of covenants between individuals such as David and Jonathan, of commercial contracts, even of pacts between various nations. What the Bible has done is to take an everyday word and give it its own special meaning.

General points

Three general points can be made about biblical covenants.

First of all, in covenants between God and man there is always a firm emphasis on God's initiative and God's sovereignty. The covenant is never a pact between equals. It is not some kind of negotiated settlement. It is always God who takes the first step. In Genesis 9, for example, the covenant with Noah is established very much in terms of God's own initiative: 'God said to Noah.' With regard to Abraham, God again makes the first approach. The redemptive and spiritual covenant always has as its background God's own grace. God announces His promises and lays down His terms. That is especially true, of course, in the Christian covenant. Man does not negotiate his own salvation with God. The whole process has its origin in sovereign grace. The covenant is a disposition arranged and announced by God and accepted by man virtually as God's vassal. This asymmetry is an essential element in the redemptive covenant.

Secondly, notwithstanding this divine initiative, the covenant is always two-sided. Sometimes the importance of God's sovereign initiative is emphasised in such a way as to minimise the importance of man's response, but a covenant is by definition bi-lateral, and when it comes to the redemptive covenant, this is no less so. It is true that God takes the initiative and that God bears the cost. Yet the human response always remains an important element. If we go back, for example, to the Abrahamic covenant in Genesis 17, we find a clear emphasis on the part played by Abraham's faith. There is no covenant without this human response. In the Christian covenant, faith remains indispensable. John 3:16, for example, tells us that 'God so loved the world'. That is God's sovereign initiative. And yet God's salvation reaches only those who believe: 'whoever believes in him shall not perish but have everlasting life.' There are forms of gospel proclamation which convey the impression that we simply announce God's unilateral, one-sided accomplishment of salvation. We are told merely to inform men that their sins are forgiven and that they are already sons of God. There is no emphasis at all on the human response. In the Bible, by contrast, there is a firm emphasis on 'whoever believes'. The indicatives are always followed by imperatives: 'The kingdom of God is at hand: repent ye, and believe the gospel' (Mark 1:15). That essential characteristic remains even in the redemptive covenant between God and man. The human response is an indispensable element in our experience of salvation.

Many theologians today tell us that covenant does not mean contract: it means something much more like a marriage agreement. Now, of course, a marriage is not commercial. Yet marriage, intensely personal though it is, is always a two-sided agreement. It involves mutual obligations. In the same way, the redemptive covenant involves not only divine input and divine imposition, but also the human response of faith and obedience. This is not to minimise the asymmetry arising from the divine initiative and cost-bearing but it is to insist, equally, on the essential two-sidedness of the covenant. 'Abraham believed God': only at that point did he become righteous.

The third general point is this: it is due to the fact of divine covenant that our human lives have a substantial element of predictability. If we contrast the people of God under the Old Testament with the surrounding nations we find that those nations worshipped a great multiplicity of gods, all of whom behaved in an extremely arbitrary fashion. They were irascible and unpredictable, given to outrageous behaviour, controlled by mood and passion. That meant that ancient man lived in an environment which was, in effect, demonised and those demons made human existence highly unpredictable. That is a great contrast to the state of things among the covenant people of God. Israel had one God and that God had made a covenant with his people which gave a great framework of stability. The first man knew where he stood with God. Adam knew that, provided he observed God's directive, he would remain in a loving relationship with his Creator. Abraham and all his descendants had the same privilege. They knew the terms of the covenant. They knew that if they kept the covenant they would enjoy the blessing of God. The same was true of Noah. He was given certain assurances by God.

In the New Testament, too, the people of God are in covenant with Him. They know the terms of that covenant. They know the great promises of God. They even know 'that all things work together for good to them that love God' (Romans 8:28). That is the foremost factor in our religious security. As we live in relation to our environment we have a confidence based on the covenant of God. As we face history, we have the same privilege. We don't know the future but we know the God of the future. We know that He is in control. We know the terms of His covenant.

Against that background we can now look at the four great biblical covenants.

The Adamic covenant

First of all, there is the Adamic covenant. God laid before the first man certain stipulations. In particular, He announced that if Adam ate a certain fruit he would face death. This is a rather peculiar covenant because, in essence, it is not so much a conditional promise as a conditional threat. God tells Adam, 'If you eat of it you will surely die' (Genesis 2:17). But enfolded within this there was total security for mankind because man knew that provided he observed this one condition he was secure with God. Bear in mind all the elements of grace: the abundance of God's provision for man in terms of all the other fruit of the garden and the ability God had given man to keep His covenant. Provided man avoided this one fruit he would continue not only to exist but to exist in fellowship with God. God did not say to man, 'The day you eat this fruit you will cease to exist.' He said, 'If you eat this fruit then you will cease to live', that is, 'in fellowship with Me.' In other words, God was giving man a solemn promise that if he avoided this one fruit then he would continue to enjoy forever this stable, loving, rich relationship with God. Man, as we know, under the devil's promptings, violated God's conditions and came under the operation of God's threat. He lost all; but he lost it covenantally. He lost it despite the tenderness and generosity of God's stipulation, despite the abundant provision of grace by which to comply with the stipulation and despite knowing exactly where he stood with God.

Some people have enormous trouble with this because they find the whole notion of a covenant of works distasteful. But it is clear beyond a doubt that the reason why man was expelled from the garden was his disobedience. There is nothing whatever inherently improper in a covenant of works. Our very salvation rests on the obedience of the Last Adam and that obedience was compliance with a covenant of works. Christ saved us by finishing the work given to Him to do (John 17:4). He was 'obedient unto death' (Philippians 2:8). 'By the obedience of one shall many be made righteous' (Romans 5:19). There were, indeed, gracious elements in the Adamic covenant. But we must accept that the primary relation between God and man is a relationship of works and obedience. That has never been abrogated. It is still true that the man who does the things contained in the law shall live by them. More important, it is still true that Christ saved us by putting His own personal obedience over against Adam's disobedience.

The Covenant with Noah
Secondly, there is God's covenant with Noah, recorded in Genesis 9. It is sometimes called the Covenant of Preservation or

the Covenant of Nature. In essence, it is God's gracious and sovereign announcement that so long as the world lasts it will never again be destroyed as it was at the time of the Deluge. It is a covenant God makes not only with man, but also 'with every living creature' (verse 10). It is important to bear in mind the psychology of this. Here was Noah in the aftermath of the Flood, trembling and quaking because he had been face to face with the elemental forces of destruction. He had seen the havoc wrought by the Flood. Here was cataclysm on an unsurpassable scale. Noah must have faced the future with foreboding. He must have been deeply distrustful of his environment. What kind of world was he living in, where such havoc could be wrought and where life in all its forms could be brought so close to extinction? Here he was in the aftermath of the trauma, with the pressure off, his taut nerves relaxing, the challenge over, peculiarly vulnerable to depression and despair. Into this situation God projected His great assurance that while the world lasted there would never again be cataclysm on this scale: 'Never again will all life be cut off by the waters of a flood; never again will there be a flood to destroy the earth' (Genesis 9:11); 'As long as the earth endures, seedtime and harvest, cold and heat, summer and winter, day and night will never cease' (Genesis 8:22).

This is a covenant made with the whole human race: 'I now establish my covenant with you and with your descendants after you and with every living creature that was with you ...' (Genesis 9:9f.). Here is a great divine pledge which is particularly and even poignantly relevant to our own troubled century, a century which is acutely aware of the perils of ecology and the pressures of conservation. We know the forces latent in the world around us and we know how delicate is the balance of those forces. We know how close we are to environmental disaster. How we need this divine reassurance as we reflect on the greenhouse effect and the threat to the ozone layer and the perils of nuclear energy and nuclear weaponry: all these things that have come out of the bottle and that will not go back into the bottle! We must live on a knife-edge of insecurity unless we recall God's great pledge that never again, until the end of history, will He allow global disruption of the seasons or the unleashing of those forces of destruction which ravaged the world of Noah's day.

But we cannot take this as a blanket comfort. The Noahic covenant does not mean that we cannot have localised famines, localised floods and localised wars of appalling ferocity and inhumanity. It does not preclude the possibility of nuclear war because we have had nuclear war already in our recent history. What it does mean is that God is promising that there will be no global catastrophe comparable to the Flood. I am not prepared to say that this gives us the comfort that we cannot have catastrophe: even nuclear war on an unimaginable scale. I do not find that that kind of faith has any warrant in the divine promise. But God is saying that, by some process or other, He is going to secure that never again will there be disruption of the seasons, of day and night, of the earth's fertility. The nuclear shadow must be limited by these divine promises. One of the great nuclear horrors we face is the possibility of a nuclear winter, involving virtually total darkness and sub-zero temperatures and the eclipse of all life. That scenario will not fit into the promise God is giving us in Genesis 8 and 9. God is promising us seed-time and harvest, cold and heat, summer and winter, day and night. These things shall not cease.

It is also interesting that at precisely this point God should bring in the whole dimension of population control, because this is perhaps the most common reaction of modern man to his environmental problems. Frank Fraser Darling, for example, who in his Reith Lectures[1] first brought ecological issues to public notice, strongly emphasised that pollution was the consequence of man's search for food. This was the real cause of such phenomena as over-grazing and deforestation. The answer, Darling argued, was to limit population and thus to limit the demand for food. 'All governments,' he wrote, 'should boldly face their responsibility to work out population and nutritional policies, not play the opposite game of subsidising irresponsibly productive families.'[2]

We may be confident that Noah was not worried at all about overpopulation, but he was probably very concerned about the kind of world he lived in and he might well have said, 'No sane man would wish to bring children into this kind of world'. That is a very common argument today. It made very good sense in the aftermath of the Deluge, just as it does in the shadow of the greenhouse effect and nuclear holocaust. At that very point, God says to man, 'Be ye fruitful, and multiply' (Genesis 9:7). It was a challenge to Noah's faith. We have, of course, no right to use our sexuality irrationally, because we are not beasts and no man should bring into the world more children than he and his wife can care and provide for. But any birth-control which is a reflection of un-faith, of a lack of confidence in the Sovereign Provider, is illegitimate for a Christian. We cannot refuse to have families simply because of ecological fears. That is what this covenant is arguing against. It is coming right into Noah's existential situation: into his fear. It also comes into our twentieth century fears: our fear of world war, of over-population, of nuclear horror, of ecological disaster. It says to us, 'Be fruitful and multiply', and our glad compliance is an expression of our faith in God and of our confidence in the future of the earth. Not for a moment does this discharge us from our environmental responsibility. We must use our environment rationally as we use our sexuality rationally. But clearly, one of the great stipulations of God's covenant is that we should not fearfully refuse to procreate.

Two more things about this covenant.

God gives His sign in the rainbow: 'This is the sign of the covenant .... I have set my rainbow in the clouds and it will be the sign of the covenant between me and the earth' (Genesis 9:12-13). God may simply have used an already existing phenomenon and given it special symbolism. In any case, the rainbow is now the great sign of God's Covenant of Preservation. There is an allusion to this in Revelation 4:3: 'A rainbow ... encircled the throne' (NIV). Here is a reminder that God's sovereignty is set in the rainbow, in the context of a covenant of peace and preservation.

He will never use His sovereignty in a way that is destructive. One day, of course, God will regenerate the universe. But that is not destructive. It is re-creative. God is a God of covenant. He has pledged Himself to maintain and preserve this world. And He has given us His rainbow as a sign that, in Christ, He is at peace with us.

There is also an allusion to the Noahic covenant in the baptism of Christ, when the Spirit of God came upon him in the form of a dove (Matthew 3:16; John 1:32). Just as the dove reminded Noah that the strife which provoked the Deluge was at an end, so here, at the very point of His publicly assuming our sins, the dove of God's peace was sign and seal to the baptised Christ that through His ministry there would be peace between God and man.

The Covenant of Redemption

The third great biblical covenant is the Covenant of Redemption. This covenant is specifically between God the Father and God the Son and should, in my judgement, be distinguished from the Covenant of Grace. There is no explicit reference in the New Testament to such a covenant and some theologians of unquestioned orthodoxy (for example, Thomas Boston) have refused to accept the idea of a separate Covenant of Redemption. However, this covenant is essential for two reasons.

First of all, it is essential if we are to understand the relation between Christ and His Father. Why is Christ in the world? He is in the world to shed His blood, the blood of the new covenant (Hebrews 12:24). He is in the world because of His specific relationship with the Father. The Father sent Him, the Father gave Him commandments and the Father gave Him promises. He was able to go to the Father and say, 'I have finished the work. Now you must fulfil your promises.'

We cannot begin to understand the relation of the work of Christ to the will of God unless we see it in the light of a pre-temporal, pre-incarnation agreement between God the Father and God the Son, in which the Son agrees to come to complete a specific task and the Father promises to uphold Him and to reward Him. That is how Christ could claim, 'I have finished the work.' His service was covenantal. He knew where He stood with God. He knew exactly what He had to do. He knew what God required. That is why He could describe Himself as the Servant of the Lord (Matthew 20:28). And that is why His work could be summed up by Paul in these terms: He was 'obedient unto death' (Philippians 2:8). Obedient to what? To the covenant stipulation.

Secondly, we need this covenant to understand the relationship between Christ and His people. He is His people's representative and substitute. He is the church's bridegroom. How does that relationship come to exist? Does it exist merely by divine decree? Does God simply announce that Christ is Head of His people? No! It comes about, surely, because there is a people given to Him and assumed by Him. He loved the church. He became by agreement the church's Head. He became their Representative, their Vicar and their Substitute. The headship of Christ cannot be understood apart from consent and agreement within the depths of the godhead itself.

The parties to this covenant are, as we have seen, God the Father and God the Son. The stipulation is that Christ will do everything that is necessary for the salvation of His people. What we receive freely in the Covenant of Grace Christ earned by His compliance with the Covenant of Redemption. For Him, it was a covenant of obedience. From this point of view, Christ did do no more than obey and fulfil the law. Laying down His life was a covenant stipulation. Sinless obedience, fulfilling all righteousness, was a covenant stipulation. The Saviour's righteousness is covenant right-eousness. The covenant-*breaking* of the First Man (and of all mankind) is covered by the covenant-*keeping* of the Last Man, the Lord Jesus Christ. 'This is the blood of the covenant' (Hebrews 9:20). And so for Him, the covenant was a covenant of works. He was righteous because He did and suffered all that the covenant required. He kept faith with God; and on the cross He cried, 'It is finished.' He had run the race set before Him.

What are the promises of the Covenant of Redemption? In

essence, everything necessary for the salvation of the church. Some of it is obvious enough: 'If you bear sin, if you atone for sin, if you endure the curse, then there is forgiveness for your people.' Christ purchased forgiveness and justification and adoption. He secured a change in our whole relationship with God. We must remember, however, that by His covenant-keeping Christ also purchased a change in our personal spiritual condition. In other words, by His cross He secured the new birth, the gift of faith, the gift of sanctification, of perseverance and, finally, of glorification.

We can put it like this: what is required in the Covenant of Grace is provided in the Covenant of Redemption. For example, God requires faith and repentance. But Christ has actually secured these for His people. Similarly, God requires sanctification. He calls upon us to struggle, to mortify sin, to grow in grace and to keep on renewing ourselves. But how magnificent it is that on the cross Christ purchased holiness for us! This does not in the least modify the importance of the struggle towards holiness. And yet, so often, the New Testament links the cross not with justification but with sanctification. Take, for example, that great passage in Ephesians 5:26,27: Christ loved the church 'that He might sanctify and cleanse it with the washing of water by the word, that he might present it to himself a glorious church, not having spot, or wrinkle or any such thing; but that it should be holy and without blemish'. On the cross, Christ purchased for His people a complete salvation. He was there as their covenant Head. He obeyed in their place. And by His obedience He secured everything they need: objectively, subjectively, forensically, ontologically; a change in relationship, a change in nature; justification, sanctification. It is all there!

The Covenant of Grace

In some ways this is the most difficult to understand of all the covenants. In particular it is very difficult to be clear as to who are the precise parties to this covenant. God is one party. But in our confessions and catechisms there is great uncertainty and even some measure of confusion as to the other. Is it God and the elect? Is it God and mankind? Or is it God and the believer? The Shorter Catechism is totally non-committal: 'God having, out of his mere good pleasure, from all eternity, elected some to everlasting life, did enter into a covenant of grace, to deliver them out of the estate of sin and misery ...' (Answer 20). A covenant of grace with whom? There is no answer. The Westminster Confession of Faith (Chap. VII) is equally silent, stating only that by this covenant God 'freely offereth unto sinners life and salvation by Jesus Christ'. Only the Larger Catechism is specific: 'The covenant of grace was made with Christ as the second Adam, and in him with all the elect as his seed' (Answer 31).

The trouble with this answer is that it does not distinguish between the Covenant of Grace and the Covenant of Redemption. My own decision (since I have to make one) is that the Covenant of Grace is between God and the believer; and I take that decision because the archetypal biblical revelation of the Covenant of Grace is the covenant of God with Abraham. The patriarch, at the point of covenant institution, is not there as an elect person. He is not there as a sinner. He is not there simply as a man. He is there as a believer.

This is surely an encouraging way of understanding our own salvation. To be saved is to be in covenant relationship with God. There is a covenant (dare I say, a *contract*?) between me and God. God is irrevocably committed to me. I may be a very humble believer, a very immature believer or a very untalented believer. But every believer is in covenant with God. It's a marriage bond. It's a treaty. It's a contract. It is totally secure because God is righteous; and God's being righteous means that God is a covenant-keeper. That is what the great Old Testament word *lovingkindness* (Hebrew *hesed*) means. God never reneges on a contract. He never breaks a promise. He never issues an idle threat.

Believers, then, are in covenant with God. They are married to Him: 'Thy Maker is thy husband' (Isaiah 54:5). This is as true on the personal level as it is on the collective and corporate level.

But what is the promise? In a word, again, salvation. But it is put in a great variety of ways.

For example, God promises the believer life. This is why the covenant is sometimes called the Covenant of Life. Alternatively, it is put this way: 'I will be God unto thee.' That's what God said to Abraham (Genesis 17:7) and although the words occur in the very first half of Genesis there is no more glorious promise anywhere in the Bible. There is commitment: 'I will be your God!' And of course, it is bilateral: 'they shall be my people.' We are for Him. We are committed to Him. We speak so often of commitment, of committed Christians. Of course, there is no other kind. But do we see our commitment in covenantal terms? We have no option but to be committed. We are contracted to be committed, because that is the covenant: 'You shall be my people.' But the glorious thing is that God is committed to us: committed to being our God, our very personal God.

Martin Luther said once that religion consists in personal pronouns. That is why Paul could say, '*My* God shall supply all your need' (Philippians 4:19). See the glory of that! The covenant promise is tantamount to God saying, 'I shall use my God-ness for you. All my God-ness is yours. All my wealth (of attributes, of prerogatives, of functions), all I have and all I am is yours.' That is God's commitment. And it is as true for each individual believer as if no other entity existed. We have God's undivided attention. He is for us in all the splendour of His resources.

Or again, we have the great promise of Galatians 3:14 that the blessing of Abraham has come upon the Gentiles. Paul explains it in these terms: We have received the promise of the Spirit through faith. What is the blessing? The promise of the Spirit. The Charismatic Movement makes a distinction between having Christ and having the Spirit and tells us that we can be Christians and yet lack the Spirit in the richer manifestations of His presence. But here is the Apostle Paul telling us that what we Christians have is the blessing of Abraham; that that blessing consists in the promise of the Spirit; and that we get that through faith. In other words, if we are Christians at all, if we are in covenant with God at all, then we have the Spirit because the Spirit is God's great covenant promise.

This is where the debate with the Charismatic Movement should be pitched, not at the point of tongue-speaking. The central issue is this: Can you be in Christ and not be in the Holy Spirit? As far as the New Testament is concerned, our relationship with Christ and our relationship with the Holy Spirit are symmetrical. We cannot divorce being in Christ from being in the Spirit. All the promises of God are yea and amen in Christ Jesus (2 Corinthians 1:20). All the promises! Because I am in Christ! The Charismatic Movement is doing exactly what the Galatian Christians were doing and what medieval Catholicism was doing: underestimating, minimising, eroding the significance of our being in Christ. The moment we are in Him we have everything: all the promises of God; everything that He has, because the moment we become believers we become heirs of God and joint-heirs with Christ (Romans 8:17).

Let us now look at the stipulation in this two-sided arrangement. The Shorter Catechism has the ideal word for it: 'God *requireth* of us faith in Jesus Christ, repentance unto life, with the diligent use of all the outward means ... ' (Answer 85). Faith and repentance are *requirements* of the covenant. That is what we must do: 'whosoever believes'. And that is what evangelism is all about. It is not about saying to people, 'Hi! all you people, you're all saved'; It is about saying to people, 'I have salvation for you if you believe in Christ.' 'What must I do to be saved? ... Believe on the Lord Jesus Christ and thou shalt be saved' (Acts 16:30 ff.). That faith is a covenant stipulation. It is something we must do if we wish to experience the salvation of God.

But let us always remember the asymmetry and the disproportion between the input of God and the input of man, between the grace of eternal love which offers its own Son, and this little thing that we bring, the empty hand that receives. There is disproportion. There is no balance and no correspondence between what God did and what God requires. And yet what God requires is an essential element in the arrangement, small and insignificant though it is.

So where does grace come in, if the human response is so

significant? We have the answer in the words of Augustine's great prayer: 'Lord, give what thou dost command and command what thou wilt.'[3] God requires faith. And yet, He also gives it. It is the gift of God, and that is where the whole tension between grace and works is finally resolved. That faith is *required*. It is *my* faith. It is my doing. I do it. And yet I do it by the grace of God: 'Give what thou dost command.' God commands faith. God gives faith.

It can be expressed in this way: the stipulation of the Covenant of Grace is faith, but that faith has been purchased for us in the Covenant of Redemption. Christ by His cross has secured that His people will believe and that His Spirit will give this grace and indeed all graces, to those in whose place He stands.

Conclusion

Lastly, it is a remarkable and solemn thing that the familiar words of the Great Commission of Matthew 28 are cast in the form of an ancient covenant. There is a preamble, 'All authority is given to me in heaven and in earth.' There is a stipulation, 'Go, teach all the nations.' And there is a promise, 'I am with you always.' What are we being told here? That the presence of God is covenantal: 'I am with you as you go and because you go.' If we divorce the promise from the stipulation, there is no presence. The preaching of the Word, the evangelising of the nations, church extension, outreach, bringing God's word to bear upon the lostness and blindness around us: it is all covenantal. That is the precondition of our enjoying the presence of God. We cannot invert the biblical order and say, 'We won't go; we're not ready; we are waiting for the presence.' It is the going church which alone enjoys the covenant promise of the presence of God.

References
1. Frank Fraser Darling, *Wilderness and Plenty*, London, 1970.
2. *op. cit.*, p. 81.
3. Augustine, *Confessions*, X.XXIX.

8

The Deity of Christ

The deity of Christ is, by any standard, a fundamental doctrine of the Christian faith. It is no mere academic matter. It is very much a religious matter because it involves the propriety of our worship of Jesus. If He is God, it is right to worship Him. If He is not God, then it is blasphemy and idolatry to worship Him. For that reason the whole of our religion is involved in this doctrine. That being so, it is hardly surprising that the doctrine has been under attack at many points in the church's history. What was probably the most dangerous phase of this attack took place in the fourth century at Alexandria when Arius began to argue that Jesus Christ was not God but a mere creature. Arius conceded that He was no ordinary creature. He was, he argued, the greatest of all creatures, a kind of median being between creator and creature, but certainly not God. He was not eternal, and there was a time when He did not exist. This heresy threatened the life of the church for some thirty years and God raised up the great Athanasius to combat it. What we call today the Nicene Creed is the result of this controversy.

The attack on the deity of Christ continues unabated in the twentieth century. It has had many manifestations not only in so-called Liberal theology but also, and most popularly, in the sect known as Jehovah's Witnesses. The most distinctive tenet of this sect is their outright denial of the deity of Jesus Christ. Their position is remarkably similar (in fact, almost identical) to that of the Arians of the fourth century. The doctrines, the arguments and the approach to scripture are in essence the same.

Arguments for the deity of Christ
In response to these attacks the church has marshalled a battery of arguments in favour of the full deity of our Lord and Saviour.

I want to emphasize, as firmly as I can, that as a matter of methodology it is a great mistake to confine our response to this attack to those parts of the New Testament which specifically describe Christ as God. There is no doubt, as we shall see, that the New Testament does very often describe Christ as God. But the proof of His deity is much wider than that. We simply must not allow Jehovah's Witnesses to limit the debate to the narrow question, Does the Bible call Jesus God? The deity of Christ pervades the entire New Testament. Let me catalogue the arguments briefly.

First of all, there are those New Testament passages which ascribe divine titles to Christ. Among such passages are those that speak of Jesus as God. But there are also others which speak of Him as Lord; yet others that call Him Son of God; and still others that call Him Son of Man. This last is particularly interesting. *Son of Man* in the Bible is not a designation of the Lord's human nature. It is a divine title, applied in Daniel 7, for example, to the pre-existent Messiah who exercises universal and eternal dominion. When Christ used the title He was saying, 'I am *that* Son of Man.'

Secondly, there are the New Testament passages which ascribe to Christ divine functions. They describe Him as Creator; as the Lord of Providence, upholding all things by the word of His power; and as Judge. All of these are divine functions. Jesus creates. Jesus preserves and governs. Jesus judges the world.

Thirdly, there are passages which ascribe to Christ divine attributes: for example, eternity and omnipotence. 'Before Abraham was, I am' (John 8:58). 'I am Alpha and Omega, the beginning and the ending, saith the Lord, which is, and which was, and which is to come, the Almighty' (Revelation 1:8). No mere creature can possess such qualities. They are uniquely and untransferably divine.

Fourthly, there are passages which ascribe to Christ divine prerogatives, especially the prerogative of worship: 'I fell at his feet as dead' (Revelation 1:17). The church consists of those who call on the name *of the Lord* (Acts 22:16). We make melody in our hearts *to the Lord* (Ephesians 5:19). The New Testament, in the most explicit fashion, portrays Christ as the object of divine worship.

My concern for the moment is to indicate the scope and breadth of the evidence. Jesus is given every possible divine designation. Jesus performs every divine function. Jesus possesses every divine attribute. Jesus enjoys every divine prerogative. These are the lines of evidence along which we have a right to argue for the deity of Christ. And note, too, that the evidence is to be found in every single layer of the New Testament. It is found not only in the Gospel of John and the Epistle to the Hebrews, the traditional quarries of anti-Arian arguments. It is found also in the Pauline epistles, in the synoptic gospels and in the book of Acts. We can even look behind our gospels and assert that the deity of Christ is found not only in the gospels themselves but in every identifiable source used by the evangelists. There is no level or segment or phase or form or source of New Testament teaching that does not portray a divine Christ.

Furthermore, that evidence is found at a very early stage in the history of the church. It is quite remarkable that there is not a trace in the New Testament of any debate about this doctrine. In the very earliest documents (*Galatians*, *First Thessalonians*, and the *Epistle of James*) taking us back to between 40 and 44 AD, we find the church already in full and unselfconscious possession of this doctrine, primarily because it was implicit in its worship of its Saviour.

This evidence is conveniently summarised in H. P. Liddon's Bampton Lectures, *The Divinity of our Lord*. Although over 120 years old, Liddon's work remains the greatest vindication of the doctrine in the English language. For a more modern treatment, you should consult the work of Hoskyns and Davey, *The Riddle of the New Testament* (London, 1958). This provides a brilliant argument to the effect that the Jesus 'of modern popular humanitarian or humanistic ideas' cannot be found anywhere in the New Testament.

It is an interesting fact that the Gospel of John, which

proclaims the deity of Christ with particular force and clarity, has, in the last 150 years, been under sustained attack by academic theologians. Indeed, most scholars today dismiss that gospel as entirely non-historical. Although there are human reasonings and scholarly arguments behind that approach it is difficult to dismiss the suspicion that it is really part of an all-out Satanic attack on the deity of our Lord. It is hardly surprising that a book which is so precious, precisely because of its testimony to Christ, should be singled out for a particularly vicious attack. That is the context in which we reflect upon this doctrine.

Jesus is God

We cannot here go into the arguments in detail, but we can devote some attention to those passages in the New Testament in which Jesus is referred to as God. As we saw, this is only part of the evidence. But it is a very important part.

Firstly, the opening words of the Gospel of John: 'In the beginning was the Word, and the Word was with God, and the Word was God.' This tells us three things about Christ. He was 'in the beginning'. He was 'with God'. And He 'was God'.

The words 'In the beginning' take us right back to Genesis 1:1: 'In the beginning God created the heaven and the earth.' John is telling us that in that beginning God did not create the Word, because the Word was already in being. John was no academic and yet he uses language with meticulous and brilliant skill, choosing the imperfect tense of the verb 'to be' to convey the idea of continuous, open-ended being. In verse 14 he says 'the Word was made flesh': the Word *became* flesh. But in the beginning He did not become. He was already in being. In fact, it was through Him that all things were made. Without Him was nothing made (verse 3).

And so we have this unlettered man writing what is arguably the world's greatest single piece of literature and in its very opening statement taking us back to the beginning of creation and telling us that when, in the beginning, God created the heavens and the earth, the Word was already in being.

John then tells us that the Word was 'with God'. The pronoun used here normally means *towards*; and this reminds us of the outgoing nature of the relations between the persons of the godhead. But the most important point John is making here is that the Word is distinct from the Father. He is not the Father, but He is *towards* or *with* the Father.

Thirdly, John tells us that the Word 'was God'. In the New World Translation, published by Jehovah's Witnesses, the rendering offered is 'the Word was a god'. Their explanation for this is that in the Greek there is no definite article before 'God', whereas if God (*theos*) were meant in the full and absolute sense it should be *ho theos*: 'God' with the definite article. But the grammatical rule is quite simply this: if the noun comes after the verb and functions as a predicate, it lacks the definite article. If John wanted to say that the Word was God, making the word 'God' a predicate of Jesus, then he did so in the best way open to him, by omitting the article.

Our second reference is in Romans 9:5. Here Paul is discussing the privileges of the Jews: 'Theirs are the patriarchs, and from them is traced the human ancestry of Christ, who is God over all, for ever praised!' (NIV). Again, the New World Translation renders it differently, putting a full-stop after the word 'Christ', thus turning the rest of the verse into a doxology and effectively eliminating the reference to the deity of Christ: 'God who is over all be for ever praised!' Again, there is absolutely nothing in the grammar of this passage that can justify such a translation (which is not confined to the New World Translation but is also found in the RSV and some other modern versions). The underlying reason for this is that in ancient manuscripts there was no punctuation and there is therefore sometimes room for debate as to how we should read particular verses.

There are two ways to respond to the argument offered here. We can say, first of all, that the majority of the early church Fathers clearly understood this verse in the sense of the Authorised Version and the New International Version. More important, the word order in this verse is quite different to that of a doxology.

If this were a doxology, the word *eulogetos* (blessed) would come at the very beginning of the sentence. Instead, it comes towards the end. This makes it virtually certain that Romans 9:5 is not a doxology.

Thirdly, we find Christ explicitly designated as God in Hebrews 1:8: 'But about the Son he says, "Your throne, O God, will last for ever and ever." ' This is an allusion to Psalm 45:6. The New Testament writer, under the guidance of the Holy Spirit, is saying that the verse refers specifically to the Messiah, who is called 'God'. Both the Authorised Version and the New International Version are quite explicit about this. There is, however, some debate among scholars as to how this verse should be translated. Many do not accept that in the original psalm God is in the vocative case and argue that the passage should be translated, 'God is your throne,' instead of 'Your throne, O God.' The only motivation for this comparatively modern rendering is the concern to evade the attribution of the title *God* to Christ. The Hebrew is not ambiguous; and the idea, 'God is your throne', is incomprehensible. Moreover, what we have here is the New Testament canon delivering itself of an authoritative interpretation of the Old Testament and telling us that this verse in Psalm 45 speaks of our Messiah and calls Him 'God'. For Christian theology that should be decisive.

These are the three verses in which, according to the Authorised Version, the New Testament specifically calls Jesus God. However, the New International Version makes this attribution rather more often than the Authorised Version does; a fact which effectively demolishes the prejudice that modern versions tend to compromise the deity of Christ. Let us look at some of these New International Version renderings in a little detail.

First of all, there is John 1:18: 'No-one has ever seen God, but God the only Son, who is at the Father's side, has made him known.' In the Authorised Version we do not have this designation of Jesus as God. The reason is that there is a textual problem. It is uncertain whether the text should read *monogenes theos* (only begotten God) or *monogenes huios* (only begotten son). The difference, as far as the Greek script is concerned, is really very small. The consensus among modern scholars is that the reading should be *theos* and not *huios* and I share that conviction, not only because of the manuscript evidence but also because it is very difficult to understand why anyone should change *son* to *God*, but easy enough to see why people should want to change *God* to *son*. The main point I want to make is that in the judgment of modern scholars, John is here calling Jesus *God*. That can hardly reflect prejudice on the part of these scholars. By and large, they are not at all partial to the idea of Christ being called God, but they recognise that in the authentic text that word actually occurs. No one, says John, has ever seen God, but 'God only-begotten' has declared Him. The Son is the Exegete of the Father.

In Titus 2:13 we find a second instance of the New International Version ascribing deity to Christ where the older versions do not: 'we wait for the blessed hope – the glorious appearing of our great God and Saviour, Jesus Christ, who gave himself for us'. There is no textual problem here. We know beyond any shadow of doubt what the Apostle wrote. But the Authorised Version distinguishes between 'the great God' and 'our Saviour Jesus Christ' and renders the phrase, 'Looking for that blessed hope, and the glorious appearing of the great God and our Saviour Jesus Christ'.

There are two reasons why the New International Version rendering must be taken as the correct one. One is grammatical: there is a rule called the Granville Sharp Rule which declares that if in such cases the definite article is not repeated before the second noun then the second noun refers to the same person as the first. That is exactly what we have here. If it was 'our God' and 'our Saviour' (two separate persons) we would expect that definite article to be repeated. But we have it only once, which means that 'the great God' and 'our Saviour' refer to the same person. That grammatical argument can be abandoned in any particular context only if there are strong grounds for doing so.

The other reason for preferring the New International Version translation is contextual. We are not expecting any appearing of our great God. We expect the *epiphany* of Jesus only, not of God the Father.

For these two reasons, grammatical and contextual, I take the New International Version to be correct.

We find a similar situation in 2 Peter 1:1. According to the Authorised Version this reads, '... through the righteousness of God and our Saviour Jesus Christ'. According to the New International Version it reads, '... through the righteousness of our God and Saviour Jesus Christ'. Again, the Authorised Version takes the passage as referring to two persons, the New International Version to one. The Granville Sharp Rule operates here with exactly the same force because once again we have two nouns linked by *and* covered by a single definite article. We find the opposite arrangement in verse 2, where there are two definite articles and where the New International Version rightly translates, '... through the knowledge of God and of Jesus our Lord'. Incidentally, notice the importance of a knowledge of Greek grammar. The man who said it was the best preparation for death spoke even better than he knew.

Jesus is Lord

All this is only a fragment of the evidence under the first heading, the ascription of divine titles to Christ. He is called God. There is a widespread impression that the word *Lord* is a much weaker title. But this is not so. When we say that Jesus Christ is Lord we are making a statement of unsurpassable significance. In the Latin culture of Imperial Rome the highest title Caesar could claim was *Lord*. It was a divine title. The same was true in Greek culture: a *kurios* was a divine being. 'There are many "gods" and many "lords",' as Paul reminds us in 1 Corinthians 8:5. But what really matters is that in Jewish theology the designation *Lord* had the very highest import. When the Greeks wanted to translate the Hebrew scriptures they came up against the distinctively Jewish name for God: *Jehovah* or *Yahweh*. How should they translate? Their solution was to render it by *Kurios* (Lord). The English versions have done the same thing. (There are, in fact, two

Hebrew words translated Lord: Jehovah and Adonai. The English
Bible distinguishes very precisely between them by consistently
printing the word for *Jehovah* in large block capitals: LORD. The
distinction is very clear in Psalm 8:1).

The importance of all this is that when the Apostles called
Jesus *Lord* they were using a Roman title of divine significance,
a Greek title of divine significance and an Aramaic title of divine
significance (*Mar*). Above all, they were ascribing to Jesus the
word used by Greek-speaking Jews as equivalent to Jehovah.
When we say that Jesus Christ is *Lord* we are saying exactly that
Jesus Christ is *Jehovah*. This may startle us by its very novelty.
But it is the truth, and there is nothing more remarkable in the
whole history of human psychology than that monotheistic Jews
of the first century, men like Paul and James, should ascribe to
a human being the title *Kurios* and go on to apply to Him Old
Testament verses which in their original context referred to
Jehovah, the God of Israel. Let us never forget this simple fact.
When we say, 'Jesus Christ is Lord,' we are saying, 'Jesus Christ
is Jehovah.' When we sing, 'The Lord is my shepherd,' we are
singing, 'Jehovah-Jesus is my shepherd.'

Bearing that in mind, we turn for a moment to James 2:1: 'My
brothers, as believers in our glorious Lord Jesus Christ, don't
show favouritism' (NIV); 'My brethren, have not the faith of our
Lord Jesus Christ, *the Lord* of glory, with respect of persons'
(AV).

There is so much happening here! For one thing, here is an
Apostle facing a very elementary problem, the problem of
snobbery in the church of God. When certain people walk in,
everyone makes a great fuss and tell others to get up and give their
seats to these important people. 'Now,' James said, 'You can't do
that. You are really saying that if Jesus had been in your church
(dressed in the garb of a poor man) you would have told Him to
get up and give His seat to Lord So-and-So. Do you have the faith
of our Lord Jesus Christ? You can't have faith in this poor
Galilean carpenter and be a snob. It's as simple as that.'

But in the course of making this very elementary point James does two other remarkable things. First, he calls Jesus 'Lord'. Bear in mind that James was the Lord's brother. He was also, by all accounts, a very strict Jew, known among his own people as James the Just because of his respect for the Law and for the beliefs and customs of his fathers. Yet here he is, calling his brother 'Jehovah': 'the *Lord* Jesus Christ'. There is nothing anywhere in the New Testament more glorious than that: that James, of all people, who had shared the same home, the same table and probably the same bed as Jesus, who had seen Him from the inside, who had lived with Him, who was so committedly monotheistic and Jewish, should call his own brother 'Jehovah'!

The second and even more remarkable thing is James' use of the word 'glory'. Its use here embarrasses all translations and all commentators because what James says is, literally: 'Don't hold the faith of our Lord Jesus Christ, *the Glory*, with partiality.' The Authorised Version gives us a parenthesis 'the Lord of glory', but the word *Lord* is no part of the original text. The New International Version, too, has faltered and simply says, 'our glorious Lord Jesus Christ'. By turning the noun into an adjective it has evacuated the word of all its force, because James is doing a remarkable thing here. He is calling Jesus the Glory, the *Doxa*, the *Shekinah*. Again, that was a great Old Testament concept. It was part of the church's Messianic hope. God had said, 'I will be the glory in the midst' (Zechariah 2:5). The church had been told to pray 'that his glory may dwell in our land' (Psalm 85:9, NIV). What does John say in John 1:14? 'We beheld his glory as he dwelt among us!' He speaks of the glory *dwelling*, reminding us of the glory that dwelt between the cherubim (see, for example, 1 Samuel 4:4; 2 Kings 19:15; Psalm 80:1). We remember that when Solomon dedicated the temple, the glory of the Lord filled it, and this glory came to be called the Shekinah, from the Hebrew verb for *to dwell*. The Shekinah was the Glory. The Shekinah was God manifested; and James is calling Jesus *the Glory*. He is not simply glorious. Nor does he merely possess glory. He *is* the Glory of God. As a testimony to the deity of Christ this is fully equal to the opening statement of John's Gospel.

I also want to look briefly at what is called the Christ-hymn in Philippians 2:6-11 and specifically at verses 10 and 11: 'That at the name of Jesus every knee should bow, of things in heaven, and things in earth, and things under the earth; And that every tongue should confess that Jesus Christ is Lord, to the glory of God the Father.' Verse 9 tells us that God gave Jesus 'a name which is above every name'. What Paul actually said was not that God gave Him a name, but that God gave Him *the* name: the name above every name. Now there is only one name that can qualify for such a description: the name *Jehovah*. It was so sacred that no Jew, not even a modern Christian Jew, will take it upon his lips. That is Jesus' name: Jehovah. Let us notice, too, that the words of verse 10 are taken straight from Isaiah 45:23, where Yahweh says, 'Unto me every knee shall bow, every tongue shall swear'. The astonishing thing is that the Apostle unashamedly ascribes those words to Jesus. Every tongue will confess that He is Lord and every knee will bow to Him. Jews did not bow to angels or to rabbis. They bowed only to God. The Lordship of Jesus must be great enough and solid enough to sustain the weight of divine worship.

Consubstantial, co-equal

As I said, there has been much discussion of this particular question down through the centuries. Two great gains have emerged from these discussions.

First of all, the exclusion from the church of the Arian heresy. To meet this heresy, the Council of Nicea (325) adopted as a test of orthodoxy a word which we still use to the present day: *homoousios*. It means 'one and the same in being'. It occurs in Answer 6 of the Shorter Catechism which describes the three persons of the godhead as 'the same in substance'. There is another Greek word, *homoiousios*, which means *similar in substance*. Some in the church would have been quite content with this word, but the orthodox fathers would have none of it. They insisted, that in relation to God, Christ was not *merely homoiousios*. He was not *just like* God. He was the same as God.

He was *homoousios*: the same in substance, the same in essence, the same in nature, the same in being. He has every single attribute and every single excellence and every single perfection of God. Everything that constitutes Godhead or Godness is found in Christ.

The second great gain we owe to John Calvin who insisted that there was no place for any essential subordination between God the Father and God the Son. There were, and there still are, many theologians who, although they proclaim Christ as the same in substance with the Father, yet regard the Father as the source or font of deity and the Son as deriving His being from Him. Calvin's answer came to be expressed in another great Greek word, *autotheos*. Christ was God in His own right. His deity was not imparted, it was not communicated, it was not derived and it was not dependent. It was from His very Self (Latin, *a se ipso*). Here is the culmination of Trinitarian thought: the co-equal deity of Christ as the one who is God in His own right and from Himself alone.

Practice

What does it all mean in practice? It means that we have the right and the obligation to bow the knee to Jesus. It cannot be emphasised too strongly that if He is not God, we dare not worship Him. If He is only Michael the archangel, as Jehovah's Witnesses allege, we dare not worship Him. If He is not God our worship is idolatry. It is blasphemy. That is why Athanasius felt so strongly that the church was fighting for its very life and that what was at stake was not a mere dogma but the future of Christianity as a religion. He kept saying to the church, 'Do you want us to go back to paganism? To worshipping demi-gods?'

If we worship Him, we worship Him as the living and true God. That is why this doctrine is so important. We adore Him and praise Him and pray to Him because we are assured that He is *Theos* and *Kurios*, *God* and *Lord*.

9

The Incarnation

The incarnation of Christ means literally His *en-fleshment*, or, as the early Fathers sometimes put it, the *en-manning* of the Saviour. The clearest biblical statement is in John 1:14: 'The Word was made flesh, and dwelt among us.' There are several points in this statement worth careful attention.

The Word made flesh

In the first place, the one who became incarnate was the Word of God. The incarnation pre-supposes both the prior existence of Christ and His divine status. His existence did not begin with His birth from the Virgin: He was from the beginning, and in the beginning He was God (John 1:1).

John's words remind us, too, that it was not the three Persons of the Godhead who became incarnate, but specifically the Second Person: God the Word, or God the Son. The Father did not become incarnate. Neither did the Holy Spirit. Neither did the divine nature. It is the Second Person alone who underwent this experience. Modern theology is often anxious to encourage a 'Christology from below', but the New Testament presentation of the incarnation always starts from above, with the pre-existence and deity of Christ. Only then does it go on to tell us that this specific Person, God the Word, became flesh. We have to express ourselves carefully on this point to avoid conveying the impression that the incarnation implies a change in the divine essence or nature. The Son of God became man, but the divine nature did not become human.

Note, too, that John speaks of Christ as *becoming* flesh. That is in deliberate contrast, as we have seen, to the earlier statement, 'the Word *was* God'. We are never told that He became God.

There is a change of tense, too, as well as a change of verb. The imperfect tense used in verse one tells us of the eternal being of God the Son: He always was, and He was always God. But *became* in verse 14 is not imperfect. It is in the aorist or punctiliar tense. The Word was not always flesh. He became flesh at one particular, decisive moment.

What did He become? He became *flesh*. That means He became man; and He became man in the conditions of accursedness and poverty which are the consequence of the Fall. This involves two things.

A human body

First, that Christ took a human body. It is a remarkable fact that the first heresy the church had to face with regard to the Person of Christ was not denial of His deity but denial of His physical humanity. The heresy of Docetism plagued the early church. We even find the Apostle John saying that anti-Christ is the one who denies that Christ came in the flesh (1 John 4:3; 2 John 7). The peculiar philosophical position of Docetists was that matter was evil, and it was therefore abhorrent that God should become incarnate in the sense of taking a body. According to this view, the physicalness, the body of Christ, was only a 'seeming' (hence the label *Docetism*, from the Greek *dokeo*, I seem). It was only an appearance, a phantasm. It was not real, three-dimensional, historical, touchable, visible, woundable flesh and blood. This is why the Apostle John, who is often accused of being interested only in the deity of Christ, is, on the contrary, fascinated by physical and geographical and topographical details. For example, it is he who tells us that when the Lord's side was pierced on the cross there came out blood and water (John 19:34), something that could never have happened to a spirit or apparition. That is why John's Gospel can be called 'the most earthed of all the Gospels'.

The great fact is that Jesus Christ, God's Son, took a human body which had exactly the same biochemical composition as our own, exactly the same anatomy and physiology, the same central nervous system and the same sensitivity to pain. It was a human body with a genetic composition similar to our own (although, of course, with a specific code peculiar to Jesus as an individual). To this genetic composition His mother made the same contribution as any human mother makes to the genetic make-up of her child. One half of His chromosomes came from His mother. The rest were imparted miraculously in the creative act of the virgin birth.

Through His mother, too, the Lord's humanness is given specificity and particularity. He was not 'humanity'. He was a first-century Jew, rooted in the culture of His people. But it is equally true that through His mother (through the umbilical cord) He was keyed in to the life-stream of the human race and to the whole created order. In the incarnation of God the Son, as we have already seen, the redemptive process has entered not merely the world of the spirit but the world of matter. That link with matter never has been, and never will be, severed. The resurrection body of the Lord is the Omega Point of the material creation: the point at which the skill and wisdom and power and artistry of God find their supreme expression.

The other side of this, of course, is that in and through His body the Lord became vulnerable to physical privation and pain, and at last, to physical death.

We stress then, unreservedly, that the Lord took a human body; and, with that, that the gospel is not interested only in ideas. It is concerned with facts and it is concerned with matter. It exists in the world of physics and biology.

A human psychology

The second factor involved in the assumption of human nature is that Christ took an ordinary human psychology. He became man 'by taking to Himself a true body *and a reasonable soul*' (Shorter Catechism, Answer 22). This truth, too, was denied by an early heresy, Apollinarianism, the product of over-sensitiveness regarding the deity of Christ. Apollinarius was so concerned to safeguard the fact that Christ was God that he minimised His humanness, and that has been a very common tendency in the church right down to the present day. His position was, that when God became incarnate He indeed took a human body, but in the place of a human soul there was simply God the Logos, the Eternal Word. There was a union between a divine nature and a human body but there was no human psychology. The church of the late fourth and early fifth century discussed this issue thoroughly, repudiated this construction of Apollinarius and insisted that just as in Christ there was complete and perfect Godhead so there was complete and perfect manhood. Nothing that was necessary to humanness was lacking to Him. Just as there was a complete human physicalness so there was a complete human psychology.

A human mind

But this fact itself contains several components. It means, for example, that our Lord had a human mind and that that human mind was limited and finite. It had to reason in a human way from premises to conclusions. It had to gather, store and organise information. Its knowledge was not (as God's knowledge is) intuitive. It was inductive and deductive. Furthermore, it was not absolute or infinite. He was not, at the human level, omniscient. There is nothing at all novel in this idea. For example, we find the Lord confessing His ignorance of the time of the Second Coming: 'But of that day or that hour no one knows, not even the angels in heaven, nor the Son, but only the Father' (Mark 13:32). Calvin discusses this thoroughly in Volume 3 of his *Commentary on a Harmony of the Evangelists*. He writes: 'There would be no impropriety in saying that Christ, who knew all things, was ignorant of something in respect of his perception as a man.' He also points out that if we refuse to accept that Christ was not omniscient we shall find ourselves in very serious difficulties when it comes to His mortality. If we are offended by limited knowledge, how will we cope when the Son of God dies?

There is a similar indication in Luke 2:52 where we are told that the child Jesus 'increased in wisdom'. He became wiser. He became better informed. He *accumulated* an ever-increasing fund of prudence and common sense. This does not mean that the Lord was fallible. Infallibility does not depend on omniscience. It depends on the ministry of the Spirit, and Jesus enjoyed that in the fullest measure, both because of who He was and because of what He came to accomplish. But it is clear that the Lord's human mind was finite and His human perception limited. He underwent normal intellectual development and learned by observing the world around Him, listening to His mother and searching the Scriptures. He was not ignorant of anything He ought to have known. God kept from Him nothing which it was good for His church to know. But there were things like the date of the Second Coming which were not the church's business and so the Lord said nothing about them. Indeed, He could not. What He knew of the mysteries of God in His capacity as Mediator He knew only as God the Father revealed them to Him through the Holy Spirit. Information as to the date of the end was not revealed. Hence His confession of ignorance. Even now, at the right hand of the majesty on high, Christ's glorified human mind does not fully understand the glory of His own divine nature. There are complexities in His own being which are still inaccessible to His finite human intellect. He is a depth to Himself.

Human emotions
Secondly, the fact that God the Son took a human psychology means that He experienced the whole range of human emotions. He knew, for example, the emotions of joy and contentment. Although we are never told that Jesus laughed it would be quite wrong to regard Him as living a life of gloom and despondency. His delight was to do the will of God (Psalm 40:8). The fruit of the Spirit is love, joy and peace (Galatians 5:22). Contentment is commanded by God (Philippians 4:6). We have every reason to believe that Christ was at peace with Himself, with His environment and with God. Nevertheless, He was no stranger to the darker side of our human emotions. He felt the sorrow of bereavement at the tomb of Lazarus (and probably earlier, on the

death of his father, Joseph). In Gethsemane he was 'sore amazed'. He was afraid. He did not simply peripherally experience those emotions. He experienced them in horrendous depth. He was very heavy. He was sorrowful, 'even unto death'. In Gethsemane he was literally so terrified of the imminent encounter between Himself as the Sin-bearer and God in His holiness that He shrank from 'this cup' (even though He knew it was the will of God) with a horror that exceeds any horror that we have ever known. Emotionally, He went to the outer limits of human endurance, so close to the absolute limit that He was almost overwhelmed. Christ was no stoic or robot. The lesson for ourselves is priceless. We are not called upon to be ashamed of emotion, or of its expression in tears. The Son of God understands and legitimises our emotional pain.

Affections

Thirdly, the Lord shared the *affective* side of our humanness. He needed human relationships. Mark tells us that He chose the twelve simply to be 'with him' (Mark 3:14). When He went to Gethsemane He took three of them with Him because He dreaded being alone. In the hour of His agony, He needs the presence of His own kind. All He asks is that they be there.

Are we ever ashamed of needing others? What is happening to our civilization (and to our Christianity) that we are ashamed of the need for relationships? Do we think we can find fulfilment by avoiding relationships? The archetypal Man, the Last Adam, needed people with Him. How often, too, we feel ashamed that there are some people we love and like more than others! Yet, it is so apparent in the life of the Lord that He was closer to some than to others: felt more at home, more relaxed with them, more at ease; drew upon them more; liked and loved them more. We see the man Christ with friends, both male and female. We see how He loved children. We see Him weep over Jerusalem. We see His spontaneous affection for the rich young man. There is no tolerance there of a detached, non-relational Christianity with its fear of getting too close and its dread of becoming too deeply involved: its fear of vulnerability. There was nobody more vulnerable than Christ. We can avoid all the pain in life by avoiding love. The Lord was prepared to so love as to be vulnerable, and He was hurt at last, cruelly hurt. One of the Twelve betrayed Him. The three intimates forsook Him and fled. In the end there was not one at the cross to offer encouragement or understanding. He knew the full horror of human infidelity and treachery.

And so there is in Christ a full human psychology, intellectual, emotional, affective, even volitional, as seen in the agony of decision making in the Garden of Gethsemane.

Dwelling among us

John also tells us that the Word dwelt among us. He not only took our nature. He came into our environment. It is possible in the abstract that Christ could have taken our nature and kept that nature in a protected, sanitised environment: kept it in Heaven, or made for it some other Eden. But in our flesh He came into our world of sin. He came into solidarity with us. Of course, that is particularised. He came into first century Nazareth. He came into Jewishness. But the important point is that He did not, as incarnate, live a life of detachment. He lived a life of involvement. He lived where He could see human sin, hear human swearing and blasphemy, see human diseases and observe human mortality, poverty and squalor. His mission was fully incarnational because He taught men by coming alongside them, becoming one of them and sharing their environment and their problems. For us, as individuals and churches in an affluent society, this is a great embarrassment. How can we effectively minister to a lost world if we are not in it? How can we reach the ignorant and the poor if we are not with them? How can our churches understand deprived areas if the church is not incarnate in the deprived areas? How can we be salt and light in the darkened ghettos of our cities if we ourselves don't have any effective contacts and relationships with the Nazareths of the twentieth century? We are profoundly unfaithful to this great principle of incarnational mission. This great Prophet came right alongside the people and shared their existence at every level. He became flesh and dwelt among us.

This means that Christ shared our experience of pain, sorrow, bereavement and temptation. None was ever so tempted as the Son of God. We always yield long before the Tempter needs to unleash his full force or deploy his every wile. The only creature who ever felt the unmitigated force of Satanic onslaught was Christ, because He alone dared him to do his utmost and stood, resisting, to the very end. He knew temptation, as we shall never know it.

And He tasted death: not only died, but tasted it. He tasted it in the accentuated bitterness of the cross, derelict, forsaken by God, fully conscious, sensitized with all the splendid purity of His moral humanity, His every nerve heightened by His perfection, His every pain exacerbated by the glory of His uncontaminated cerebralism, because here was mind and intellect and brain such as the world had never seen, all of them *now* accessions to His glory, but all of them *then* accentuations of His pain. Let us never imagine that God does not understand. God's Son took our nature. He entered into our experience. He knows what physical pain is. He knows what emotional and spiritual pain is. He knows what the loss of God is. He stood in the outer darkness: in the place where there is no comfort; in the place of the absolute 'Why?' where, needing God as no man ever needed God, He cried and God was not there. Bearing a burden such as the world has never known, and left comfortless. We never go beyond His pain. Our darkness is never more intense than His. Our 'Why?s' are never more bewildered. Sometimes, when we have to ask, 'Why me?' part of *His* answer is, 'Me too!' There is good reason to believe that it is part of the reality of God that just as God the Son suffered the loss of His Father, so God the Father suffered the loss of His Son. Which was worse: For the Son to cry, 'Why?' or for the Father, powerless to help, to hear it from the Far Country?

What a great lesson there is in Hebrews 4:15: 'For we have not an high priest which cannot be touched with the feeling of our infirmities; but was in all points tempted like as we are, yet without sin.' He remembers we are dust and he knows our frame (Psalm 103:14). He knows our nature from the inside. He's been where we are. He has walked through the Valley of the Shadow of Death. He has fought with Apollyon. He's been in the Darkness where there's no light. He can look down on us in all our struggles, turn to His Father and say, 'I know exactly how that woman feels!' He is not only Shepherd but Lamb, and what He saw and felt and suffered here is etched indelibly upon His memory, sustaining a sympathy we can never outreach.

Philippians 2:5-11

Paul gives us further insight into the incarnation in his great 'hymn' in Philippians 2:5-11. He starts with the prior existence of Christ (verse 6): 'who, already existing in the form of God'. The Greek word *morphe* (form) refers to visibility: what an observer sees. Here it means that Christ possessed the image of God and the likeness of God and the glory of God; everything that made God God; everything that made the angels adore Him. He had the splendour of God.

That is the starting-point. But the context here is fascinating: a church in difficulties because of human power-struggles. Every member knew who he or she was. Everyone knew who she was equal to and superior to. Each knew his own precise position in the pecking order: 'I'm an old Christian.' 'I'm a deacon.' 'I'm an elder.' 'I'm a missionary.' 'I'm a professor.'

Paul takes their squabbles to the foot of the cross and asks , 'How do we look now, in the light of Calvary?' Christ was in the form of God and equal with God. But did He cling to it? Did He say, 'I must not let this glory go'? Did He say, 'I will go into the world, but only provided my glory goes with me and provided you give me a proper coach and a chariot so that everyone knows who I am. I want to go with appropriate protection and in dignity and style. They must know who I am'?

Heauton ekenose: literally, 'himself he emptied'. Some theologians argue that in becoming incarnate Christ emptied himself of the form of God and that the incarnate Christ was consequently an attenuated, depotentiated, reduced Christ who had divested Himself of Godhead and contracted and shrunk to the proportions of a mere man. That idea is probably widely prevalent even in evangelical circles. But the answer to it lies in this passage itself because the exact wording is, 'himself he emptied, *taking*': *ekenose, labon*. What a marvellous paradox! Christ emptying Himself by taking! It was what Christ took to Himself that humbled Him, not what He laid aside.

But what did He take?

First, He took the form of a servant. In identity He was the Lord, the Master and Sovereign of the Universe. But He became a servant, 'made under the law' (Galatians 4:4). Men saw Him as a slave. Nor was this a mere seeming or a pretence. It was the truth. He was the servant of God. He was the One who washed the disciples' feet.

Secondly, He took the likeness of men. The interest here is in what Christ looked like, what people saw. If you had seen him, Paul says, He would not have turned any heads. There was no halo. There was no shining face. I don't suppose he was conspicuously elegant or handsome or that He had those attributes the glossy magazines commend to us today as archetypal masculinity. He was just a man. There was nothing to betray who He was.

Thirdly, he took the cursed death of the cross. Part of the glory of this is the reminder that the humiliation of Christ was not a point, but a line. 'He made himself nothing' (NIV), He 'made himself of no reputation' (AV), both versions struggling to express the meaning of 'he emptied himself'. But even after He took the form of a servant and became man He went lower still, as if the Manger weren't low enough. What did the angels think of it all? One day they blinked in astonishment as they saw their great Creator in a manger in Bethlehem. They must have found the spectacle incomprehensible. Then as the days and years moved on they saw a drama unfold which must have over-loaded every circuit in their computers. One day word came that their

Lord was in Gethsemane, and one of them had been sent to strengthen Him. Hours afterwards there came even more astonishing news: He was bleeding on the cross of Calvary. That, surely, was the bottom: the very worst! But no! The next thing was, The Father had forsaken Him. The God whose whole impulse it was to wash away the tears from the eyes of His people not washing away the tears of His own Son! That's how it was from beginning to end of the earthly life: down! The tremendous step from throne to stable, and then the incredible journey from the stable to the cross and beyond it the journey on the cross itself from the immolation to the dereliction. The angels must have been saying, 'Will this never, never end? How low is He going to go? How low does He have to go?'

> And when I think that God His Son not sparing,
> Gave him to die, I scarce can take it in;
> That on the cross, my burden gladly bearing,
> He bled and died, to take away my sin.

Luther and Calvin used two great words of similar import to express this aspect of the incarnation. Luther spoke of the divine *incognito*; the unknown, un-recognised Christ. Calvin spoke of the *krupsis*, the hidden Christ, because on Calvary His glory was obscured by a veil which was impenetrable. There was nobody there, with one possible exception, able to understand who He was because His identity was buried beneath layer after layer of humiliation: beneath servanthood, beneath humanness, beneath death, beneath cross and curse and dereliction. This was the last place in the whole wide world where a man would look for God. There was nothing that looked less like God than that thing on the cross! There was nothing that looked less like a divine act than that transaction on the cross! He is so obscure that His disciples do not recognise Him: they lose their faith and their hope. His glory is so obscured that at last even He himself is not sure and for once (and only once) in His entire life He prays to God without calling Him 'Father'. There is no, 'Abba! Abba!' Only, 'Eloi! Eloi! My God! My God!'

Who was the one possible exception? The youngest believer in the world, the terrorist who said, 'Lord, remember me when you come into your kingdom.' The faith of the child penetrates the obscurity and calls the immolated, bruised and bleeding Saviour 'Lord' and 'King'. Was there ever greater faith than that!

There are three final points to bear in mind.

First, the sinlessness of Christ. Close though He came to our humanness and thoroughly though He assumed it, it is always a humanness without sin. This does not mean that He was without temptation or that He lived in a sanitised spiritual environment. On the contrary, He was plunged into the world of the flesh. And yet there was in Him no propensity to sin nor affinity with sin; and there was certainly no stain of sin on His reputation.

Secondly, the uni-personality of Christ. Although truly divine and truly and perfectly human He was (and is) one Person. The essential point here is that whatever He did was done by the Son of God. *He* made the world and *He* died on the cross. A nature did not do it. *He* did it. *He* bled, and died to take away my sin. He gave, not merely His sufferings, not only His human nature: He gave Himself.

Lastly, how often is this fact of the incarnation brought before God's people as their chief incentive and inducement to service and obedience. Paul urges us to think the way Jesus thought. He humbled himself. He made Himself nothing. He said, 'I don't matter'. There is scarcely a month that a church is not wrecked by Somebody. That is the whole problem: there is always a Somebody. If we were willing to be nobodies the church would not be wrecked. That is what the church needs: nobodies who have crucified their egos and left them on the far side of that great word of Jesus, 'Let a man deny himself' (Mark 8:34).

Similarly, in 2 Corinthians 8:9 Paul reinforces the obligation to give to the collection by saying, 'You know the grace of our Lord Jesus Christ, that though he was rich, yet for your sake he became poor.' When we think that our giving is costly, let us ask ourselves, Could God afford his own Son? And could the Son afford to give Himself?

'If I have washed your feet you should also wash one another's feet' (John 13:14). The God who washes feet! It is the greatest vision of God ever given to mankind. The God who became flesh, who dwelt among us, who made Himself nothing, who washes feet. Think the way Christ thought! If He had thought differently there would have been no incarnation, no cross, and no salvation.

10

The Atonement

The atonement is God's answer to human sin and the most important preparation for studying it is a sense of personal sin and spiritual need. The outstanding treatment of the topic is that of Anselm (*Cur Deus Homo?*), who responded to criticisms of his doctrine by saying, 'Ah, but you haven't pondered the gravity of sin.' All shallow views of the atonement are the consequence of shallow perception of sin and superficial awareness of spiritual need. If we know something of the depth of our own depravity and the extent of our own guilt we shall readily appreciate God's provision in the blood of His Son.

The facts
We must always begin with the facts, that is, with the sufferings of Christ. These sufferings began, not at the cross of Calvary, but at the very inception of the Lord's life and ministry. He came into this world at the lowest end of the social scale. He was born 'in a low condition' and His whole life was homogeneous with that low beginning. He was the Man of Sorrows, acquainted with grief. Throughout His life there was poverty, deprivation and homelessness; pain, thirst and weariness; misunderstanding and rejection by those He came to save. All those sufferings were intensified as the Lord moved into the shadow of Calvary. In the great struggle of Gethsemane He became sharply aware of the impending crisis, when He, as the Sin-bearer, would answer for the sin of His people. As He brooded on the imminent collision, He experienced the darkest and deepest human emotions. He was overwhelmed with sorrow. He was 'sore amazed and very heavy' (Mark 14:33). He felt overwrought and overborne. He began to ask, maybe for the first time, whether His frail humanity

130 _A Faith to Live By_

could cope with the unmitigated reaction of God against sin.

There are moments in our experience, too, when we wonder whether we can cope. But in the goodness of God's grace the experiences we dread are seldom as awful in the moment of experience as they are in expectation and contemplation. For Christ the opposite was the case. In the Garden His perception of the agony was limited. No human imagination was really able to grasp what it was going to mean to be the Sin of the world in the presence of God. And Gethsemane, awesome though it was, was only a pale shadow of Calvary. On Calvary, Christ moved into unmitigated physical pain and into total social isolation. He experienced all that Hell could do by way of darkness and onslaught and temptation. Above all, He experienced the agony of being forsaken by God His Father and becoming, as the Bearer of the world's sin, the Great Outsider. There is a sense in which no being was less prepared and less apt for the dereliction than God's own Son. The very closeness and perfection of the bond between Him and His Father made the desolation more excruciating. He had never known in the remotest degree what the loss of God was. In the story of Abraham and Isaac there is a striking emphasis on the fact that father and son went up to Mount Moriah 'both of them together' (Genesis 22:6). That was the way it was with God the Son and God the Father. As they went up to Calvary they went 'both of them together'. This is why Jesus could say, 'I am not alone, because the Father is with me' (John 16:32). Yet in the moment of the Son's greatest need and greatest pain, God is not there. The Son cries and is not heard. The familiar resource, the ultimate resource, the only resource, is not there. The God who was always there, the God who was needed now as He had never been needed before, was nowhere to be seen. There was no answer to the Son's cry. There was no comfort. Jesus was left God-less, with no perception of His own Sonship, unable for the one and only time in His life to say, 'Abba, Father.' He was left with no sense of God's love and no sense of the operation of God's purpose. There was nothing but that '_Why?_', trying vainly to bridge the Darkness. He was sin. He was lawlessness, and as such He was banished to the Black Hole where lawlessness belongs and from which no sound can escape but, 'Why?' That was the Son's only word in His final agony as He reached out to the God whom He needed so desperately but whom as Sin He couldn't discern and from whose presence He was outcast. There could be no accord. 'God His Son not sparing'! He had to be dealt with not as Son but as Sin.

This was not only a moment in the experience of the Son. It was a moment, too, in the experience of God the Father. There was a loss in the Father corresponding to the loss in the Son. We are on the outer parameters of revelation here, but we have to accept the New Testament's constant emphasis that the cost of our redemption was borne not only by God the Son but by God the Father (see, for example, John 3:16 and Romans 8:32); and that carries with it the fact that the divine compassion is never simply the compassion of the Son but equally the compassion of the Father.

The impression is often given that the evangelical understanding of the cross, our doctrine of the atonement, somehow increases the pain of the Saviour. But it is not a theory that constitutes the pain of Christ. The pain was in the facts: that on the cross He suffered in body, suffered in soul, suffered from Heaven and from earth and from Hell. The fact is, Christ died. The fact is, He paid the wages of sin. The fact is, He was dealt with as sin deserved.

There are three further facts that accentuate this central fact of the suffering of Christ.

First, His sinlessness. He died. It is a great pity that we are so little conscious of the anomalousness of that: that He who knew no sin should die; that He who had never sinned should receive the wages of sin; that 'the only perfect innocent in the Universe should be the greatest sufferer in the Universe', as John Duncan said. We are so familiar with the cross, with the death of the sinless One, that we do not appreciate the anomaly. Why is the sinless One suffering the wages of sin? The problem does not lie in the theory, it lies in the facts.

Secondly, the One who receives the wages of sin is the Son of God. Again, we have heard that so often we completely miss the paradox. The soldiers at the cross watched Him there (Matthew 27:36).

> Who is he on yonder tree?
> Dies in grief and agony?
> 'Tis the Lord, O wondrous story!

What is He doing on the cross? What is He doing between two thieves? What is He doing taking the wages of sin? What do you think the angels thought? Which things the angels peer down to see (1 Peter 1:12)! They can understand human mortality because human beings are sinners. But what is He doing on the cross? We can imagine the whispered voices going through Paradise: 'Have you heard? He has borne the wages of sin! He has died! His blood has been shed, the blood of the Son of God!' Watch HIM there: God's own Son, the sinless One, receiving the wages of sin.

The third twist in the paradox is that the cross is the act of God the Father: 'God so loved the world, that he gave his only begotten Son' (John 3:16). He did not spare His own Son but delivered Him up for us all (Romans 8:32). It was not Pontius Pilate who sacrificed Him. It was not Judas Iscariot. It was not the Jewish powers. It was not even Jesus Himself, the Great High Priest. There is a priesthood that stands above and beyond the priesthood of the Son. There is an agency that goes beyond even the agency of the Mediator. Of course, Christ was Priest on the cross. He was giving Himself voluntarily, prompted by His love for His people. But there was a higher agency still: the agency of God the Father. He, his Son not sparing, gave Him to die.

We really must learn to see the cross as a gigantic problem, a problem of mind-boggling proportions. We must see the scandal of it. We must say, 'What is this ugliness? What is this blot on the moral universe? What is this when God the Father is crucifying His own Son, when the righteous God is exacting from the Sinless one the wages of sin? What is this horrendous anomaly, this thing that we cannot understand, this offence, this hateful, wretched, ugly thing?'

The twentieth century has seen many chilling manifestations of evil. But the cross of Jesus Christ is a greater scandal to faith than Belsen or Auschwitz or Aberfan because here is the Omega-point of the demonic and the irrational: God's own Son is being dealt with by God in the way that sin deserved. 'Can there in the Highest be knowledge of things below?' (Metrical Psalm 73:11). Does God know what He is doing? Has God blown His mind? Has He flipped?

It wasn't the theory that caused the Lord's pain. It wasn't Anselm's doctrine of the atonement that caused His grief. It was these facts of history, in time and space, on a 'green hill far away, without a city wall'.

The doctrine

What is the New Testament solution to the problem? It is this: that the death of Christ was a sacrifice. It was not an accident. It was not an act of divine malice (although that interpretation is a very plausible one because the cross looks malicious and malevolent). No, says the Bible, it was a sacrifice: 'Behold, the Lamb of God, who takes away the sin of the world!' (John 1:29); 'For by a single offering he has perfected for all time those who are sanctified' (Hebrews 10:14). That is how the New Testament sees the death of Christ. As the apostles looked through the eyes of God's Spirit at the event and the facts of Calvary they were led to say, 'This is the fulfilment of the Old Testament sacrifices. This is the consummation of that instinct in the universal human heart that has led to sacrificial and piacular religion.' This became for the apostles the master-concept of the atonement, the category under which they could subsume, and through which they could understand, the death and suffering of the Lord Jesus Christ.

But what did it mean for Christ to be a sacrifice: to be the 'lamb without blemish and without spot' (1 Peter 1:19)? It meant that He was the One to whom sin was imputed. In the Old Testament ritual the offerer put his hand on the head of the sacrifice, confessed over it the sins of which he was guilty and thus transferred them symbolically to the victim. In the Christian doctrine of the atonement Christ is the One to whom sin is transferred, not only by the imputation of God, but also by His own *assumption* of it. He loved the church, and *took* her liabilities and debts to himself (Ephesians 5:25). The New Testament's language on this is bold in the extreme: 'He made him who knew no sin to be sin for us' (2 Corinthians 5:21). Christ on that cross took His identity from sin, bearing all it deserved. He became the sin of His people. He came to be identified with their guilt and liable to their punishment. And because He was Sin, He became a curse (Galatians 3:13). There was no mitigation and no sparing. There was only the absolute recoil of God from the sin His Son was. He was *katara*: cursed, banished. He was His Son, but His sonship was obscured by the *anomia*. The Son belonged in His bosom; the *anomia* belonged in the Black Hole. God put the whole universe, and more, between Himself and the Son of His love. He banished Him to the farthest edges of reality; and even beyond, because the Black Hole is what lies beyond reality. It is, absolutely, Outside (Revelation 22.15): the place of Outer Darkness (Matthew 8.12) where the Sin borne by the Lamb is out of sight of the God who is of purer eyes than to behold iniquity (Habakkuk 1:13).

There are some theologians who are quite magnificent on the doctrine of the incarnation but then mar it all by telling us that the incarnation is itself our atonement; that all that matters is that God took our nature and by uniting it to Himself transformed it. Others tell us that Christ made atonement by means of a vicarious repentance: an Amen! in the human heart of Christ to God's condemnation. But when God saved the world the process did not stop at Bethlehem, or at Gethsemane. If sin could have been atoned for by incarnation, the Lord could have returned to Glory from the cradle in Bethlehem. If sin could have been dealt with by an Amen! to God's condemnation He could have returned to Glory from Gethsemane. But sin was such, the offence against God such, the depravity such, the guilt such, that the salvation could not be completed until Christ had gone into the Black Hole.

The Son of man came 'to give his life a ransom for many' (Matthew 20:28; Mark 10:45). He did not come simply to take our nature. He did not come simply to say Amen! to our condemnation. He came so that on the cross He would endure what our sin deserved: He was 'obedient *unto death*' (Philippians 2:8). He came to be the great sacrifice, the Lamb without blemish and without spot, the Lamb who bears the sin, the Lamb who is dealt with as sin deserves. He came to be the Passover Lamb who secures our immunity to destruction; the Scapegoat who bears our sin to a place where God cannot see it, and from where it will never return; the Holocaust, the burnt offering, left totally vulnerable to the exactions of God's righteousness, not spared, but totally exposed to all that sin deserved.

The fact is, He received the wages of sin. People speak with horror of 'the penal theory of the atonement'. But what happened to Christ on the cross? He died! And what is death? It is the penalty for sin! The question of whether Christ endured the penalty for sin is not a question of theory. It is a question of fact. On that cross He was dealt with as sin deserved. The glory of it is, it wasn't His own sin. It was our sin. He bore the sin of the world (John 1:29). John Duncan once said that the best expression of the gospel he had ever heard was the simple and unforgettable statement of a black American Christian: 'Either *I* die, or *He* die. *He* die, *me* no die.' He was the sacrifice, without blemish, who bore our sin and endured its penalty.

What did the cross achieve?

What did that sacrifice achieve? What did the cross, contemplated as an act of the Father's high-priesthood, in which He offered His Son as a sacrifice for the sins of His enemies, achieve?

First, there was the effect of the cross on sin: it *expiated* sin. The word means, primarily, to cover. The sacrifice of Christ, the sacrifice of His obedience, covers sin: 'as by one man's disobedience many were made sinners, so by the obedience of one shall many be made righteous' (Romans 5:19). Our disobedience is completely covered by the obedience of the Son of God. Not that the cross was a work of supererogation. On the cross Christ did all that was necessary for our salvation: but no more than was necessary.

Secondly, the effect of the cross on God. There are three words to be used here.

The cross *propitiates* God. The reality of God's anger was dealt with by the curse-bearing of His Son. What covers sin removes the ground of the Wrath and effects appeasement.

Again, the cross *reconciles* God. Reconciliation presupposes enmity. It is not merely that our human hearts and intellects had something against God. God had something against us. He had sin against us and this sin really mattered. God always loved His people, but He did not proceed directly from loving them to being at peace with them. Between His love and His peace there lay the terrible process described in 2 Corinthians 5:18ff.: He made him who knew no sin to be sin in our place, so that we might become God's righteousness in Christ. It is only when we become God's righteousness that God is at peace with us. And how righteous are we? As righteous as Christ! How righteous is Christ? As righteous as God! When the church of God pleads, confessing sin, praying for forgiveness, it does not address its prayer to the divine clemency or the divine pity but to the divine righteousness. He is faithful and righteous to forgive us our sins (1 John 1:9). Grace reigns through righteousness (Romans 5:21). We are so righteous in Christ that the great Advocate can demand our forgiveness, and insist upon it, because we are righteous with all the righteousness of God Himself. There is absolutely no condemnation to those who are in Christ Jesus (Romans 8:1).

It was Luther's discovery of this great fact – not only of justification but of the atonement that lay beneath it – that liberated Europe from the bondage of an evil conscience. It is a such a pity that many of us in the Reformed tradition, Luther's heirs, know so little of the exhilaration, the sheer sense of emancipation, that should come from this knowledge. God has nothing against us. All He had against us has been dealt with between Himself and His Son in a way we can never fully understand.

The cross also *satisfied* God. *Satisfaction* is not a biblical term but the word, under proper controls, has its own value. It means that on the cross Christ did all that was necessary. There is nothing left to do. There is no need to supplement it or to make good the imagined deficiencies of a 'Saviour's obedience and blood'. He cried, 'It is finished!' (John 19:30) and it was finished. The whole glory of faith is that it is so completely satisfied with Christ. That is the very nature of faith. In the great words of William Guthrie: 'Less cannot satisfy, and more is not desired.'[1] If we have faith we 'close in' with Christ. He is all our salvation and all our desire. Our souls rest because the cross that satisfies God satisfies our consciences also.

> Just as I am, and waiting not
> To rid my soul of one dark blot,
> To Thee, whose blood can cleanse each spot,
> O Lamb of God, I come.
>
> Just as I am, poor, wretched, blind -
> Sight, riches, healing of the mind,
> Yea all I need, in Thee to find
> O Lamb of God, I come.

Thirdly, the cross's impact on the sinner: it redeems him. It ransoms him and loosens him and sets him free. It is a great emancipation. We are redeemed from the curse of the law; redeemed from the guilt and power of sin; redeemed from the fear of death; redeemed from 'the doctrines and commandments of men'. But we are not only redeemed *from*: we are also redeemed *to*. We are redeemed to God. We are a people for a possession (Ephesians 1:14). We are God's inheritance (Ephesians 1:18). We are not our own. God has bought us with his own blood (Acts 20:28). Indeed, we are now so much God's property that we must never surrender our Christian liberty, because 'for freedom, Christ has set us free' (Galatians 5:1). When Luther found justification by faith and redemption by the cross of Christ he also found 'the freedom of a Christian man'; and he told the whole world, 'I cannot be any man's slave or any church's slave!'

How can we, for whom Christ paid such a price, undo His work by enmeshing ourselves again in human addenda to the law of God?

Fourthly, the effect of the cross on Satan: it *conquered* him. Christ has disarmed the principalities and powers and made a public spectacle of them (Colossians 2:15). He destroyed the one who had the power of death (Hebrews 2:14). That is not part of our future, it is part of our present. Of course, Satan is still active. But his tyranny is broken. He no longer holds the Gentiles in thrall (Revelation 20:3). He no longer has dominion in the lives of believers (Romans 6:14). How seldom we do justice to this great fact of victory! So often we are conquered by sin, because we expect to be conquered. We think it only natural. But the Bible tells us that 'we are more than conquerors through him who loved us' (Romans 8:37). Christ was not only a Prophet proclaiming God's love and a Priest making atonement for sin. He was also a King conquering Hell. There is a magnificent passage in Hugh Martin's peerless work on *The Atonement* where he speaks of 'earth, and hell, and heaven thus in conspiring action against Him, unto the uttermost of heaven's extremest justice, and earth's and hell's extremest injustice'. 'What,' asks Martin, 'is the glory of the Cross, if it be not this; that with such action conspiring to subdue His action, His action outlasted and outlived them all, and He did not die subdued and overborne into dying, He did not die till He *gave* Himself in death?'[2] Hell did its utmost to extinguish the commitment of God to man and to divert the stream of His grace. But Christ's action conquered and Satan was routed. We must pour into our whole missionary endeavour at home and abroad the resources of that great fact: we are now evangelizing a world that no longer belongs to Satan. It belongs to Christ.

We have seen the facts. We have seen the fundamental explanation for those facts in the idea of sacrifice. We have seen what that sacrifice achieved: its impact on sin, on God, on sinners and on the powers of Hell. But the question remains, How can Something which Someone else did 2,000 years ago bring spiritual benefit to me?

We may put it another way: What right did God have to sacrifice His Son ('it pleased Jehovah to bruise him; He hath put him to grief', Isaiah 53:10)?

The answer to both questions lies in the connection between the believer and Christ, a connection which cost Christ dear and which is expressed in two great New Testament prepositions.

First of all, there is the preposition *for*. He became sin *for* us. In *my* place condemned He stood. He is not only the Advocate, the Attorney, acting for us. He is the Victim, suffering in our place. All our sin was placed on Him. He became the One for us. That is God's right to bruise him. That is the justification of Calvary. That is why Calvary itself is finally not a Black Hole, but the iridescence of the love of God. Without the *for,* the cross becomes the supreme argument that God is not love; that God is mad and the universe is mad; that there is no God. But with the *for* it is the light of the world.

Secondly, there is the preposition *in*. We are God's righteousness *in* Him (2 Corinthians 5:21). It is the *in* of spiritual identification. We are members of the Body and branches of the Vine, and it is the safest place in the universe. The gospel invitation is to all men, but the assurance of salvation is only for those who are in Christ. Only those who have made the journey to Him find rest. We simply must make that journey. But that journey is as nothing compared to what God did. Faith and atonement are not symmetrical. He gave His own Son. What do I do? I believe. I make my little journey, my reasonable journey, which takes me to be in Christ. Once I am there, I have everything. We are complete in Him (Colossians 2:10). In Him we are justified. In Him we are consecrated. In Him we are filled and baptised and sealed with the Spirit of God: 'complete in Him'. That is why He is all our salvation and all our desire.

References
1. William Guthrie, *The Christian's Great Interest,* 1951 edition, p. 43.
2. Hugh Martin, *The Atonement*, 1882 edition, p. 83.

11

What is Faith?

The sixteenth chapter of Acts reminds us of the wide variety of people who are touched by the gospel of Jesus Christ. There is Lydia, a respectable middle-class woman of public piety, who hears Paul preach and whose heart the Lord opens with the result that she becomes a disciple. There is the young slave girl, probably a profligate, again touched by the gospel and delivered from the power of evil by the grace of God. Then there is the jailer, a man of rough and barbaric past life, brought to a sense of his spiritual need and led by Paul and Silas to a knowledge of Jesus Christ. As human personalities they are all remarkably different. Yet the gospel is relevant to each of them.

The requirement God imposes on all of these is the same: 'Believe in the Lord Jesus Christ!' Paul and Silas knew nothing of the jailer's past, nor of his inward spiritual condition. They didn't know whether he was convicted of sin, whether he was a seeker, whether he was born again or whether he was elect. Yet they confronted him at once with the imperative, 'Believe in the Lord Jesus Christ!' (Acts 16:31).

This is one reason why the topic before us, *What is faith?*, is so important. It encapsulates God's directive to all of us. It is what God requires. But it is important too, because all of us should be able to answer such questions as: How do I become a Christian? What does believing in Jesus mean? We should be able to introduce people to Christ by explaining what we mean by this great step of faith.

The nature of faith

What, then, is faith in Jesus Christ? It involves two basic elements.

First of all, it means belief, or assent. It is an intellectual commitment: the submission of the mind to the truth of the gospel. It presupposes that God has given us some knowledge of the truth. We have heard the message. We have heard the report of the Word of God. We have heard that God is, that God became incarnate in Christ, that Christ is able to save us, that Christ offers to save us, that Christ pleads with us to come to Him for salvation, that He died for our sins, that He rose again and that we are justified by faith in His name and in His sacrifice. That is the message. And faith, at the most basic level, means that we believe those facts to be true. We accept those great doctrines. Our minds are convinced. Faith will lead to emotions and to decisions, but those emotions and decisions are based on convictions and the convictions presuppose knowledge. In this sense, faith is rational. It is not rationalistic but it is an act of reason. It always involves an act of the mind. We believe the report. We receive this great tradition that speaks of the lordship, incarnation, death and resurrection of the Son of God.

Similarly, our first concern in evangelism is to propel into the minds of our hearers the convictions which lie at the foundation of our own faith. That is where all faith begins. It presupposes a hearing of the word of God and an acceptance of what we hear.

Secondly, faith is trust. It begins with belief, but it is always more than belief. It is a personal commitment to God in Christ. That has sometimes been disputed. The Sandemanians in eighteenth century Scotland held that faith was simply a matter of the intellect: a matter of believing that things happened as the New Testament recorded. They said that it simply meant belief of the truth or acceptance of the propositions. This reflected the commitment of these men to the doctrine of justification by faith alone. They were very suspicious of the preaching of men like Whitefield and Wesley because it seemed so emotional and laid such stress on commitment and decision. 'No!' said the Sandemanians, 'faith is simply a matter of intellect. It means believing the apostolic message with the top of your mind.' The same concern has been found in Roman Catholicism, which equates faith with accepting implicitly whatever the Church teaches.

We can, of course, over-react to this and dismiss altogether the intellectual side of faith. We must be very careful about this because that is precisely what lies at the heart of Modernism: anti-intellectualism, the anti-dogmatism and the suggestion that religion resides primarily in the emotions. On such a construction faith is divorced from doctrine and piety from theological belief.

We have to walk between these two great perils: on the one hand, the Sandemanian error which says that the intellect is everything and, on the other, Modernism which says that the emotions are everything and the mind is nothing. Over against these we must say that faith must begin with the mind but must go on to become a personal trust in God and in the Lord Jesus Christ. The Reformers emphasised those two components firmly. They spoke of *fides* or belief on the one hand; and *fiducia* or trust on the other. Only where these two exist in combination is there a real faith: that is, such persuasion of the mind as leads to personal trust in God our Father and Jesus Christ our Saviour.

Trust is emphasised firmly in the New Testament. With the heart we believe and because we believe we come to Christ. We turn to Christ and we look to Christ. Our faith is directional. It is dynamic. It is mobile. It is faith *in*; it is faith *into*; it is faith towards; it is faith *upon*. Faith is a leaning grace. It leans on God. Faith is a grace that wraps the soul around its Saviour, not all that far removed from love. It is a personal relationship. It begins with the belief that, in the light of all the information we have, Christ is trustworthy. That is a proposition: 'Christ is trustworthy.' But my faith moves on from that to the actual commitment, and that is brought out fully in many of the biblical metaphors. We trust God as we trust our father. We trust Christ as a flock trusts its shepherd. We trust Christ as we trust a physician. We trust our doctor because we know certain things about him. He has been trained; he has studied; he has experience; he has skills. Our trust is not divorced from these propositions. If we trusted just anybody to perform surgery our faith would be mis-placed and irrational, but because our faith is based on implicit propositions it is reasonable and well warranted. We start with the proposition,

'Christ is a great high priest' (Hebrews 4:14) and from that the commitment follows. We trust Him with our souls.

The object of faith

What, or who, is the object of this faith?

First, our faith is directed towards the Bible as the Word of God. We believe that the Bible *is* the Word of God. We have to remember, however, that in the Bible, as the Westminster Confession (XIV.2) reminds us, there is a wide variety of materials. For example, there are commandments, threatenings, doctrines and promises. Now faith responds to these in quite different ways. Faith responds to commandments with obedience. Faith trembles before the threatenings. Confronted by a solemn and sombre divine warning faith is not ecstatic, but tremulous and afraid, responding to the Bible in accordance with the quality of the material presented to it. Faith meets a doctrine – say, some great truth about the incarnation of Christ – and it responds with belief and conviction. And faith meets promises and rejoices in them: all the great promises of preservation, provision, help, sanctification, glorification and transformation. It also turns these promises into prayers. It has been said that every promise in the Bible is an invitation to prayer. In fact, every promise is a command to pray, because if God promises us something He is directing us to ask for it. Prayer is always bounded by the promises of God. We can only pray for what is divinely warranted; and what is divinely warranted is what God has promised. This relationship between prayer and promises must be retained inviolate.

Secondly, faith has as its object the person and work of Jesus Christ. But here, too, faith is manifold. Precisely because Christ is so many-sided faith itself is many-sided. For example, it responds to the fact that He is 'very God of very God' by bowing the knee in adoration and worship. Wherever there is such worship there is faith, even though we may not have been through any great conscious spiritual crisis. In the same way faith responds differently to each of the three mediatorial offices of

Christ as Prophet, Priest and King. It has been a fault of the Reformed churches, going back to Luther, that we have often seen faith exclusively in terms of the priestly activity of Jesus. We have thought of it only in relation to forgiveness and justification. Of course, that is an indispensable element in all faith, but it is not the only element and it is not the point at which every Christian has his or her first experience of faith. It may well be that someone first meets Christ, not in His priestly office, but in His prophetic office or in His kingly office. A sense of guilt is certainly not the point where God's grace invariably first touches the soul. Faith has other responses besides its response to the priestly victim on the cross of Calvary.

For example, faith in Christ as Prophet means that we believe whatever He teaches because He teaches it. Why do I believe in the infallibility of the Old Testament? I believe it because Jesus Christ said, 'The Scripture cannot be broken' (John 10:35). Faith means the submission of my mind to Christ.

Faith in Christ as King means submission to His commandments and confident repose in His protection. In the twentieth century the human soul is much more preoccupied with insecurity than with the question of guilt. Does life have meaning? Is there purpose? Is there someone in control? It is very important in our twentieth century witness to focus on the sovereignty and kingship of Christ and to ask for a faith that is directed in the first instance not so much towards the sin-bearing sacrifice as towards the cosmos-bearing sovereignty. He's got the whole world in His hands.

Faith in the Prophet means, then, that my mind submits to him. Faith in the King means that I obey and trust Him. And faith in Christ as sacrifice means that to Him, to His cross, to His death, to His blood, I bring all my sins, because He says, 'Come unto me, and I will give you rest' (Matthew 11:28). In the Old Testament, if someone sinned he had to bring his sacrifice to the Holy Place. Christ is our Holy Place. At Him we confess our sins. With our hands on his Head we confess our sins, and resting our case entirely and exclusively on what He has done we ask that

God would forgive and cover our past. The sign of such a faith is peace of conscience: the unshakeable persuasion that our sin has met its full answer and found its full remedy in the obedience of our Saviour. In God's judgment nothing is relevant to our spiritual standing but what He has done and suffered. Faith, here, means that we add nothing to Jesus.

Faith, then, is many-sided, depending on what aspect of the Word or what aspect of Christ we are responding to. Because of the infinitely varied types of human personality one faith-activity predominates in one person and another predominates in another. In some Christians the predominant manifestation of faith may be worship. In others, it may be the total absence of worry because God is in control. My protest is against the notion that faith always has the same access point, the same kind of origin or the same kind of manifestation. What predominates will depend both on our own temperament, on our own experience and on our particular exposure to the Word of God.

The Warrant of Faith

There is a third question: What about the warrant of faith? Who has the right to believe? Who has the right to come to Christ? That question has been discussed very thoroughly in Reformed theology and the answer has been unambiguous: every human being, without any exception whatsoever, is entitled to come to Christ and to take Him as his own Saviour. Every man as a man, every sinner as a sinner, the foulest, the vilest, the most vicious – it was put in the strongest possible terms – had the right to come.

This was based on certain clear emphases of the Word of God itself. For example, God commands every human being to believe. No one is exempt from that command. We have the right to come to Christ, whoever we are, because God commands us to come to Christ.

We have the right, secondly, because of God's offer and invitation to come to Christ. 'Look unto me, and be ye saved, all the ends of the earth' (Isaiah 45:22); 'Come unto me, all ye that labour and are heavy laden, and I will give you rest' (Matthew

11:28); 'Let the wicked forsake his way ... and let him return unto the Lord' (Isaiah 55:7). The offer was absolutely universal.

Thirdly, there is a universal divine promise: if we believe, we shall be saved. That is God's promise. Now it is a conditional promise. The reward is conditional upon our believing. But God's promise is made categorically: if we turn to God in Christ we shall be saved. Alternatively, it can be put in these terms: the warrant is universal because it arises from the fact that the Bible explicitly states that there is no price to be paid. This salvation is utterly gratuitous (Isaiah 55:1). We receive the water of life freely (Revelation 22:17). We take it without money and without price (Isaiah 55:1).

Some Reformed preachers went to great lengths to express this fact that every human being, no matter how sinful, has the right to come and take Christ as his Saviour. They were predestinarians of the deepest dye (men like Thomas Boston, John Duncan and Martin Luther) but they believed equally firmly in the free, universal offer of the gospel. John Duncan put it most succinctly: 'Sin is the handle by which I get Christ.' 'I don't read anywhere in God's Word that Christ came to save John Duncan,' he said, 'but I read this: He came to save sinners and John Duncan is a sinner and that means he came to save John Duncan.' Luther argued in the same way. He said to the devil, 'Thou sayest I am a sinner and I will take thine own weapon and with it I will slay thee and with thine own sword I will cut thy throat because sin ought to drive us not away from Christ but towards Christ.' The Bible and Reformed theology have taught us to come – just as we are.

> Just as I am, and waiting not
> To rid my soul of one dark blot,
> To Thee, whose blood can cleanse each spot,
> O Lamb of God, I come.

Now it may be that in Reformed theology there is no theological answer to the question, 'How can it be simultaneously true that only the predestinated are saved and that God commands all men to believe?' All we can say is that both horns of the dilemma are equally valid. For the moment, our concern is with only one aspect of the truth: every human being is warranted to come to Christ. The great thing here is that the universal becomes the particular. If all are warranted, each is warranted. If each is warranted, *I* am warranted. This is supremely important in relation to those who are tempted to spiritual despair: the backslidden, those who were once bright, shining Christians, but from whose lives the glory has gone and who feel that for them there is no hope. Wherever we stand, we have the warrant to believe.

Conclusion

Three points of general interest in conclusion.

First, the possibility of varying degrees of faith: greater faith and lesser faith. The disciples prayed, 'Lord, increase our faith' (Luke 17:5). Of course, faith varies from person to person. It also varies in our own lives from time to time, What we must always remember is that it is not great faith that saves, but real faith. And yet: why should our faith remain little? We should feed it. Sometimes we try to feed faith on faith, giving it a diet of teaching about faith, teaching about assurance and analysis of the grace itself. What feeds faith is a sight of the glory of the Word of God and above all, a sight of the glory of Christ. Often, faith is little, faith is malnourished, because it is starved of Jesus. It is a terrifying possibility that there may be Christians who are firmly within the bounds of orthodoxy and starved of Christ. Faith needs to feed on the full range of His glory: as human and divine, Prophet, Priest and King. We should treasure and value those means of grace, those sermons and discussions and books that bring the Lord closer to us, because that is where our faith grows. The most magnificent definition of faith ever penned was the one implicit in the great words of William Guthrie describing a man who has come to faith in Christ: 'Less would not satisfy and more is not desired.' That is faith! Thrilled with Jesus. It cannot think of any way in which He could be improved. The New Testament is full of Christology. Let our reading and our meditation be full of Christology. Then our faith will grow.

Secondly, there are the Lord's words to the disciples during the storm on the Sea of Tiberias: Where is your faith? (Luke 8:25). How pertinent that often is! We can have the beliefs and we can have the convictions and we can quote all the great promises of the Bible and thrill to the sound of the words and yet, when we are struggling away down in the seaweed with Jonah, where is faith? The Lord does not deny its existence or its reality or its availability. But is it being applied in our current situation?

Thirdly, Will there be faith in heaven? I raise this question not because of any prurient academic interest but because in many ways it raises the whole question of what faith is. Some argue that there won't be faith in heaven because then faith is swallowed up in sight (1 John 3:2). Faith, they say, is what gives substance to things hoped for and evidence for things not seen (Hebrews 11:1) and when we see Him as He is we won't need faith. But the Bible uses the idea of faith with a slight ambiguity. Sometimes it contrasts faith with direct knowledge of what is before is our eyes. In this sense, certainly, faith will one day give way to sight. But I come back to my basic definition: faith is trust. And I ask, Will there be trust in heaven? Will we trust God in heaven? Will we trust Jesus in heaven? Surely one of the glories of heaven is the great prospect of the consummation of trust! Then we shall trust Him implicitly. Here the image of the Lamb shepherding the flock is very significant (Revelation 7:17). We shall follow the Lamb because faith is the bond, the trust between the soul and its Saviour, and that bond will never be broken. It is consummated on the threshold of glory and it will move on to ever higher levels of commitment and intimacy as the millennia go by, allowing us to penetrate the being and the life of the Saviour in some such way as His life penetrates that of God His Father. Heaven without faith has no attraction. Indeed, it has no credibility. Heaven is the place where doubt in all its forms gives way to complete trust. 'There shall be no night there' (Revelation 21:25; 22:5).

12

Full Assurance

The question of assurance is important for at least two reasons.

First, because the lack of assurance has often been a serious problem for Reformed Evangelicals. Not only have we lacked assurance: we have even tended to cultivate the lack of it. This is most marked in the North of Scotland, but the same phenomenon is found, for example, among Dutch Calvinists. It is all too easy to assume that lack of assurance reflects real humility and, conversely, that assurance is a mark of spiritual pride.

Secondly, because it bears very directly on the quality of our Christian lives. Without assurance it becomes very difficult to serve the Lord. Without assurance it is hard to cultivate sanctification or to mortify sin. Without assurance there is no joy in our discipleship, and joy, remember, is the lubricant of obedience. I suspect that many of the most pressing problems in the church today stem from the lack of assurance. Wordsworth defined poetry as 'the spontaneous overflow of powerful feelings'. Whether that is a correct definition of poetry is not for me to say, but these words certainly express a fundamental principle of our Christian faith. The quality of our witness, our worship, and our whole service of God depends on the depth and power of our feelings and affections; and primary among these is this fact of assurance. Our service is driven by the persuasion that God loves us.

Summary definition

In summarising the doctrine I want to follow the excellent statement in the Westminster Confession, Chapter 18.

The Confession reminds us, first of all, that those who are hypocrites may nevertheless enjoy some kind of assurance. These are people who are not converted and yet have an invincible assurance that they are God's children, secure for time and eternity. The Bible itself bears abundant witness to the fact that this is entirely possible. The Old Testament Jews, for example, said, 'We have the temple of the Lord. We have Abraham for our father. We don't need to be baptised or to be born again' (see Jeremiah 7:4; Matthew 3:9; John 3). The Pharisee was thankful to God because he wasn't like other men: he wasn't a sinner (Luke 18:11). Similarly, down through the centuries men have looked at their national connections, their liturgies and their various rites and ceremonies and assured themselves that they were true children of God.

This raises the whole question of presumptuous assurance. How can we distinguish spurious assurance from true spiritual assurance? If I am limited to one sentence I would simply say this: Spurious assurance is always accompanied by spiritual pride. It is always based on something egotistical and personal. In its very essence it is legalistic. It is based on my own morality, my own religiosity, my own sincerity, my own kind and quality of conversion, my own faith, my own conviction of sin, my own repentance, my own love for the brethren, and (maybe most often) my own zeal for religion. It is always based on something inherent: on something personal to myself. The man who is spiritually proud is a complete stranger to what the Lord calls poverty of spirit (Matthew 5:3). By contrast, the blessed man has no spiritual self-confidence. He comes to Christ and says, 'Nothing in my hand I bring.' Boasting is excluded (Romans 3:27). Was it David Dickson who said, 'I cannot bring my best work to the touchstone of God's law!'? The true believer is ashamed, not only of his evil deeds, but of his righteousness. He stands boastless before God, his whole identity contracted to the point where he is nothing but *the sinner* and he says quite simply, 'Lord, be merciful to me' (Luke 18:13). That is something the hypocrite can never begin to understand.

The Confession teaches, secondly, the possibility of a real, spiritual assurance. It insists that the true believer, who sincerely loves the Lord Jesus Christ and endeavours to walk in all good conscience before Him, can have an unshakeable confidence that he is in good standing before God. Sometimes, as we have seen, it has been a badge of orthodoxy to lack assurance. But if we deny the possibility of assurance, if we play down its importance, our position is, by Confessional standards, heretical. It is heresy to say that the child of God cannot have assurance. It is heresy to say that assurance is not important. The Confession insists that it is absolutely normal, and even obligatory, for the Christian to be confident that God is his Father. It certainly gives no countenance to the view that if one has assurance one's conversion must be highly suspect. I have heard, too often, the idea that if you didn't doubt your conversion, others should doubt it for you. Such reasoning is light-years away from the teaching of Luther and Calvin and the Westminster Confession. I can recall finding things very difficult as a young Christian because I didn't have the requisite doubts; and I still remember the pressure to have the humility that everybody else seemed to have. It was virtually mandatory to lack assurance. People said, 'When I was converted; that is, *if* I was converted ....' It simply wasn't *kosher* to be sure of having had this saving experience. I think that ethos is now behind us, although we can be sure that it will one day return in some other form to trouble the church. For the moment, I simply want to say to anyone tempted to go back to it, that it is a violation of Confessional teaching.

What does the Bible say?

But what does the Bible say? It lays down very clearly that it is perfectly normal for a Christian to be assured of his own salvation. In fact, it is very difficult to find in either the Old Testament or the New any instance of a child of God doubting whether he/she is a child of God. There are possibly some instances of doubt in the Old Testament, but they are very hard to find. It is surely quite remarkable that in the pre-Pentecost age, when the Spirit was less intimately active in God's people than He is today, we should find such boldness and confidence on the part of believers. The Psalms especially breathe the language of

`assurance. For example: 'The Lord is *my* shepherd' (Psalm 23:1).
'I am poor and needy; yet the Lord thinks of *me*' (Psalm 40:17).
'I know that *my* Redeemer lives' (Job 19:25). That's the way
these Old Testament believers thought of their relation to God.
We're back to Luther – religion consists in personal pronouns: in
being able to say, '*My* God!' These Old Testament saints could
certainly say that.

We find the same assurance in the New Testament. 'We know
that we have passed from death to life,' says the Apostle John (1
John 3:14). 'We know that nothing shall separate us from the
love of God,' writes St. Paul (Romans 8.39). The same Apostle
Paul was able, in the gloom of his Roman dungeon, to say, 'I have
finished the race, I have kept the faith. Now there awaits me the
crown of righteousness' (2 Timothy 4:7-8). He faced death with
total confidence because he was certain of his own relationship
with God.

Clearly, then, it is the teaching of both the Old and the New
Testaments that Christians are to be absolutely certain that God
loves them. Imagine how a human parent would feel if a child
expressed doubt as to his affection! How would we feel if a son
or daughter said, 'I don't know if my father loves me.' We would
surely be most disturbed! And is it not improbable in the extreme
that God should want His children not to know who their Father
is and not to know whether He loves them? Surely if God is our
Father He wants us to know it! He wants us to be sure that He
loves us. The Shorter Catechism, when defining the benefits
which flow from justification, lays down at the very head of the
list, 'assurance of God's love' (Answer 36). It is a remarkable
tribute to our tendency to disjoin theology from experience that
generations of Scottish Christians reared on the Shorter Catechism
thought it spiritual pride to have peace of conscience, assurance
of God's love and joy in the Holy Spirit!

How do we come to assurance?

The third thing we see from the Confession is that this assurance
is produced by two specific factors: the inward evidence of our

graces, and the witness of the Holy Spirit.

First: assurance arises from our finding in ourselves the inward evidence of those graces to which God's promises are addressed. At first glance, this seems a rather convoluted statement, but the reason for this particular form of words is simple. The divine promises are infallible: but they are addressed not to the whole human race nor to named individuals but to a specific class of people. The question is, Do I belong to this class? Am I one of Abraham's children? Am I a believer? Do I have the characteristics of the blessed man, as laid down in the Beatitudes?

Sometimes we make this inordinately difficult. For example, we look for marks of faith when it might be easier to look for faith itself. Faith is something we do with the conscious part of our mind and, other things being equal, we should be conscious of its workings. It is doubtful whether any other mark (for example, love for God or love for the brethren) is any more detectable than the act of faith itself. I am personally very conscious of my belief, particularly at an intellectual level, because I have known the pain and the agony of doubt; and I am also conscious that I find Christ attractive as I find nothing else and no-one else attractive.

This is the crucial question: Do we find such beauty in Christ as to desire Him (Isaiah 53:2)? Do we want Him? Faith, as we saw, is not simply assent. It is such a perception of the glory of Christ as makes us long to have Him for ourselves.

Alternatively, we can put it this way: What arguments do we use when we pray? These arguments are very good indicators of what our faith relies on. If we go to God and say, 'Lord, accept me because I am a very good man', our trust is in our own goodness. But if we go to God and say, 'Lord, accept me because of Jesus' blood and righteousness', our trust is in Jesus' blood and righteousness. If anyone were to tell God what great progress he had made, what spiritual fruit he bore or what graces adorned his life, this would be clear proof that his faith was not in Christ but in himself.

What, then, is our argument before God? Is it something we have done? Something we are? Something we feel? Or is it something Jesus Christ has done?

All this means that we should be directly conscious of our own faith. It is also true, however, that this faith has certain marks. For example, it revolutionises our social preferences: 'We know that we have passed from death unto life, because we love the brethren' (1 John 3:14). We love our fellow Christians. That is not always easy, but the Apostle John attaches great importance to it. It may be that in the very church itself some people cause us indescribable pain. Do we love them? Do we love those who persecute and hate us? That is a very great test of our whole relationship with God.

Or, take another mark: Do we know poverty of spirit? Do we know this persuasion at the very core of our being that our lives are indefensible and that we are spiritually powerless? We have nothing to offer to God; and because of that we are meek and we are merciful to others and we positively hunger and thirst after the righteousness we know we don't possess.

As I indicated before, there is no verse in the Bible that says, 'So-and-so is saved!' But there are verses that say that believers are saved; that those who see beauty in Christ are saved; that those who pray in the name of Christ are saved; that those who love the brethren are saved; that those who love their enemies are saved; and that those who are poor in spirit are saved. Do I find in myself those graces that distinguish the people of God?

The witness of the Holy Spirit

The second factor in assurance is the witness of the Holy Spirit to our own hearts. This has caused endless discussion among theologians. There is a sense in which the objective possession of the Spirit is itself the evidence. In other words, we are sealed with the Spirit. God attests His children by putting His Spirit in their hearts; and the Spirit in turn gives us filial feelings. He makes us cry, 'Abba! Father!' This ability to say 'Abba' to God is quite remarkable. One can search the whole of the Old Testament and the whole of rabbinical literature and never find a single instance of a believer addressing God as 'Abba!' When

Jesus Christ called God 'Father!' He was inaugurating a theological revolution. This had never before been done in Judaism. God had been seen in terms of power and holiness and the instinctive response had been one of fear. But Jesus called Him Abba! And when we talk about fellowship with Christ, that is a very important element in our fellowship: we share the Spirit that says 'Abba! Father!'

Let's return to the natural relationship between parents and children. It is very doubtful whether any of us has gone through a logical process in order to come to the assurance that our father is our father. Similarly, scrutiny of the marks of grace is not the normal road to the assurance that God is our Father, any more than analysis of the theistic proofs is the road by which we normally come to believe that God exists. As George Gillespie said, 'All thy marks will leave thee in the dark.' We have all known Christians who have borne very clear marks of a work of grace and yet have no assurance of salvation. Of course, without such marks assurance is presumption. But it is never enough to have this inward evidence. We must also have this work of the Spirit of God in the depths of our hearts, giving us this ability to go to God in all His holiness and all His heavenliness and all His grandeur and still say, 'Abba!' It is in the language of such assurance that the Lord Himself taught us to pray: 'Our Father, which art in Heaven.'

Daily experience of God's love

There is a third factor in assurance, not mentioned specifically in the Confession, but still of enormous importance: our daily experience of God's goodness and mercy. Here, again, there is a clear parallel with ordinary life. How, for instance, does a husband know that his wife loves him? If he is of a juridical cast of mind he can turn every day to his Marriage Certificate and say, 'Here is the proof that my wife loves me. This piece of paper certifies that we are married, and that she vowed to love me!' I doubt if that's how it works in practice. The assurance normally comes in the context of a living, daily relationship. Unfortunately, a good deal of Christian discussion on assurance closely resembles the practice of going back to check if the Marriage Certificate is in correct form, forgetting that confidence between parents and children, between husband and wife and, above all, between the believer and his Saviour is a matter of a living, ongoing, daily relationship. The multiplicity of loving acts, tolerances and forgivenesses is what fosters and strengthens assurance. No real marriage needs to go back to the title deeds for assurance. In the same way, it is our daily experience of the goodness of God that fosters our sense of His love. We cry to Him and He answers. We bring our needs to Him and He supplies. Things we hardly dare dream of, God gives us. The things we have done, God overlooks. Sometimes, of course, it is so demoralising, so humbling, to find that God is so kind. Sometimes, in our perverseness, we wish that God would not be so loving. Then we could stand up and argue with Him and get some of our ego back. But no! The constant flow of acts of goodness and mercy fuels the assurance. There is nothing particularly mystical or dramatic about it, any more than family life is mystical or dramatic. But it is there: God listening to us, God hearing us, God answering us, God supplying our needs, not in some niggardly way but according to His own riches in glory by Christ Jesus.

Let's not be going back constantly to the Marriage Certificate (or the Birth Certificate) to see if God really loves us. Let's look, instead, at the way He treats us.

Think again of my earlier point about the child who says, 'I don't know if my father loves me.' What kind of father does he have? And what impression do we convey to men of our Father? What impression do we convey to the angels when we doubt our Father's love? I am almost prepared to say that for a Christian such language is blasphemous. Are we saying that God hasn't shown us much kindness? that He hasn't shown us much love? that He is not very good to us? These would be the normal, logical deductions from the way we often speak! But it is surely a travesty of the truth, because God's mercies are new every morning. That's how we know He loves us.

Assurance not of the essence of faith

So far, then, we have seen three things. We have seen that hypocrites can enjoy some kind of assurance; we have seen that God's people can and should enjoy assurance; and we have seen the grounds of that assurance. Now we see, fourthly, that assurance is not of 'the essence of faith' (Westminster Confession, XVIII:2). In other words, a believer can lack assurance. Now, I am very conscious of the danger of such teaching. There are, and there have always been, Christians who react at once by saying that if we don't know whether we are converted, then we are not converted. Spirit Baptism, they say, is a conscious, unforgettable experience and once we've had it it remains impressed indelibly on our memories.

That can be put in terms of a pastoral problem. If this teaching is correct, nobody who doubts his conversion is a Christian. What then do we say to that relatively large number of men and women who lead lives of exemplary godliness and yet have no assurance of their own salvation? 'Rabbi' Duncan was tormented day after day by what he called, 'The same old question: Is John Duncan born again?' Similarly, C. H. Spurgeon often experienced deep spiritual depression. Are we to conclude that these men were not Christians? And are we to say that those people who come to almost every pastor in Scotland doubting some part of their experience are by definition not Christians?

Whatever that is, it is not Confessional theology. The Confession is crystal clear that assurance is not of the essence of faith. That doesn't mean that assurance is not important. It is so important that its absence is always a sign that there is something wrong. The norm is that a Christian should have assurance. Nevertheless, assurance is not of the essence of faith in the sense that every Christian has it and has it always.

The Confession puts that in two ways.

First, it lays down that a true believer may wait long for assurance (XVIII:3). He may come to assurance only a long time after his conversion. Again, I am not saying that this is the norm. I am not commending it, or encouraging it. I am simply saying that the possibility exists that a man may be in a converted state and not know it. He can be in a converted state and be tormented for months with doubts as to his own salvation. His assurance and his conversion do not coincide. In the context of modern Charismatic theology, this can easily lead to misunderstanding. Many people who claim to have had a subsequent Spirit baptism are, in fact, people in whose lives there has been a hiatus between conversion and assurance. They may easily feel that in the moment of assurance they have had some second overwhelming experience. It is very important that I should not deny the experience. I am simply denying the label. It is not Spirit Baptism.

There are so many instances of people who are converted and then go days or weeks or months or even years before they enjoy assurance! Sometimes, those involved in pastoral work may even have to confront some person with the possibility that he or she is a Christian. The person may not have assurance, and therefore doesn't feel bound to live like a Christian, and doesn't have the joy of a Christian. But what he needs may be to be brought to the point, not where he *becomes* a Christian, but where he *knows* he is a Christian.

This may not be a common experience, but it is certainly a possible one. For example, someone brought up in a tradition where there is great emphasis on dramatic conversion-experiences may conclude that because he has not had such an experience he cannot be a Christian at all. Take the case of John the Baptist. He never had any Damascus Road experience. But suppose he had been brought up in a tradition where people were always 'giving their testimonies' and where every testimony he ever heard followed an unvarying sequence (a life of debauchery, followed by an episode of conviction and then a moment of great spiritual deliverance). He would never have understood these testimonies. And if he had been told that that was the only way to become a Christian he would have said, 'Well, I'm not one, because I've never had that kind of experience.' There are as many conversions as there are Christians, each one different.

Losing our assurance

Secondly, the Confession tells us that we can have our assurance 'shaken, diminished, and intermitted' (XVIII:4). In other words, we can lose it. There are several factors that can contribute to this. One is the possibility of direct Satanic attack. The devil can, in a moment, and without any rational argument, take from us our faith that God exists or our faith that God loves us. Our joy, our peace and our confidence disappear and we cannot give any reason why it happened. There was no argument. It was simply taken away.

Again, we can lose our assurance because of our own temperament. There are people with a predisposition to depression, and this depression tends to feed on the most solemn aspects of religion. The temperament of some Christians is such that their thoughts are always on hell or on the unforgivable sin. It is not that the Bible's teaching on these matters creates their depression. It is rather that their depression gravitates towards the teaching on hell and towards the more sombre aspects of Calvinism, and ignores heaven and grace and comfort and divine pity and love. Experience shows that argument and biblical quotations can seldom shake such people out of their depression. We have to fall back on the Lord's own counsel: 'This kind comes forth by nothing but prayer and fasting' (Mark 9:29).

Sometimes, then, lack of assurance is a symptom of clinical depression. But it can also be due to bad teaching. Luther declared that the article by which a standing church is distinguished from a falling church is justification by faith alone. That is a very familiar form of words, but the doctrine itself is not all that common in the church today. Legalism always tends to creep back into our preaching, if not in the form of salvation of works then in the form of salvation by religious experience. People see that their lives are indefensible and they then conclude that they are not Christians. Or they find themselves being defeated, and come to the same conclusion. If they were receiving sound teaching, however, it would make unmistakeably clear that the fact that one is ungodly is not proof in itself that one is not a

Christian. It is indeed a very sad thing to be ungodly. It may be proof that a man is a very poor Christian. But God's people need to be taken into that glorious area where their acceptance before God is a matter of sheer grace: where the believer is able to make the most appalling accusations against himself, and yet know that he is accepted by God. The Apostle Paul did it: 'O wretched man that I am!' he said (Romans 7:24). But he also said, 'Nothing shall separate me from the love of God in Christ Jesus' (Romans 8:35ff.). It is a difficult art, to nourish the sense of wretchedness that is itself so necessary to a Christian and at the same time to nourish that assurance of God's love that is equally necessary to a Christian. The guiding principle must be that our acceptance with God does not depend on the quality of our own spiritual lives.

But lack of assurance can be caused not only by unsound teaching but also by *unbalanced* teaching: particularly teaching that centres on the marks of grace. It is important, of course, that people should examine themselves. But it is a complete betrayal of biblical proportion and balance to have people constantly looking at themselves and taking their own spiritual pulses. That produces spiritual hypochondriacs, and Scotland has produced many such. If people are brought into an area where their minds are imprisoned by the principle of radical doubt they will never get out of it. The great French philosopher, Descartes, began to doubt whether he himself existed. He wanted proof of his own existence. But if someone doubts his own existence he is not able to move. He is immobilised. Sometimes we get so immersed in the marks of grace and so introverted that we become paralysed. We raise a radical doubt as to our own salvation; and once the doubt is raised, there is no way out of it. 'That way madness lies' (King Lear, Act 3, scene 3). We shall never get anywhere if we become obsessionally preoccupied with the marks of grace. It is always a matter of proportion and balance, of course. Christians need to be criticised, they need to engage in self-examination and they need to take spiritual inventories now and again. But they cannot be fed on that kind of diet Sunday after Sunday.

Most sadly of all, however, we sometimes lose our assurance through our own sin. We do something which completely disrupts our relationship with God. This often happens on the human level. A member of a family does something which disrupts the whole relationship. God, too, has children who sometimes do things that make it imperative that He should not smile on them or talk to them or favour them with blessings: things that force Him to withdraw his Spirit and take from us the confidence to say, 'Abba, Father.'

Practical

What does assurance mean on a practical level? How important is it to our Christian lives? It is often said that it is the doubter who is spiritually active. In a way, the person who doubts his salvation is active, of course. But is he active for God and for His kingdom? Bunyan's Pilgrim was active, in a sense, when he went back to look for the Roll he had lost. But he had to turn his back on where he was going. He had to give up all his other activities to go back and find the roll. That is what happens when we lose our assurance. We have to go back. We are taken out of the action. We cannot witness and we cannot evangelise.

Where, may I ask, do we find the New Testament parallel to a man who is 'exercised' day in, day out, about whether he is saved or not? whose whole spiritual and psychic energy, not to say his physical energy, is directed towards looking for his parchment? What the Confession says is that, so far is Christian assurance from 'inclining men to looseness' that it is the stimulus to diligence in 'the duties of obedience' (18:3). Real assurance gets us working for God. 'The love of Christ constrains us' (2 Corinthians 5:14). 'I love the Lord, because my voice and prayers he did hear' (Psalm 116:1). The great men who did so much for God (for example, Martin Luther, John Calvin and John Knox) were never found prostrate with doubt as to whether God loved them. They knew that God loved them. That was their dynamo. That was what kept them going. Andrew Bonar, converted in 1830, recorded in his *Diary* in 1889, 'The Lord has enabled me to lean upon Christ, day by day, for sixty years .... and has never once left me in darkness as to my interest in Him all that time.'

We must have sympathy with doubt, but we must also get away from the idea that there is something meritorious or humbling in doubt itself. There is nothing that humbles a man more than knowing that he is precious to God. That is what makes us feel small. That is what makes us feel debtors to mercy alone. Such assurance produces not looseness or slackness but a deep, driving sense of gratitude to God.

> When I survey the wondrous cross
> On which the Prince of Glory died,
> My richest gain I count but loss,
> And pour contempt on all my pride.
>
> Were the whole realm of nature mine,
> That were an offering far too small,
> Love so amazing, so divine,
> Demands my soul, my life, my all.
>
> (Isaac Watts)

13

Be Filled with the Spirit

We move on now to ask what happens when someone believes. The primary answer is that in the very first moment of faith we are united to the Lord Jesus Christ. We come to be in Christ and Christ comes to be in us. That is the foundation of our salvation in all its developing aspects, and in and through that union with Christ we enjoy justification, the forgiveness of all our sins, adoption into the family of God, consecration and transformation. All this happens the very moment we come to believe.

We are also, in that moment of faith-union with Christ, filled with the Holy Spirit. This privilege is one of the core elements in our initiation as Christians. It is something that happens through faith in Christ and it happens immediately we come to be in union with Him. It is as much part of the meaning of being a Christian as justification, adoption or sanctification.

Terminology

The first thing we need to look at is the question of nomenclature or vocabulary. Efforts are often made to distinguish between being *filled with the Spirit* on the one hand and being *baptised in the Spirit* on the other. To add to the confusion some Christians also say that to *have* or to *receive* the Spirit is one thing but to be *filled* with the Spirit is something quite different; and still others draw a similar wedge between being *sealed* with the Spirit and being *filled* with the Spirit.

We have, then, these various terms: to be *filled*, to be *baptised*, to *have*, to *receive*, to be *sealed*. Can we draw distinctions between them? And can we use them as labels for distinct experiences?

I hold very firmly that it is impossible to draw any clear

163

distinction between these terms and that, in fact, they describe, more or less indiscriminately, the same experience. To be *baptised* with the Spirit is the same as to be *filled* with the Spirit, is the same as to *receive* the Spirit, is the same as to *have* the Spirit, is the same as to be *sealed* with the Spirit.

The main reason for my saying that is that virtually all of these terms are used to describe what happened on the day of Pentecost. In Acts 1:5, as the Lord foretells the events of that day He describes as a being *baptised*: 'In a few days you will be baptised with the Holy Spirit.' That promise is a clear allusion to Pentecost. Yet in the account of Pentecost the phrase 'baptised with the Spirit' is not used at all. Instead what is said is that they were all '*filled* with the Holy Spirit' (Acts 2:4). In other words, the great promise of being *baptised* with the Spirit is fulfilled in terms of being *filled* with the Spirit. In Acts 10:47, on the other hand Peter, referring to what happened in the house of Cornelius, declares, 'They have received the Holy Spirit just as we have.' The Pentecost experience is defined here in terms simply of *receiving* the Spirit of God.

Clearly, then, Luke is not using these words to draw precise technical distinctions between various levels of experience. To *receive* the Holy Spirit is to be *baptised* in the Holy Spirit; and to be *baptised* in the Spirit is to be *filled* with the Spirit. No-one *receives* who is not *baptised*, and no-one is *baptised* who is not *filled*.

This idea of being filled with the Spirit is worth lingering over. There are two points to be borne in mind.

First, to be filled with the Spirit is always something we owe either to God the Son or to God the Father. It is God Himself who fills us with the Holy Spirit. It is not so much that we are baptised by the Spirit or filled by the Spirit or even sealed by the Spirit. Instead, the Spirit is the medium in which we are baptised or the element with which we are filled. He is not the Baptiser. He is not the Agent. He is the one *in* whom God the Father or God the Son baptises, pouring Him out upon us until we are drenched.

The second point is precisely that: the baptising always

amounts to a filling or to a very full experience of the Spirit of
God. The reason why that has to be said is that the Holy Spirit is
a Person and therefore there is no possibility of our receiving
simply part of the Holy Spirit. We are filled with the Spirit. We
are baptised in the Spirit. We receive the whole Holy Spirit, in the
fullness of His divine personality and in the fullness of His
activity. The Holy Spirit does not do a half job or undertake only
some of His functions or engage in a partial ministry in the life
of any Christian. He comes in all that He is to do all that He can.

His ministry is described most comprehensively as a ministry
of encouragement. In detail it means that He comes to lead and
comfort His children, to sanctify them, to mortify sin and to stir
up all His own gifts within them. It really is a most glorious fact
about Christians, that the Holy Spirit, the divine Person, lives in
each one of us; and in each one of us engages in a full ministry.
God does not give the Spirit by measure (John 3:34), doling Him
out in some limited way. He gives Him in abundance. We often
find it difficult to believe this. We ask, How can Someone as
great as the Holy Spirit live in our puny personalities? and
starting from that point we begin to impose limits and constraints
on the gospel. The simple fact is that God does come into our
puny lives in the whole of His personal glory, with the result that
we become temples of the Holy Spirit (1 Corinthians 6:19) and
experience the whole range of the Spirit's ministry. But is this
experience shared by all Christians? Or is it the privilege of only
some, and possibly of only a minority?

The Charismatic Movement has as its central tenet that the
experience of Spirit-baptism or Spirit-filling is not enjoyed by
every single believer; nor is it usually given in the moment of
conversion. It is, they say, a post-conversion, second-tier
experience granted by God only to some of His children. In other
words, you can be a believer and yet not have been filled with the
Spirit. You can be born again and you can be saved and you can
be united to Christ and yet you can lack the experience of Spirit-
baptism.

Now, I respect the character and lifestyle and missionary zeal of many who hold this point of view. But I believe that they are profoundly mistaken. I also believe that their mistake is a serious one. People who have not been baptised in the Spirit are not Christians at all. To deny that is to leave room for so-called carnal Christians: religious people who live on a very low moral and spiritual plane and yet claim to be Christians, lacking only the second-tier experience of the Spirit.

Why do I hold that Spirit-baptism or Spirit-filling is something enjoyed by all Christians?

First, because according to Acts 2:4, 'they were all filled with the Holy Spirit.' That is the story of Pentecost. Verse 1 tells us that when it happened 'they were all together in one place'. They were not doing anything particularly important or exciting. They were simply there. It was not what is sometimes called a 'tarrying meeting'. There was no great importunity. There was no heightened atmosphere. They were simply there, and while they were there the Holy Spirit came on every one of them. The whole church of God was there: and they were all baptised. No one was left out. There is a strong suggestion, too, that this is to be the model for the New Testament age: 'In these last days, this is the way it is going to be. I will pour out my Spirit on all people' (Acts 2:17). All people: young men and old men, sons and daughters and servants, the whole body of Christ. The whole stress falls on the universalness of the experience.

Secondly, there is the sequel to Pentecost. At the conclusion of Peter's sermon the 3,000 converts are given the promise of 'the gift of the Holy Spirit' (Acts 2:38). Peter tells them, 'Repent (which is simply, Be converted) and be baptised and you will receive this gift.' He does not say, 'Be converted and wait for some other experience.' They are converted, they submit to baptism, and the Holy Spirit is given to them.

The same teaching is laid down very explicitly in 1 Corinthians 12:13: 'We were all baptised by one Spirit into one body.' The language here is exactly the same as that of Acts 1:5: 'You will be baptised with the Holy Spirit.' In both instances the Greek preposition is *en* (*in*). What is promised in Acts 1:5 is declared to be universal in 1 Corinthians 12:13: all believers are baptised in one Spirit. This is confirmed by the words which come later in this same verse, although they have caused translators some perplexity. What we read in the older versions is that, 'we were made to drink of one Spirit'. But modern scholars are fairly confident that what is being said here is that we were all *irrigated* or *drenched* in one Spirit. The term is a horticultural one. We are all plants in God's garden and we are all irrigated simply because we *are* plants in God's garden. It cannot be that the Great Husbandman leaves some of His plants un-irrigated. This is equally clear if we return to Paul's original metaphor. When he says that we are all baptised into one body, he means that if we are in the body of Christ at all then our mere participation in that body involves our being baptised in the Spirit of God. Otherwise we end up with the very danger Paul was so concerned to avoid: a schism in the body between those baptised in the Spirit and those not baptised.

A medical metaphor may be helpful here. The body, medical people tell us, has its own complex irrigation system, which carries fluids to every limb, every organ and every cell. It is fatal for any part of it to suffer dehydration. Paul was probably not conversant with those medical marvels but the comparison is still interesting. If we are in the body of Christ then the irrigation systems of the spiritual body are as efficient as those of the natural body. This great Spirit, this power, this enablement, this water of life is carried to every single cell. One cannot be in it and not profit from the irrigation. Similarly, one cannot be a plant in the Lord's garden without having the same experience. Jesus spoke of Himself as the vine and His people as the branches (John 15:5). There again the irrigation from which the vine profits must affect every single branch. Otherwise there is no life or productivity. So the explicit teaching here is that every convert is baptised in, or filled with, one Spirit.

This may seem coldly dialectical, but in truth the notion that baptism in the Spirit is limited to some believers violates the most fundamental elements of the Christian doctrine of salvation.

It was the great distinctive of Reformation theology, for example, that by faith alone one came into possession of all the glories of salvation. Now the Roman Catholic Church believed in faith, too, and stressed its importance, but it would never allow that faith alone secured salvation. It had to be faith plus all kinds of other things. But the Reformation said, 'No! By faith alone you are justified, adopted, and share in the priesthood of all believers; and by faith alone you have the Holy Spirit.' But this modern teaching comes and says, 'By faith alone you don't really have the Holy Spirit. You have Him in some partial way but not in a full way: not in complete measure!' What is happening is that *sola fide* is once again being truncated. Galatians 3:2 tells us explicitly that we receive the Spirit simply by the hearing of faith. But I am now told that faith does not secure this gift for me. On the contrary, it brings me only a partial salvation and a limited experience of God's Spirit. That, surely, is a severe limitation of faith.

In the same way the Charismatic doctrine of Spirit-baptism strikes at the notion of union with Christ. If we look at Ephesians 1 we find time and time again the apostle using the phrase, *in Christ*. We have everything in Christ. In Him we have our adoption and our predestination (verse 5), our redemption and our forgiveness (verse 7). In Him we have every spiritual blessing (verse 3). How can we say that we have every spiritual blessing in Christ if we can be in Him and lack the baptism and sealing and filling of the Spirit of God? In actual fact that blessing is itself utterly central: 'You were sealed with the Holy Spirit of promise' (Ephesians 1:13). To miss out on this sealing is to miss out on the whole Christian inheritance.

Again, the idea of a limited Spirit baptism truncates the Christian doctrine of the atonement. Some of the boldest and most powerful language in the Bible is in Galatians 3:13: 'Christ redeemed us from the curse of the law by becoming a curse for us.' God's Son made a curse for us! Why did He do it? What did He achieve by this terrible atonement? What was the point of this dreadful experience? 'That the blessing promised to Abraham might come to the Gentiles through Jesus Christ, so that by faith we might receive the promise of the Spirit' (Galatians 3:14).

Why did Christ die? What does it mean, to have the blood of Christ sprinkled upon us? It means that we have the promise of the Spirit. By faith Christ died. By faith we have the Spirit of God. We cannot say, 'We benefit from the atonement, but we don't have the Holy Spirit.' By faith alone we have the Spirit. In Christ we have the Spirit. By the blood of the cross we are filled and sealed. We cannot go on to say, 'The cross alone does not secure that!'

The Charismatic Movement is essentially perfectionist because it always wants more than faith, more than being in Christ and more than the blood of the cross. It is not happy with the ungodly man who has nothing but that he believes in Jesus and that he is united to Christ. Yet that is the gospel. Such a man has no *plus*. There is nothing I can do in addition to being in Christ. There is nothing I *must* do in addition to having faith and being sprinkled with the blood. There cannot be something over and above the blood, the simple blood of Christ, that secures Spirit baptism. There is not something I must do, like tarrying; or renouncing all known sin; or really, really, really, believing; or really submitting; or fully surrendering. All those adverbs! And the devil comes in and says, 'You're surrendered, but are you fully surrendered? You believe, but do you really believe?'

It all comes back to the same thing: that unless we are special, second-tier Christians, we don't have this blessing. That is why I say that this is all so fundamentally unevangelical. It compromises the gospel because it says that faith alone and Christ alone and the blood alone are not sufficient to secure that great promise to Abraham which is the very core of our salvation.

It is a great pity that the debate with the Charismatic Movement is so often fought on the basis simply of tongue speaking. That is a peripheral issue. It can at least be said in favour of tongue-speaking that it was practised within the New Testament church. But it cannot be said that only a minority of the early Christians had received Spirit baptism, and it is on that issue that the debate must be conducted. Even if we could grant that tongue-speaking still exists today, that is not the issue. The issue is whether the charismatic is correct in his claim that such tongue-speaking is proof of Holy Spirit baptism. It certainly wasn't in the New Testament. Many spoke in tongues who did not have Spirit baptism; and many of those who did have Spirit baptism gave no sign of speaking in tongues.

This debate is about the Christian gospel. It is about the significance of being in Christ. It is about the significance of faith alone. Above all, it is about the significance of the atonement. Does the cross give us a full salvation? Does it secure the promise? Does it give us every spiritual blessing? Does it give us the ministry of the Holy Spirit of God? I think it does. It is the glory of Reformation and biblical teaching that we are complete in Christ (Colossians 2:10). That is the greatest truth imaginable! In Christ, with nothing else to commend us or to describe us, we have everything. In Him we have every spiritual blessing. In Him we are filled with all the fulness of God (Ephesians 3:19). It is that precious truth that Charismatic theology jeopardises.

There are, however, passages in the book of Acts that seem to contradict this position. For example, the so-called Samaritan Pentecost (Acts 8). Philip evangelised, the Samaritans believed and then they were baptised; John and Peter came and found that the converts did not have the Holy Spirit. Is this an instance of believers who do not have the Spirit?

There are two things to notice.

First, it is quite possible that they were not believers in any genuine sense. The language used is very strange: they believed Philip's preaching (Acts 8:12). They believed the message. There may have been nothing of personal trust in and commitment to Christ.

Secondly, this was a totally a-typical situation. It was the first time the gospel had gone beyond the Jewish community into a different constituency altogether and there was a real danger of a separate Samaritan church emerging, claiming independence of the church in Jerusalem. God deliberately created a hiatus in the order of redemption so that these believers did not receive Spirit baptism until the apostles arrived and fellowship was established with the church in Jerusalem. The whole event is an emphatic statement to the effect that only in the one church of Christ, only in union with the apostles, is the gift of the Spirit going to be experienced.

The other passage of some consequence is in Acts 19, the account of the Ephesian believers who had never heard of the Holy Spirit. These people were, in fact, disciples of John the Baptist (Acts 19:3). They had some little knowledge of the Lord Jesus, but they had no experience of the Holy Spirit. They had never even heard of Him (Acts 19:2). The crucial thing is this: with those believers an apostle did something we never see done on any other occasion in the New Testament. He re-baptised them. That clearly indicates that Paul was not happy with their condition. They were really Old Testament believers, followers of John the Baptist, who had never been baptised in the triune Name. Paul, therefore, baptised them in the appropriate way and the Spirit came on them (Acts 19:6).

We move on to consider on a more practical level what the Bible means when it says, 'Be filled with the Spirit' (Ephesians 5:18). This is an imperative addressed to all Christians. Furthermore, the tense used in the Greek is the continuous present, which means that this is not a punctiliar, single-moment, once-for-all experience. What Paul is actually saying is, 'Keep on being filled!' It is not only possible for someone to have more than one filling: it is imperative. Peter was filled with the Spirit at Pentecost (Acts 2:4). In Acts 4:8 he was filled again. Stephen was 'a man full of faith and of the Holy Spirit' (Acts 6:5). That was his habitual state.

God's directive to us, then, is to keep on being filled with the Spirit. Our concern as Christians must be to go to Him and say, 'Keep on filling me with your Spirit. Keep Him there and grant me His ministry in every single area of life.'

This means, first of all, that we must avoid whatever grieves the Spirit. Whatever we pretend to the contrary, there is usually little mystery about the ebb and flow of our spiritual lives. The loss of dynamism and the lack of love are easily explained. We can go back and find that somewhere we have violated God's commandment. We have gone off God's road and grieved His Spirit. If we want to keep on being filled with the Spirit there must be a studious, sensitive care to avoid anything that grieves Him.

Secondly, being filled with the Spirit means abiding in Christ. Of course, there is a definitive moment when we make our initial commitment to Christ, and too often Christians think, 'Well, that's it. I was saved on such and such a day.' It's all in the past! But the Bible keeps on saying, 'No! It must be continuous. It must be present.' We not only receive Christ and take Him for our Saviour. We abide in Him. We cling to Him. We bind ourselves around Him with tenacity. And we keep on doing it day after day, manifesting the stickability of faith.

Thirdly, it means that we 'keep in step with the Spirit', to use the language of Galatians 5:25. The word used here was used in Greek for formation dancing. In such dancing it is very important that everyone keep in step. Similarly, being a Christian means that we stay in formation: we keep in step with the Spirit of God.

Ultimately, it all comes back to this: Does it really matter to us? All the ebb and flow of our Christian lives can be explained in terms of these principles: that we have sometimes run the risk of grieving the Spirit; that we have sometimes not been concerned to abide in Christ; and that we have sometimes broken formation and not kept in step with the Spirit of God.

Supposing that we do keep on being filled with the Spirit, what are the effects? How does it show in our lives?

First, it has the exactly opposite effect of alcohol: 'Do not get drunk on wine, which leads to debauchery. Instead, be filled with the Spirit' (Ephesians 5:18). This passage is often abused. People speak of being 'drunk with the Holy Spirit', 'drunk with God', being 'a God-intoxicated man'. They give the impression that a really religious person is intoxicated, in a state of ecstasy, in a religious frenzy, drunk with the Spirit, intoxicated with the love of Jesus. Far from it! What the Bible says is, Do NOT be drunk!

A drunken man has no self-control, neither physical nor emotional. He is out of touch with reality because of what alcohol has done to his brain. To have the Spirit of God, on the other hand, is to have a spiritual mind and thus to be exercising self-control. Time and again the Bible speaks of moderation and sobriety. We are to have our appetites, our emotions, our lusts and our instincts under control.

We sometimes tend to think that if we had the Spirit we would find it easy to approaching total strangers about the gospel, because we would be totally uninhibited and tact would not matter. On the contrary, that's when it would matter. Then we would speak in the most loving, tactful, self-controlled and creative way.

The Holy Spirit imparts control. There is not a single recorded instance when Jesus appeared like a drunken man. He was never too loud, or emotionally uncontrolled. Of course I want the most prodigal zeal for Christ. I want enthusiasm. I want emotion, love, urgency, agony. But these are rational. The Spirit-filled man is mentally disciplined. He walks into a place and is totally aware of his audience and of his environment. He handles the situation wisely precisely because he is sober. There is nothing uncouth, uncontrolled, barbaric, insensitive, impersonal or egotistical about such a man. He is the very opposite of drunk because his brain is under the Spirit's control and working at its maximum efficiency.

Secondly, if we are filled with the Spirit the effects will be most apparent in the moral and ethical sphere. Paul makes this clear in Ephesians 5. The great, overall result of being filled with the Spirit is that we submit to one another (Ephesians 5:21). The context also speaks of Spirit-filled praise and gratitude, but it is marvellous to see the Apostle move from the principle of being filled with the Spirit to detailed ethical instructions about husbands and wives, parents and children, masters and servants (Ephesians 6). Being filled with the Spirit shows itself first and foremost in our relationships: in the kind of husband we are, in the kind of wife, in the kind of parent, in the kind of child, employer or employee.

Above all, it shows itself in submission. Surely the great thing here is this: the transformation of attitudes so that I never, never approach a problem or a relationship from the standpoint of my own rights. I approach it from the standpoint of my obligations. That is the value of the whole idea of submission. The natural man, the non-spiritual man, knows his rights. He knows what everybody else owes him. But to the Christian, the only person who has rights is the other person. Paul doesn't tell the husband, or the child, or the employer his rights. He tells every one of them his obligations. It would work wonders in the church if we had that kind of spiritual attitude, concerned not with what people owe us but with what we owe them.

In other words, the primary effect of Spirit baptism is not in the realm of the emotions (inducing ecstasy). Nor is it in the realm of gifts (giving us spectacular powers). It is in the realm of personal living, transforming us so that we live in accordance with God's Word and, in particular, in accordance with His principle that we are always to submit our own interests to those of others.

14

Holiness

The Shorter Catechism contains many superb definitions of the fundamental doctrines of the Christian faith. We must not forget, however, that it is a human document and as such liable to occasional lapses. In its definition of sanctification, for example, it makes a deliberate distinction between sanctification and justification. Sanctification is a *work*: justification an *act*. The difference was important to the divines. Justification was instantaneous, whereas sanctification was an ongoing process.

The distinction may have some merit. The problem is, it does not reflect the way the concept of sanctification is used in the New Testament. There the stress falls not so much on sanctification as a process, but on sanctification as the moment of transformation that lies at the beginning of the Christian life.

This point was brought out very clearly by the late Professor John Murray in an important article on *Definitive Sanctification*.[1] In this article, Professor Murray drew attention to the fact that most of the relevant biblical texts referred not to ongoing transformation but to definitive and instantaneous transformation. That does not mean that the old approach is erroneous. It means that the old approach is inadequate, and that in future we must always analyse sanctification from the two points of view: on the one hand, *definitive sanctification* and, on the other, *progressive sanctification*. In other words, we have two facts brought before us in the Bible: all Christians are holy and all Christians are becoming holy. Unless we emphasise both of these, our doctrine is defective.

Definitive sanctification

The idea of definitive sanctification is, as we saw, simply a matter of faithfulness to the Bible's own use of this term. In

1 Corinthians 1:2, for example, those addressed are defined as 'sanctified in Christ Jesus and called to be holy'. The emphasis, surely, is that they are already sanctified in Christ Jesus. The tense is a punctiliar one, referring to the point at which they came to be in Christ Jesus and indicating that at that same point they were sanctified. As a result, they are already saints.

We find the same thing in 1 Corinthians 6:11, where Paul contrasts the present state of these believers with their former state. They had been thieves and drunkards and sexually immoral, 'but you were washed, you were sanctified, you were justified in the name of the Lord Jesus Christ and by the Spirit of our God.' The very same language is used of sanctification as is used of justification. All agree that justification is a once-for-all experience at the commencement of our Christian lives. The same must be true of sanctification. These Corinthians were sanctified at the same time as they were justified. In this respect, sanctification and justification are co-ordinates: the two different aspects of what happens to us as a result of our union with Christ. There is a once-for-all change in our whole position.

There are three things to note concerning this change.

Change in relationship

First, definitive sanctification involves *a change of relationship*. The word *holy*, particularly in the Old Testament, does not refer in the first instance to a moral state, but to a relationship. There were holy cities, holy vessels, holy buildings. When the Old Testament spoke of Jerusalem being holy, for example, or the nation being holy, it did not mean that they were good or morally pure. It meant that they stood in a special relationship to God. They were set apart from a common to a holy use. They were consecrated. They were separated to God. Something holy was, literally, cut off. In fact, the idea was not very far from the idea of something being cursed. Something cursed was devoted to God for destruction; something holy was devoted to God for His use and for His enjoyment.

That is one of the great primary ideas in definitive

sanctification: Christians are set apart from a common to a holy use. They are no longer common or profane. They belong to God. That in turn is rooted in the idea of redemption. In redemption we have been bought: therefore we should glorify God in our bodies and in our spirits (1 Corinthians 6:20). They are for God's use. Indeed, everything we are and everything we have has been set apart from a common to a holy use. We are 'separated unto the gospel of God' (Romans 1:1). God has called us out. He has set us apart. We are His 'peculiar people' (1 Peter 2:9): his special possession.

Transformation
Secondly, definitive sanctification means *transformation*. What we are is radically altered. Our whole being is changed. Our humanness undergoes radical transformation. It is put most dramatically in these New Testament terms: 'If anyone is in Christ, he is a new creation' (2 Corinthians 5:17). If we are in Christ the 'old man' is crucified, the 'old man' is dead, the 'old man' is done away with. We become new creatures in Christ Jesus.

Of course, that does not mean that 'the flesh' is destroyed. Nor does it mean that there is no indwelling sin or that we have no more spiritual struggles or spiritual problems. But it does mean that we are new. We are not the people that we were. The person, the proclivities, the prejudices and the incapacities that used to mark us no longer exist.

This poses a serious challenge to much traditional theology, which has sometimes been too willing to accommodate everything to the notion of indwelling sin. It has been perilously easy to say in the midst of our own guilt and our own failings, 'Ah! That's only the Old Man! That's the Old Adam!' This was one reason why John Murray gave such emphasis to the notions both of definitive sanctification and of the destruction of the 'old man'. That old unregenerate person is no longer there. That man that we used to be cannot be blamed for anything we do. It is we ourselves, the new man, who sins. It is the regenerate self. It is this man in Christ, this man filled with the Spirit. That is why the doctrine is so important. It has such great moral leverage because God has done this mighty thing: He has destroyed the man we used to be and He has turned us into new creatures.

Now, of course, this new man has continuities with the old man. He has the same temperament. He has the same physical body. He has the same IQ. He may have the same bi-polar depression. He may have much of the old introspectiveness or the old extrovertness about him. Yet, at the same time, there is so much that is new. The problem for Reformed religion has been that we have been so busy reacting to perfectionism that we have found it hard to do justice to the change effected in definitive sanctification. The New Man has a whole range of new powers: things he can now do which he could never do before. We have been down-playing these, minimising their importance. This new person can believe. This new person can repent. This new person can love God. This new person can love the people of God. This new person can loathe sin and struggle against sin. This new person sees beauty in Christ. This new person hungers and thirsts for God. This new person has patience under the mighty hand of God. This new person has a concern for the souls of the lost that she never had before.

We do Christianity a disservice when we minimise the significance of these new forces and abilities. We are not what we used to be. We cannot go back and blame that 'old man', because he is dead and a dead man cannot be blamed. What we face is this terrible teaching of St. Paul that *we* sin; and we sin in union with Christ. We sin as those indwelt by the Spirit of God.

But the idea of definitive sanctification also means that when we are faced with the startling demands of the Christian ethic (for example, to turn the other cheek and to go the extra mile) we cannot plead that, 'It's impossible because we're human and we still have the "old man"!' God's indicatives always go before God's imperatives. The Sermon on the Mount is addressed to people who are called 'saints': people whom God has transformed and who as new creatures possess the resources and the capacities

and the abilities to cope with the law of God. They cannot turn
to God and say, 'Lord, You haven't given me the resources!' On
the contrary, God has given them everything they need for life
and godliness (2 Peter 1:3).

Union with Christ

The third point about definitive sanctification is this: it is all a
matter of *union with Christ*. That is the fundamental thing about
a Christian. He is in Christ and Christ is in him. Besides, this
Christ is the risen Lord; and we, therefore, are united to the power
of His resurrection (Philippians 3:10). We are 'wired' into Jesus.
We are branches; He is the vine. We are members of His body;
He is the Head. He is the nerve centre, and the control-centre, and
all the energy stored up in Him is available to us. We are rooted
and built up in Him (Colossians 2:7). 'I live,' said St. Paul, 'yet
not I, but Christ lives in me, and I can do all things in the one who
strengthens me.'

Today we hear much about self-image. In sport and industry
and public life, so much depends on personal confidence. Even
preaching the gospel is, to some extent, a question of confidence:
confidence that we have something worth saying and that by
God's grace we can say it, even though at the same time we
tremble. If I begin to doubt that what I am saying is worth saying,
or to doubt that God will help me say it, then I get tied up in knots
and I can't do it. That is equally true in the whole area of the
Christian life. Many of us are defeated before we start because we
have an unbiblically low self-esteem. It is not a matter of natural
egotism. It is a matter of taking God at His word. He says we are
the light of the world and the salt of the earth (Matthew 5:13,14).
And of course we say, 'Who? Me, Lord? You mean US?' Yes!
He means us! We are new in Christ Jesus and if He tells us to
climb that mountain or carry this load or bear this temptation,
then we can do it. 'We are more than conquerors through him
who loved us' (Romans 8:37). There is nothing that God demands
of us which the Christ in us cannot do.

Progressive sanctification

But the Christian experiences not only instantaneous, definitive change, but also progressive transformation. By grace we move ever closer to complete Christ-likeness (Romans 8:29).

This progressive sanctification involves, first of all, *mortification*. We have to mortify sin. There is a great treatise by John Owen on this subject, based largely on Romans 8.[2] St. Paul's teaching there is so categorical! 'If you live according to the flesh, you will die, but if you mortify the deeds of the body you will live' (Romans 8:13). The versions obscure the force of Paul's language. What he says, literally, is this: 'If you murder sin, if you club it and batter it to death, then you will live.' He is not referring simply to sin in the abstract. It is very easy to live with sin in the abstract! But the Bible asks us to be interested not simply in sin, but in *sins*: in the deeds of the body, in the works of the flesh, itemised and individualised so that we know precisely those things in our own lives that we have to murder. And if we don't mobilise ourselves against these enemies the result is going to be fatal. Mortification is not something that happens to us automatically and unconsciously, merely by regularly attending church or being in Christian company or having regular seasons of prayer. It is not a process of osmosis. It is something we must do deliberately and consciously to our own sins.

Yet it is never something we do on our own. We do it as those who are led by the Spirit of God. It is the Spirit who leads this great death-squad as it goes about its business of searching for sins and clubbing them to death. We are terribly deluded if we imagine that we are being led by the Spirit while at the same time we are cavorting with sin. Being led by the Spirit means we are at war with sin; and not only with the grosser and more carnal and more obvious sins, but with the inward sins of envy, pride, malice, hypocrisy and self-righteousness. We are at war with everything that leads us to feel superior to others; and with all that tempts us to walk by on the other side when we stumble on the lost and the wayward. We need the Spirit of God to take us into those areas of self-knowledge where we are up against the truth about ourselves: face to face with our own guilt and our own failure. If we do not live at that interface, then God's Spirit is not dealing with us at all. We must ask God, 'Lord, show me myself. Give me *your* view of me.' And when He shows us something He finds obnoxious, we have to act as executioners and bludgeon it to death.

Renewal

The second element in progressive sanctification is *renewal:* 'we are renewed in the whole man after the image of God' (Shorter Catechism, Answer 35). In the New Testament this renewal is invariably progressive rather than definitive. Romans 12:2 is typical: 'Be transformed by the renewing of your mind.' It is also total: a renewal of the whole man. Every single aspect of the human personality is affected. Before conversion, we are totally depraved. After conversion we are totally sanctified. This affects our desires, our ambitions and our emotions. It is never merely a matter of the intellect. It is certainly not a matter of simply adopting a new set of beliefs.

Yet there can be no doubt but that the New Testament places very special emphasis on renewal of the mind. This is not simply a matter of what we think. It is more a matter of *how* we think. In his book, *The Christian Mind,* Harry Blamires argues that Christians often attack problems in exactly the same way as non-Christians. Their judgements on political issues, their attitudes to professional problems and their approaches to ethical dilemmas are often no different. Surely there is something wrong here. If we are Christians, shouldn't we approach a problem differently? Shouldn't we approach it from the Bible's point of view? Our instinct should be to ask, What would Jesus do? How would He see this particular problem? If we are Christians, both our starting-point and our method of approach are different because our minds are different.

All this comes out very clearly in the account of the disciples' reaction when Jesus told them He was to be crucified (Mark 8:31). They were horrified! But what did Jesus say? That they were thinking of the cross from a perspective that was entirely human: 'You do not have in mind the things of God, but the things of men' (Mark 8:33).

We have to learn, instead, to look at everything from God's standpoint, asking Christ's questions and presenting biblical challenges as we face every dilemma in our own lives.

This renewal has a template. We are to be renewed according to the image of Jesus (Ephesians 4:24). This depends, again, on how we see this Christ. For me, the essential thing is Christ as the Servant: the One who made Himself nothing (Philippians 2:7). Holiness is Christ-likeness, and Christ-likeness is service. Holiness is the mind of a servant, the mind that says, 'I have no rights; I have only obligations.' That is the Bible's teaching. It challenges the medieval legacy: the Christ of the icons and the tapestries; the great, imperial, dominant, grand, terrifying figure. To many of us a 'holy man' is an august, unbending, judgmental person. Such a paradigm cannot stand in the light of Christ: this Christ who never condoned sin, yet is always there for others.

So much of my Christianity is only a pale reflection of the real thing. The real thing was the Man who was willing to be crucified between two thieves on the garbage heap outside the city walls. The pilgrimage I am called to is not along a road lined with acclaim or power or influence or ease or comfort. It is routed along the *Via Dolorosa*, where nothing is easy and nothing is comfortable, because we have no right to use our divine sonship to claim favours.

Growth

Thirdly, *growth*. It is, after all, *progressive* sanctification. We start from a position of spiritual infancy and childishness and grow up into spiritual maturity. We grow in grace: in graciousness, pleasantness and beauty. The Christian gets lovelier and lovelier. At least, that is the way it should be. Growth does not mean that the Christian becomes more and more austere in relation to others, more and more remote, more and more terrifying, more and more witch-doctor-like . He becomes lovelier and lovelier: gracious, pleasant, beautiful. He grows in knowledge. He grows in his ability to resist temptation. He grows in the ability to fit into the body, to be part of the Christian social organism (Ephesians 4:16). How dreadfully difficult that is! So many of us are tempted to conclude that we can only have freedom and only find spiritual space if we become individualists. But growth means being compacted, co-ordinated into the body, becoming more adapted, more adaptable, more useful to the body itself. We are not meant to function except as members of the body of Christ. We have no right to be growing away from the body of believers. We should be growing into it.

Responsibility

In sanctification a great deal of the *responsibility* devolves upon ourselves. In the New Testament there is considerable emphasis on the fact that it is God the Father who sanctifies us, God the Son who washes us and God the Holy Spirit who renews us. What a magnificent thing it is that the three Persons of the Godhead are busily employed around each believer's life, sorting it out, renewing it and cultivating it. Yet, at the same time there is constant stress on our own personal responsibility. *We* mortify the deeds of the body. 'Everyone who has this hope,' the apostle John says, 'purifies himself, just as God is pure' (1 John 3:3). 'These are the ones,' the same apostle says later, 'who have come out of the great tribulation and washed their robes' (Revelation 7:14). They've washed their own robes. They've done it themselves.

I emphasise this because a growing number of Christians seem to regard sanctification as simply an experience. It is something God does to you in some quick, painless operation, as if you were under anaesthetic. Holiness, they seem to say, is something you get: a Second Blessing in which the Christian is as passive and non-contributing as he is in the new birth.

There is a very pertinent word on this from Dr. Martyn Lloyd-Jones in his exposition of Romans 6:13, 'yield yourselves unto God'.[3] There are people, he says, who seem to spend the whole of their lives trying to surrender themselves, but that is not what we have here. What we have is an appeal to the will. The church is not a clinic, but a parade ground. What we all need is not a doctor, but a sergeant major shouting out commands: 'Let not sin reign in your mortal body'. Stand up and do your exercises! Practice your self denial! Get on with this business of sanctification! God doesn't allow us to sit in bed taking our own spiritual pulse and saying that we're not very well spiritually. He tells us to get up and do something about it: to take our medicine, eat our food, do our exercises, get on with washing our robes and purifying ourselves. The holy men of the past were holy because they wanted to be. They worked at it.

In a way, Roman Catholicism has often been closer to the truth on this than much of our Protestantism. It has stressed spiritual discipline and spiritual exercises. In fact, I have a vivid memory of preaching once in Northern Ireland on the text, 'Work out your own salvation with fear and trembling' (Philippians 2.12) and being approached immediately afterwards by an extremely angry man who told me in no uncertain tones, 'That was a Catholic text you had tonight.' But, of course, it was not. God commands us, unequivocally, to work away at the great business of mortification, renewal and growth.

References
1. *Collected Writings of John Murray*, Edinburgh: the Banner of Truth Trust, 1977, vol. 2, pp. 277-284.
2. John Owen, *Works*, Edinburgh, 1850-53, vol. VI, pp. 2-86.
3. Martyn Lloyd-Jones, *Romans: An Exposition of Chapter 6*, Edinburgh: The Banner of Truth Trust, 1972, pp. 163-175.

15

Under Law?

There is no doubt that the law has been a problem for Christians ever since New Testament times. There have always been those, first of all, who have made too much of the law and have had a legalistic view of the Christian life, and indeed of man's whole approach to God, holding that salvation depends upon observance of various laws and ordinances.

Secondly, there have been those who turn the gospel itself (particularly its invitation to believe in Christ) into a new kind of law. From this point of view, faith itself becomes a 'work', or at least some kind of meritorious individual act.

Thirdly, there have been those who have held out against the law and said that it no longer has any place in the lives of Christian believers. We see from Romans 6:1 that this problem was present in the New Testament church itself. There were those who said that Christians should 'go on sinning, so that grace may increase'. A similar position was often taken by the early Gnostic sects. They said that the law had no place at all in discipleship and even suggested that the way to mortify the flesh was to indulge it unreservedly and thus exhaust it. In seventeenth century England, too, there was a considerable group who were both hyper-Calvinists and antinomians.

But far more important than these have been the Dispensationalists. They divide the history of salvation into six or seven great dispensations and then go on to argue that since we now live in the Age of the Church and await the Age of the Kingdom the law has no place in our lives. It belonged to the Age of the Law and that Age is now past. Those who hold this view allow no place today for Old Testament law such as the Sabbath; or even for the Sermon on the Mount, since it belongs to the coming Age of the Kingdom.

These three views may be summarised under three labels: legalists, who lay too much stress on the law; antinomians, who are opposed to the law; and neo-nomians, who turn the gospel's call to believe into a new kind of law. The existence of these three parties is itself a reminder of the difficulty of finding the truth in this area.

Not under law

Romans 6:14 is the key verse, setting the parameters of the discussion: 'You are not under law, but under grace.' These words remind us very clearly that in some sense, whatever that sense is, Christians are no longer under the law. In fact, that is true in four different senses.

It is true, first of all, in the sense that *we are no longer bound by what is broadly called the ceremonial law of the Old Testament*. Alongside the Ten Commandments, which enshrine eternal principles of conduct and have permanent validity, there was a large corpus of additional law and it is this additional law that we say no longer binds the Christian. There was a great deal of liturgical law, bound up with the Temple and its ordinances. There was also a great deal of civil and political law. These laws were temporary and transitional. They depended on the Temple itself continuing to stand, on residence in the land of Palestine, on the wilderness journeys and on the fact that one day Christ would come and fulfil the symbolism of Old Testament typology.

None of this is any longer binding: not the specific body of law that dealt with Temple ritual; nor the law that pre-symbolized Christ; nor the law that related to the church's wilderness journeys; nor the civil statutes relating to ancient Israel. Some of the penalties laid down by the Old Testament had clearly been discontinued before Jesus came. For example, the law that demanded capital punishment for sabbath-breaking was no longer binding in the age of the New Testament. Besides, there was also a corpus of law which was merely the application of the Decalogue to specific instances. It was illustrative of how the law would work in a given society, but did not last beyond that society itself. To quote just one example: the Pentateuch laid down that if a man built a house he must erect a parapet round the top of the wall. That was a humane provision: a safety regulation. But it was not one to bind the people of God at all times and in all places. The obligation to think of a neighbour's safety is absolutely binding, but those in our Scottish Highlands who built their Black Houses a hundred years ago were not bound to put a parapet around the roof. Such a law, in its own time and place, was a culturally conditioned application of the sixth commandment, 'Thou shalt not kill.' We must make our own applications.

In addition to the Old Testament ceremonial law there was also a great body of Jewish law which arose through rabbinical tradition. That law is found today in the Talmud. It never had divine sanction. It was a purely human commentary upon, and expansion of, the law that God had given to His people. Yet it was a grievous burden. Indeed, it is difficult for us today to imagine just what a relief it was for the people of the New Testament age to be given this great deliverance both from Mosaic law and from Rabbinical regulations. It was a yoke which men were unable to bear. When they became Christians they were free from Moses and they were free from the Rabbis. No wonder Paul cries out, 'Stand firm in the freedom with which Christ has made you free!' (Galatians 5:1).

Secondly, we are not under law in the sense that *our justification no longer depends on compliance with the law*. There were those in the early church who wanted to say that justification did depend on works of the law. Their position was not at all clear and simple, because they were not opposed to justification by faith as such. They thought that faith was very important. But they also thought, and taught, that in addition to faith men must keep the law of Moses; and they insisted that this was true not only of those born as Jews under the law, but also of Gentiles. Gentiles who came to faith in Christ must be circumcised and keep the law of Moses. Otherwise, said these Judaisers, there could be no justification.

It was providential that this problem arose in the early church because this meant that the apostles were still on hand to deal with it and to lay down with great clarity that by the works of the law no flesh could be justified. It was impossible to be justified by the law, because the law demanded 'personal, entire, exact, and perpetual obedience' (Westminster Confession, 19:1). It was no use observing the law most of the time. It was no use almost observing the law. It was no use observing the law through somebody else. It had to be personal, permanent and exact and, as Paul proved to the point of over-kill, no human being had the capacity to give the law that kind of honour and obedience. All the law could do was condemn, and so Paul says, 'By the law no flesh is justified' (Romans 3:20; Galatians 2:16). The law was weak 'through the flesh' (Romans 8:3). The law could say, 'Do this!' but the law could never secure compliance with its own demands.

This was the great discovery Luther made when, faced with the shadow of final, personal judgment, he tried to make himself right with God and went where his conscience told him to go: to the law! He began to try to obey the law in order to find peace. He endeavoured to keep the Ten Commandments and even to go beyond the rigours of the Ten Commandments into the whole discipline of monasticism and works of supererogation. He found that the harder he tried the more he fell short of the law's demands. The law (in the shape of his conscience) simply flogged him, lashed him, scourged and tormented him.

Until he learned this: that we are justified by faith, and not only by faith, but by faith alone; that Christ has endured the law's curse in our place and that Christ has met the law's demands in our place. To use the language of the great Covenant Theologians, we are no longer under the Covenant of Works as the way to life. Our acceptance before God does not depend on our having kept the law.

It's the great question: Whom does God justify? At the point of forgiveness, at the point of acceptance with God, at the point of adoption into God's family, what kind of people are we? We are, astonishingly, ungodly men and women! We are people who have not kept the law. The gospel (God's Great News) is that God justifies the ungodly (this man who has broken the whole law) through faith in Christ. What a marvellous discovery that is! Even though we have broken the law, we are no longer under the law! Christ has kept the law for us. We are ungodly and yet justified.

Thirdly, we are no longer under law in the sense that *it is not from the law that our motivation comes*. I lay that down as a principle according to which we *ought* to live. It is not a statement of fact as to the way Christians do actually live, because very often our motivation does come from the law and that gets us into serious spiritual trouble. Our Fathers in Scotland, and in England too, gave a great deal of thought to this problem. There was what they called a legal repentance: that is, a heart broken by the law, broken by the fear of God and by fear of judgment. And there was a legal sanctification, where one mortified sin because of the dread of God, because of fear of His sanctions and fear of His chastisements. These older theologians said it should not be like that with God's children! In fact, they said, you will never get real repentance or real sanctification if your motivation comes only from the law. That is servile: a craven fear inducing compliance with God's requirements.

And so men like John Colquhoun spoke of an *evangelical* repentance, which is not a response to the terrors of law but a heart broken by the love of God. The Westminster Shorter Catechism grasped this, too, although that is not often appreciated: 'Repentance unto life is a saving grace, whereby a sinner, out of a true sense of his sin, and *apprehension of the mercy of God in Christ* ... turns from it unto God' (Answer 87). It is this assurance that God is merciful which leads to grief and hatred of our sin and to our turning from it to God.

This is brought out magnificently in the story of the Prodigal Son. He went back to his father not primarily because he was tormented by an accusing conscience but because he was driven by the hope of mercy.

This is equally true of our sanctification. Walter Marshall, a late English Puritan, has bequeathed to us a great book called *The Gospel Mystery of Sanctification*. The title itself indicates Marshall's concern. To him, sanctification was a *mystery*. It was a response to the gospel. It was not something legalistic, as if holiness were the product of fear or doubt.

Today, Marshall is suspect in some Puritan circles for this very reason, that he seems not to lay enough emphasis on the law and on the more dreadful aspects of God's revelation. Let's do full justice to the biblical proportions here. Our God is a consuming fire. But Marshall's essential thesis is correct. To a large extent, he says, sanctification is the product of assurance. It is the persuasion that God loves me that sanctifies, sweetens, and mellows my soul.

Marshall, living in the wake of a legalistic movement, was well aware that some folk said the exact opposite: that it is the doubts, the fear that you are not saved, that keeps you spiritually active. Marshall disagreed. He said sanctification is love. To be holy is to love the Lord, and we can only love Him as a response to His own love. Sanctification, therefore, is a gospel thing. It is a response to mercy: a response to the love that God is showing us. Many Christians know at an experiential level the truth of that. Sometimes, when we have doubts and fears service is not easy. We also know that nothing humbles us so much as the persuasion that God loves us.

For a Christian, motivation does not come from the law. It doesn't come from fear or from doubt. It comes from the assurance that God loves us.

It has been said that in Christianity, theology is grace and ethics is gratitude. To be a disciple is to respond with thankfulness to all that God has done for us. A slave does not serve as a son or daughter serves. He does not have the inward compulsion, or the affection that a child has for his father. Thank God that our potential for obedience cannot be measured merely from the force of the law. The law can come with clarity, with threats and with sanctions, but God comes with the motivation of His love and the inward working of His Holy Spirit. It is not the law that keeps us holy, but grace; and that grace is God's strength made perfect in our weakness (2 Corinthians 12:9).

The law and the gift of the Spirit

There is one thing further: *we do not depend on the law for our experience of Spirit baptism or for the gift of the Holy Spirit.* Again, this has become a serious issue. The Charismatic Movement proposes a view of our experience of the Holy Spirit which is essentially legalistic. Its preachers and teachers tell us that the church is in a dreadful spiritual state and the answer to the problem is Holy Spirit baptism, which can be 'got' by going through various steps such as believing in Christ, renouncing all known sin, thirsting for God, praying expectantly and so on. There are variations on this theme but the core technology remains: there are things we have to do.

Furthermore, if the poor believer comes back and says he has been through all these steps but nothing has happened, he is then asked, 'But have you really gone through all these steps? Have you really renounced all sin? Have you made a surrender of your will to God – an absolute surrender? Have you really, really thirsted?'

Of course, the poor Christian says, 'Well, maybe not!' But this is pure legalism: the gift of the Spirit depending upon our personally attaining some kind of higher life.

Paul deals with the problem directly and specifically in Galatians 3. 'Did you,' he asks, 'receive the Spirit by observing the law, or by believing what you heard?' (verse 2). The gift of the Spirit is as much a matter of *sola fide* (by faith alone) as is justification. The New Testament preaches a glorious gospel. But when we tamper with it and add bits to it in the interests of moralism we create all kinds of problems. If our receiving the gift of the Spirit depended on our doing something, on the quality of our believing or on the strength of our religious desires, we would never have the Spirit.

There is a very interesting textual variant in the story of the baptism of the Ethiopian in Acts 8. The Received Text, which we have in the Authorised Version, says, 'If thou believest *with all thine heart* ...' (verse 37). That language is not found in any of the ancient manuscripts. There is no such condition as, 'If you believe with all your heart.' It is something the scribe put in to protect the gospel from abuse. He did not want to make it too easy.

We have been putting in those fatal words, *with all your heart*, ever since, to torment the people of God. It is as ungodly men and women that we are justified; and as ungodly men and women we receive the gift of the Spirit of God. It is pure grace. It comes on exactly the same terms as justification and with the same safeguards. God builds in His own safeguards. It is a total absurdity to say that making the gift depend on grace alone encourages antinomianism and destroys the gospel. He is a Holy Spirit and no-one can live an unholy life after He comes in. Grace will not let people be antinomians. Grace will not let people live as they please. It will not allow folk to be carnal and unspiritual. Grace can look after itself. For far too long and far too often men have been trying to protect grace from itself. Grace only operates in union with Christ, through an indwelling Holy Spirit, and God makes total provision to guard against antinomianism by uniting us to Christ and by filling us with the Spirit of holiness. And that's all that we need.

The purpose of the law
In those four great respects, then, we are not under the law. But what, in the words of Galatians 3:19, is the purpose of the law? What is the use of the law if we are no longer under the law?

This immediately suggests that we cannot say unconditionally that we are not under the law. Indeed, the idea that a Christian, or anybody else, can be completely free from the law is an absurdity, because it would mean living without law and a life without law is a sinful life. Sin is lawlessness (1 John 3:4). A life completely without law is a life totally abandoned to sin.

It is inconceivable, therefore, that a Christian can be free from the law in this unqualified sense. Luther and Calvin gave sustained attention to this question and between them they came up with a well thought-out doctrine.

They said that the law has, in perpetuity, a three-fold function. First, there is *the political use of the law*; secondly, there is *the pedagogical use*; and thirdly, there is its use as *a rule of life*.

As far as the political use of the law was concerned, Luther and Calvin were thinking very much in terms of the relationship between civil government and divine law and arguing that government is bound by the law of God. Just as an individual is bound by the whole of the Decalogue so is any human corporation, not least the state. Indeed, the only protection we have against an absolutist state is the concept of the state as the servant of God, or the *deacon* of God, as Paul calls it in Romans 13:4. The Reformers insisted that when the state enacts laws, those laws must correspond to the law of God. Where the state enacts penal sanctions, those penalties must correspond to the law of God. The state is God's minister, the avenger of God's wrath (Romans 13:4). The magistrate is not there to express his own personal view of human behaviour. He is there to express God's view of human behaviour. He is there not to express his own assessment of the gravity of the crime but God's assessment of the gravity of the crime. He has no right to approach these problems simply from the standpoint of social utility, asking what kind of laws our society is prepared to accept, or what kind of penalties our society needs.

People tend to imagine that the moment we move away from biblically controlled legislation we will get more freedom and more tolerance. That is not the lesson of history. What we will get is more inhumanity, more barbarism and more savagery. We will get exemplary sentences. We will get naked revenge. This is a serious issue for Christians at the present time. How should we treat offenders in the light of the Word of God?

The political use of the law means that in all its legislation (for example, marriage laws, industrial legislation, Sunday trading) the state must be conscious of God looking over its shoulder. It never has the right to pass autonomous legislation divorced from absolute divine norms. Sadly, a new legislative tradition is now firmly established. We have moved from God's standards to considerations of mere social convenience. The inevitable outcome will be laws which degrade and dehumanise.

The law as our 'schoolmaster'

Secondly, the Reformers spoke of the *pedagogical* use of the law. This terminology comes from the Greek word *paidagogos*. The *paidagogos* was the slave who took the child to school. It is misleading to equate the law with the teacher in this connection. The teacher, in Paul's thought, is Christ Himself. The law is the servant who performs the humble function of taking the child to Jesus or bringing the soul to Christ. Luther was particularly interested in this. The law could not justify, but it could bring the soul to Christ. Luther explored this with passionate intensity and often very movingly, particularly in his great *Commentary on Galatians*.

What does the law do as a pedagogue? Well, one thing it does is to multiply transgressions. The Old Testament church could hardly move without falling over some legal trip-wire. When they ate food, when they sowed their seed, when they made their clothes, when they went to war, when they sold, when they bore children, they were for ever falling over rules. The effect of all this was to heighten the sense of sin.

Augustine went further and said that sometimes the law itself caused sin. He was, in fact, building on Paul's comment, 'I would not have known what it was to covet if the law had not said, "Do not covet" ' (Romans 7:7). It is brilliant psychology: the prohibition itself prompting the disobedience. Augustine describes in his *Confessions* how as children they lived near an orchard full of pears and, although they hated pears, just because they were banned, every day they broke in and stole them. But it is not simply psychology: it is biblical teaching. Those who are in charge of young people are surely aware that very often the well-intentioned intent to forbid or ban something serves instead to suggest the idea of a sin never before present in the child's mind.

But the chief thing, of course, is that the law brings us to Christ by giving us a bad conscience. It is by the law that there comes the knowledge of sin. Christ came to call sinners, not the righteous, to repentance (Luke 5:32) and the function of the law is to create that sense of need, that conviction of sin, out of which alone can faith be born.

The law as a rule of life

Thirdly, there is the use of the law as a rule of life for believers. It defines the way in which he is supposed to walk – 'not after the flesh, but after the Spirit' (Romans 8:4). He is not justified by keeping the law, but having been justified, he keeps the law. He walks according to the Spirit and by doing so he fulfils the righteousness of the law. That is why a huge proportion of the Bible is law; and that, too, is why the bulk of the Bible's enunciation of law is aimed not at politicians or at unconverted people, but at Christians. The Ten Commandments were not for the Assyrians or the Babylonians but for the people of God. Similarly, most of the Lord's own ministry was concerned with expounding the great principles of conduct. The Sermon on the Mount is law from beginning to end; and it is law for the people of God. We find the same thing in the epistles of St. Paul, where the usual pattern is, first, doctrine, then law. 'Here,' he says, 'is the truth. And this is how you are to live it.'

Christians, then, need guidance as to how they are to live. Let me offer a few comments on that.

First, in God's order the indicatives always go before the imperatives. That is, God's work of redemption always comes before His exposition of obligations. This is illustrated quite superbly in what we know as the *Preface to the Ten Commandments*. 'I am the LORD your God, who brought you out of Egypt, out of the land of slavery. You shall have no other gods before me' (Exodus 20:2-3). The great thing is that God did not take them out of the land of Egypt *because* they kept the

Ten Commandments: they were to keep the Ten Commandments because God took them out. Similarly, the Sermon on the Mount is not about how to become a disciple of Christ: it is about how to live once God by His grace has made us disciples.

We come back once more to Augustine's principle: 'Lord, give what Thou dost command and command what Thou wilt.' God saves us first. He gives before He commands. Before He says, 'Live the Beatitudes!' He unites us to Christ, fills us with His Holy Spirit and makes us new creatures. Of course, the non-Christian is also bound by the Sermon on the Mount, but it binds him only because every man and woman is bound to be a Christian. We cannot say, 'I don't want to be a Christian, but I want to keep the Sermon on the Mount.' It can be kept only if the indicatives have happened: only if God's grace has taken over.

Secondly, there is no room in the Bible for an antithesis or tension between law and love. There can, of course, be legalism without love. But we cannot set law against love as was done in, for example, Situation Ethics. The antithesis is inadmissible because it is the law itself that says, 'Love the LORD your God with all your heart' (Deuteronomy 6:5). The law itself commands love. Indeed, love alone fulfils the law (Romans 13:10). The Christian cannot just stand before that great hymn to love in 1 Corinthians 13 and say, 'It's a marvellous idea, but it's unattainable!' Instead he says, 'That great description of love binds me. It is law, just as much as every other commandment. Indeed, it is the sum of all the commandments. If I'm envious, or conceited, or easily provoked, or rude, or self-seeking, I'm breaking the law.'

It cannot be said of a man that he is great at keeping the law, but he has no love. Love is the fulfilling of the law; and, conversely, if we love God we keep His commandments. That is how we show our love. The bond between the believer and God is a bond between lovers. They love one another and so they want to please one another. There is no doubt that God acts to please us, to do what's good for us and to assure us that He loves us. Do we show that we love Him? We wouldn't hurt somebody we loved: if we loved God, would we hurt Him? Would we do what God forbids? or what God condemns? Jesus was no legalist. But it was He who said, 'If you love Me, keep My commandments' (John 14:15).

Thirdly, no matter the clarity of the great biblical principles, every Christian needs special wisdom to apply the law in particular situations. It is very well to have a gut-reaction against situation ethics. Yet all of us know that life is often a moral struggle, and that in any given situation the exactly right thing to do may be far from clear. The choice before us may not be a matter of black and white. I don't want to take the rigour out of these dilemmas. The principles laid down in the Ten Commandments express absolute, inviolable sanctities. Lying is always wrong. Covetousness is always wrong. Blaspheming is always wrong. There is no situation in which such things are not sin. And yet, armed with precise knowledge of all that the Bible says, there can still be situations where we do not have clear answers. We have to accommodate and adjust.

There are situations, for example, where the principle of the sanctity of truth is in conflict with the principle of the sanctity of life and where it is impossible both to tell the truth and to save or safeguard a life. Similarly, there are situations where it is impossible to save two lives simultaneously. One life has to be sacrificed. Again, there are situations where it may be impossible to save life without taking away somebody else's property.

We may think we know it all. Tonight is Halloween: what do we think of Halloween? We may have all the principles but how do we adjust them? There is no text in the Bible about Halloween and so all we can do is work out the principles. Does the mere fact that something began with a satanic association mean that we can never again use that occasion for any sanitised or wholesome purposes? Do I say that all those masks are simply childish, or is there something more serious going on: something satanic or demonic?

The example merely illustrates that sometimes we have to try to apply to a precise situation a wide series of principles. God Himself accommodated to what Calvin called 'the rudeness of His ancient people'. For example, He sanctioned a divorce law which fell far short of His own ideal for monogamous marriage (Deuteronomy 24:1-4). He made an adjustment to suit the situation.

The obligation to live under law has been intensified by our redemption. But the great thing is that whatever God commands He also enables us to do. He gives what He commands. If we keep in step with His Spirit He will show us how to apply biblical principles in every situation that confronts us.

16

Christian Liberty

'It is for freedom that Christ has set us free.' These words of Galatians 5:1 remind us that our liberty is not something peripheral or secondary; it is one of our most basic privileges in the gospel of Jesus Christ. It was, in fact, to secure this freedom that our Saviour died. Christ shed His blood to redeem us, that is, to set us free; and that means that our liberty is something that is quite fundamental to our whole position as the people of God. It is something to hold fast, to cling to, to cherish for ourselves and to respect in others. It is not something we can negotiate on or dispense with. It is not something that lies on the margins of Christian privilege. 'Not at all!' says Paul, 'the price of our freedom was nothing less than the blood of the Lord Jesus Christ.' That means that when we begin to behave as slaves instead of sons (Galatians 4:5ff.) we are expressing contempt for redemption and for the blood of the Lord. It means that when we infringe the liberty of others we deny them a redemption privilege purchased by the blood of the Saviour. Paul, therefore, insists that liberty is one of the foundation privileges of the children of God.

From what, then, are we free? What is the content of this liberty which we have in Jesus Christ? First, we have freedom *from the Mosaic law*. In those first days of Christ's church the law was an enormous problem. There were those who wanted to impose on the community of believers all the law of Moses: circumcision and all appurtenances and also the whole content of the yoke of rabbinism. That was a very great burden on God's people and it was felt by them to be such an emancipation to be freed in Christ from the Mosaic yoke and from rabbinical obligations.

That may not seem to be very relevant to us today, but there is a movement known as Theonomy, which wants to impose on the churches of Christ all the legislation of the Old Testament. It has its origins and roots in North American Calvinism, and is a reminder to us that the mentality which wants to go back to law, even to the whole of the Mosaic ordinances, is really endemic to human nature. It is very difficult to eliminate and that is why I begin by insisting on this: that in Christ we are free from the Mosaic yoke and free from the bondage of Old Testament ordinance.

Secondly, we are free *from the curse of the law*. We are not free (as we saw) from the law itself. We are bound by every single imperative that God has given to His church; to all the great sanctities of truth and life and marriage and so on; but the law no longer has the authority to accuse the child of God or to instil in his heart the fear of final condemnation.

Thirdly, we are free *from the dominion of Satan and sin*. Many people find that difficult to believe and accept. We are not free from sin; nor are we free from Satanic influence. Sin still rages in the believer. Satan still has access (and sometimes in backsliding it is even true that Satan has us: see Matthew 16:23 etc.). But Satan does not dominate. We are not his slaves. In our natural state our wills were enslaved. They were in a state of bondage. They were absolutely incapable of 'any spiritual good accompanying salvation' (Westminster Confession, IX:3). No matter how sombrely we paint the power of indwelling sin in the child of God, it is a betrayal of the grace of God and a contravention of biblical teaching to suggest that the believer (that is, the saved man and the saved woman) is absolutely incapable of any spiritual good. That is simply not true of a child of God. Certainly there is indwelling sin. Certainly there is the flesh. Certainly sin rages. But it does not reign. It has been a historic weakness of Reformed theology that it has been too prepared to accommodate sin in the life of a Christian. The believer is not dominated by sin. He is able to believe. He is able to repent. He is able to love God. He is able to love his neighbour. He is able to see beauty in Christ and to desire Him. He is able to show spiritual stamina and sobriety and to experience spiritual growth. All that happens to a man in whom there is indwelling sin, in whom there is still the flesh but, as I said, it is a betrayal of biblical teaching to suggest that because of indwelling sin he is still in bondage to Satan and utterly and totally enslaved to sin. Thank God that in our conversions the dominion of sin has been broken! Our wills have been liberated and God has given us an ability to render to Himself that which is a true obedience even though it is not a perfect obedience.

Fourthly, we are free *from 'the doctrines and commandments of men'* (Westminster Confession, 20:2). In other words, we are free from human tradition. We are free from all merely human authority. We are not bound by any merely human taboos. This is the core of the doctrine in Reformed thought and it involves two distinct elements.

First, we are free from every human principle that contradicts the Word of God. This applies unconditionally and universally. It is true in every area of our lives that no man can be required to do what God's Word forbids. The principle is not confined to the religious sphere. It is true in the military, in the commercial, in the professional, in the medical, in every single sphere of life. I cannot be required by any human authority to contradict the will of God. That can produce or precipitate some very serious problems. For example, a military commander has no right, in any circumstances, to require someone to violate the will of God; and if divine law is contradicted, it will be no defence to plead that it was done in obedience to a higher command. That was a great principle behind the Nuremberg war trials where it was established that the mere fact of a command which came from the supreme Nazi authority could not be alleged as an excuse for the perpetration of atrocities. It is not vested in any military or political authority to require what God forbids. That is even true in the domestic sphere. A parent has no right to command a child to do what God forbids, and to do so can put a believing child in a very difficult situation. No authority, no matter how lawful, has the right to require anyone to do what God's Word forbids: to take a life, to steal property, to falsify.

The second principle is more difficult: We are free from every human directive which is additional to scripture 'in matters of faith or worship'. There are directives, of course, which are supplementary to the Word of God but are perfectly legitimate (speed restrictions and the Council Tax being just two examples). But in the realm of the spiritual and the ecclesiastical we are free from not only what contravenes God's Word but also from what supplements it. In the area of faith and life in the church of God no member of that body can be bound by a taboo or a directive which lacks the sanction of scripture. This is a crucial area because in the church of God there has always been a tendency to multiply directives, restrictions and taboos. These are what Paul called 'beggarly elements' (Galatians 4:9). The difficulty is that not only do human authorities (for example, ministers and elders) have a tendency to multiply directives but there is something in the believer himself, an element of childishness, that craves the security of such taboos. We want to go back to the womb. We want someone to tell us what is wrong. We want a list of taboos. And so very often we find the church is asked to give pronouncements on a whole range of topics. For example: Can we belong to a Masonic Lodge? Can the young folk go to a dance? People want the church to say Yes and No to such things. In every tradition there is a long list of taboos: on smoking, on drinking, on dancing, on make-up, on football matches, on pop-music. The list has certain standard elements and it also has certain variables. Some of those things are right or wrong in given situations. But none can claim the sanction of scripture; they are imposed simply on the basis of human tradition. The whole point here is that as believers we are spiritually adult and we are free from the doctrines and commandments of men in the area of faith and life. No Christian can impose any unbiblical taboo on another Christian. The Confession says that it is unacceptable because these things have only a human authority. Our Puritan forebearers deemed this principle sufficiently important to put it into the Confession. There are many things not mentioned at all in the Confession. It consists only of primary and fundamental doctrines and in the judgment of these men, the believer's liberty in the gospel of Christ was a basic and fundamental doctrine. So we ask ourselves, Is this taboo a biblical one? Is this law, this form of worship, imposed by the Word of God?

A second main question is this: What is the basis of Christian liberty? It is based on three principles.

It is based, first of all, *on the fact that we are members of the family of God*. We are sons and daughters of God. Paul brings out that point very beautifully: 'God sent his Son, born of a woman, born under law, to redeem those under law, that we might receive the full rights of sons' (Galatians 4:4-5). There is a very intricate movement going on there. God's Son became a slave so that we who are slaves might become sons with all the rights of God's children. Now the crucial thing there is that no outsider has the right to interfere with the internal workings and affairs of the household of God.

In practice, it is not from outside the problem comes. The problem comes often from those who think they have authority or prestige in the church of God itself and who therefore feel that it is within their power to interfere with the liberty of God's own children. But in the church of God all the authority is ministerial. The most senior office-bearer is only a servant whose duty it is to implement God's law. He has no right to interfere with God's children and, by implication, find fault with the laws God has given. He is suggesting that God has been too lax and that men must make good the deficiencies by laying down taboos. Men are saying they could have done it better than God. They are saying He should have forbidden dances, smoking, going to football matches and so on. But those whom God has made stewards in His household never have the right to lord it over the younger and less experienced members, and to allow them to do so is to betray the cross itself. Loyalty to the cross requires that we refuse to let men lord it over our consciences. Christ has purchased the right to be our only Master.

Secondly, our liberty is based on the fact of the sufficiency and finality of scripture as the Word of God. We all know that. The Word 'is the only rule to direct us' (Shorter Catechism, Answer 2). The only rule. There is great lip-service paid to that principle in our churches. In some contexts it is imposed with great vigour and rigour. A particular form of worship is imposed on a church because it is 'the biblical rule'. Hymns are not allowed 'because they are not in the Bible'. That is perfectly true. The same establishment insists on clerical collars. Is that in the Bible? We have such enormous difficulty being consistent! We are again saying, 'This should have been in the Bible, but it isn't, so I'm putting it in.' We are finding fault again. We are saying the Bible is not enough. Some churches have prophets: because the Bible is not enough. The Roman Church has an infallible teaching office: because the Bible is not enough. We Protestants do the same thing with our own tradition. We say the same thing exactly: the Bible is not enough; and we must have more rules and more taboos than there are in the Word of God itself.

The third principle is that 'God alone is Lord of the conscience' (Westminster Confession, 20:2). Conscience is not autonomous. It is not the final court of appeal nor is it self-regulating and self-monitoring. Conscience has a Lord. Every human conscience is only an inferior court. There is a court superior to conscience; namely God Himself. But God is the only Lord of the conscience. There is nobody else. No human authority, no church authority, can lord it over the consciences of men and women.

I want to make it as contemporary as I can. We have witnessed in this decade a remarkable and unexpected florescence of passionate conviction religion. There is observable a world-wide fundamentalist (in the broadest sense of the word) phenomenon affecting not only Christian faith but also notably, Islam. This has been utterly unexpected and it raises huge problems; because Islam has, for example, shown in its response to Salman Rushdie that it is prepared to invoke the power of the sword to suppress certain opinions. It is prepared to force conscience. And we say, How horrible! But are we, in our own traditions, so very far removed from that same attitude? For example: If there is a proposal to build a mosque in the heart of a predominantly Christian community, is it right to say that the Muslims of that community enjoy liberty of conscience and we therefore must not interfere with their freedom to worship God as they themselves wish to? If Islam preaches and practises intolerance and we Christians also practise intolerance we are facing disaster on an appalling scale. The only hope open to us is that we espouse the principle of toleration with passion and conviction. We have to allow to others the freedom that we claim for ourselves. We have no right to invoke the power of the sword against Muslims. The power of the sword? Surely we Westerners would not execute them? The fact is, the whole philosophy of legal process is based on coercion. Defiance of the law ultimately results in arrest and imprisonment and if Muslims were to go ahead and build a mosque in a community which forbade them to do so the police would be called in and arrests would be made. That is coercion; that is the sword. Do we believe our own principle that the gospel is not to be advanced by carnal weapons? That other men's consciences are as important as our own and that they will answer to God, not to men? Therefore here, at the heart of Reformed theology, at the heart of Protestant religion, is a principle that deserves our passionate commitment. It deserves to be asserted with zeal, with total spiritual energy. Paradoxically, only if we transfer the passion of militant fundamentalism to the principle of toleration will this world of ours have a chance in the decade to come. Otherwise those faiths will grind each other to powder.

So God's people are free. But is that all? Is there anything else that comes in to control and qualify the exercise of our Christian liberty? Again, there are three general principles.

First, *our liberty is qualified by civil power, lawfully exercised.* The qualification is important because civil power is not always lawfully exercised. But when competent, lawful government passes competent laws the Christian conscience is bound by these laws, even though they are supplementary to the Word of God. This is particularly important when government passes bad law. There is a monumentally important distinction between bad law and incompetent law. It is possible for a lawful government to pass a competent law which is nevertheless a bad law and the badness of the law is never itself justification for infringing that particular law. Whatever our views are on particular laws we are still bound to obey and to comply with them because however bad a law is it is not incompetent. It is imposed by a lawful government and revenue from it (if it is a tax) is being used for lawful and beneficial purposes.

Secondly, *our liberty is qualified by ecclesiastical power, lawfully exercised*. Here again the qualification is important. This speaks of the church using its power in a competent way; that is, enacting, implementing and applying God's own rules. That can be extended slightly to show that sometimes those who lead the church have to make decisions for which they cannot claim the direct sanction of revelation. They can claim its general sanction and beyond that they can claim that they are acting on the basis of Christian prudence and common sense. For example, a Christian church might decide to pronounce a certain day a fast day or a thanksgiving day. In doing so it is 'compelling' the attendances of all its members. That is what is seen as a competent and lawful exercise of ecclesiastical power. There is a general principle that it is good to have fast days and thanksgiving days; but the decision as to what particular day and what time of day is a matter simply for local church office-bearers. Their decisions can be said to restrict or limit our Christian liberty.

Thirdly, and most importantly, *our liberty is qualified by the principle that whatever we do we must do it to the glory of God* (1 Corinthians 10:31). The historical context of that particular principle was precisely this question of Christian liberty. Eating and drinking was a very specific reference to the problem that faced those early believers in Corinth. What were they to do at a meal or a feast where food was served that had been offered to idols? Was it right to eat it? Paul's answer was that, in general, that is completely indifferent. The principle was, Do it to the glory of God. It depends on the circumstances. Do the God-glorifying thing in a particular situation. Sometimes you eat, sometimes you don't eat. Sometimes you drink, sometimes you don't drink. Always do what will glorify God. Now that admits of many applications. It really is never enough to say, 'I am free to do this; therefore I shall do it.' We could not, of course, cram into one lifetime all that we are free to do; so we have to make judgments. I am at liberty to do something; but is it expedient? That means even when I face something which really is a matter of what is called indifference, I have to ask the general question, What is the God-glorifying thing in this situation? But I have also got to ask supplementary questions such as: What is for the benefit of God's church in this particular situation? What would edify the church? What would build up the church? I must always be governed by concern for the people of God. Will this divide the people of God? Will this mislead them? Is this good for them? I have also to ask, Is this for the good of the gospel? Contextualize, Paul said. He was willing to 'become all things to all men' so that by all possible means he might save some (1 Corinthians 9:22). Among the Jews he lived as a Jew. Among the Greeks he lived as a Greek. He accommodated to Jewish and Greek food laws, habits of dress, social customs. William Chalmers Burns did the same in China. He chose to dress like the Chinese for the good of the gospel. There is no doubt at all that in many cultures if a Christian is known to frequent football matches or dances that that is the end of his or her witness. So we ask: What is this doing for the gospel? If I do this will it make my witness to Christ less acceptable, less credible?

Then we ask: Will this be beneficial to my own spiritual life? Sometimes there are things that are not sins but which are weights or impediments. The writer to the Hebrews says, Lay them aside (12:1). Not only the sins that beset us but the weights, the things that hold us back.

Someone recently has made the disturbing claim that nobody ever achieved anything really significant who had hobbies. In an age when there is so much pressure on men to have hobbies and distractions to prevent them from burn-out and breakdown, there is something very searching in this idea that those people who have achieved significantly have tended to be men of one consuming passion. I am not sure but it is one of the devil's current devices for the church's impoverishment to get us ever more involved in a wide variety of leisure pursuits, none of them in themselves wrong or trivial, some of them restorative and in the true sense recreational, but perhaps also a threat to professional, and especially spiritual, achievement. We have to weigh up our own temperaments and our own inclination to addiction in different directions. It may be perfectly right for every other preacher in the world to play golf; but for one it is not because for this one it would be an obsession.

We also ask ourselves this: Will it make men praise God? The difficulty with so much that is lawful is its sheer vanity and futility. How much of our time do we spend doing things that are simply vain and empty? Of course, we cannot keep the bow taut all the time. We need to relax. There are ways of relaxing and all of us must find out for ourselves what is right for us. Something may be lawful that is trivial and vain. Is it so trivial and so vain that it doesn't make people glorify God? Much in life is inevitably vain in the sense of lacking existential significance. It depends on the quantity of vanity that we cram into our lives, the proportion of nothingness, of futility, of the ridiculous and the absurd that we tend to fall a prey to.

So there are always these considerations. And these are always considerations for me. I never, never have the right to say to somebody else, 'That is not expedient for you.' If he is free, then he himself is the only judge of expediency. Otherwise I am making it obligatory and non-free. It was said of 'Rabbi' Duncan that he had a long creed for himself and a short creed for others. We would do well to remember that. It is very important to us that we should allow others their freedom. If people want to go to hear Bob Dylan or play golf then I say, 'Yes! I protect and respect your liberty to make those decisions.' But I ask myself a series of different questions and I make my own decisions. I am content with my Gaelic music. That is no doubt equally vain and no more meritorious than non-Gaelic music; but we make our own decisions and we leave others space, and that is something that the Reformed churches have often found very difficult to do.

In the last analysis, there is nothing indifferent. We have a list of things indifferent, and yet in the actual agony of decision making there is nothing that is indifferent. We never are faced with moral choices with regard to which we can say, 'These are equal.' There is the right thing to do not in terms of clear categorical imperatives but what is right for me, in my situation, at a precise moment in my experience. Without due care and attention we find ourselves very quickly into antinomianism. It is perilous to trivialise Christian liberty. It is a great burden to be free. This is why the presupposition of this liberty is that we are adult children of God and we can handle it. We are led by the Spirit of God: that is the context in which we are free.

17

Christian Baptism

Baptism remains a controversial subject on which, tragically, Christians are deeply divided. There are three general comments to be made at the outset.

First, I have little hope of convincing my Baptist friends on this issue. I don't despair of truth or even of Baptists' logical powers. But this is a long-standing disagreement and all that can be said has already been said on both sides.

Secondly, I don't regard this debate between Baptists and Paedobaptists as a debate about fundamentals. There is no doubt that in practice it is difficult to have the two points of view co-existing in one church or denomination, but that is a practical, not a theological, difficulty. The divergence itself is not one between Christians and non-Christians. It is very much an in-house division, dividing for example, men such as C. H. Spurgeon and John Kennedy, who on all fundamentals were agreed.

The third comment I want to make is that those of us who adhere to the doctrine of infant baptism are not necessarily sacramentalists. We do not believe that baptism, by itself, mechanically and invariably effects a saving change in children. We certainly do not administer it in the belief that it automatically regenerates.

Having made these general comments we move on to ask three questions: What is the meaning of baptism? What is the correct mode of baptism? Who are the subjects of baptism?

The meaning of Baptism

First, the meaning of baptism. What is the import of this ordinance? 'Ordinance' it certainly is. Christ Himself instituted it and He has commanded all His people to submit to it as the prescribed form of initiation into His visible Body. At its most fundamental, it signifies union with Christ. It is baptism in the name of Christ, identifying us with Him and incorporating us into Him. It signifies our being one with Him and seals our participation in His crucifixion, burial and resurrection. It attests and consolidates both our covenant union and our spiritual union with the risen Lord. We live with Christ. We are built on Christ. We are rooted in Christ. We share His status and privileges. We enjoy His inheritance. We have His rights.

It follows from this that baptism represents to us all the blessings that flow from union with Christ. Specifically, this means three things.

First, the remission of sins. The water points to the washing away of guilt, reminding us that in Christ we are clean. There is 'no condemnation' (Romans 8:1).

Secondly, the renewal of our nature. In this respect, baptism is 'the laver of regeneration' (Titus 3:5), not because it mechanically and invariably transforms but because it represents, seals and furthers our spiritual renewal.

Thirdly, baptism attests our baptism by the Holy Spirit. At Jesus' own baptism this was reinforced by the advent of the dove, symbolising the Holy Spirit. The dove did not represent the Spirit's initial descent on Christ. Christ had the Spirit before His baptism. But the baptism and the dove were attestations to the Lord of what had already taken place. Similarly, in our baptism there is an attestation of the fact that we have already been baptised in the Spirit of the Lord Jesus Christ.

We may note, in addition, that baptism is the sign and the pledge of our being in covenant with God. It is our public acceptance of Christ as our Lord, and our public affirmation of ourselves as His servants. It is our confession that we are His: His property, His slaves, His pupils.

How?

Fundamentally, then, baptism signifies our union with Christ and our sharing in all the benefits that flow from that union. The second question is, What is the mode of baptism? How ought it to be administered?

In Presbyterian and other Paedobaptist churches the position taken is that the actual mode doesn't much matter. The most common practice is to baptise by sprinkling, but we may also baptise by pouring the water from some kind of vessel or even by immersion. Any of these three modes is valid.

Baptists take a different position. They argue that immersion is the only proper mode. I use the word 'proper' advisedly, because there is some disagreement among Baptists themselves on the issue. The position commonly taken by some Baptists is that baptism by any mode other than immersion is irregular and unsatisfactory, but is not necessarily invalid. But there are others who regard baptism by any mode other than immersion as entirely invalid. That means that they would not only insist on re-baptising those baptised by mere sprinkling, but that they would not allow them into church membership (or, if they are logical, admit them to the Lord s Table).

These attitudes obviously constitute a serious problem for inter-church relations. In effect, the Baptist position un-churches the rest of Christendom. But it has to be said again that there is considerable difference of opinion among Baptists on this issue. That is why some Presbyterian and Anglican ministers have been able to preach in Baptist churches and Presbyterian members have sat at the Lord's Table in Baptist churches.

The Baptist argument is that the Bible itself lays down that baptism must be by immersion. This is based on certain claims they make as to what the verb *baptise* and the noun *baptism* actually mean in Greek. The natural, normal, non-symbolical meaning of this word, they say, is to *immerse*; and therefore every instance of baptism in the New Testament is an instance of immersion.

We accept that sometimes it may mean that. We accept that immersion is a valid and regular mode of baptism. But we would also argue that there are instances in the Greek scriptures, both in the Old and in the New Testament, where the meaning *immerse* or *immersion* is impossible in the light of the context. Without going into detailed analysis we can look at some examples.

First, Leviticus 14:6. The background here is the ritual for the cleansing of a leper. The priest is to use two birds. One bird is to be slain and drained of its blood, and the living bird is then to be 'baptised in the blood of the slain bird'. It would surely be a very difficult exercise to immerse a living bird in the blood of another bird of the same species. It is possible to sprinkle the bird. It is possible even to dip the bird. But it is, I think, impossible to *immerse* it.

Secondly, Daniel 4:33. This occurs in the context of the account of Nebuchadnezzar's insanity. He lived in the open like a wild beast and his body was 'baptised with the dew of heaven'. It is very difficult to see how this can mean that he was *'immersed* in the dew of heaven'.

Thirdly, Luke 11:38. A certain Pharisee was astonished that Jesus did not wash before dinner. The verb 'wash' (*baptizo*) is, literally, to be baptised. There is no evidence that the Jews of this period insisted on immersion before a meal. Nor is there any evidence in the Old Testament of any rite of this kind. What Luke is referring to is the Rabbinical insistence that before a meal a Jew must wash his hands. There was very stringent rabbinical legislation as to just how far up the arm that washing had to go; but there was no insistence whatever that the Jew must immerse himself before dinner.

In Hebrews 9:10 we find a similar reference: 'various ceremonial washings (NIV). The Greek word here is *baptismois*. It is difficult to think of any prescribed *immersion* which the writer could have had in mind. The Old Testament laid much emphasis on sprinkling (the sprinkling of blood, for example), but seldom, if ever, did it insist on immersion.

It seems to me impossible, then, to sustain the argument that baptism must be by immersion. The symbolism is safeguarded if we use the element of water, which, sprinkled upon the individual, is itself an appropriate reminder of the washing away of guilt and corruption and of the outpouring of God's Spirit.

The symbolism is safeguarded by the element itself, not by the manner of its application. We may be sprinkled, we may have the Spirit poured upon us, we may even be 'drenched' in the Spirit, to use the language of 1 Corinthians 12:13, but I cannot see any need to insist on immersion.

I know that in Romans 6:3-4 the symbolism of union with Christ is discussed by the Apostle in terms of our 'going down into the water' and Baptists are very confident that that symbolism is only safeguarded by immersion. The difficulty with this is that baptism is also a symbol of burial and it would be difficult to carry the symbolism of immersion quite as far as that. Also, of course, in the same context (Romans 6:5) there is a different symbolism where we are 'planted together in the likeness of his death'. My point is, that going down into the water is an adequate symbol of the Lord going down into death, but it is not an adequate symbol of burial (or more precisely, of entombment, because Jesus was not buried, He was entombed); and it is no symbol at all, in my judgment, of being planted in the likeness of His death.

I am not in the slightest diminishing the validity of the Baptist mode of baptism. I respect immersion, but I am asking that there should be a place for our mode too. There is no stress in the New Testament on the mode of baptism, any more than there is any stress in the case of the Lord's Supper on the fact that the bread used was unleavened bread.

Who ought to be baptised?
The third question is, Who ought to be baptised? One's instinctive answer is, Those who are believers! That point needs no demonstration. It is plain enough in the New Testament that adults were baptised on profession of faith. But the Reformed Confessions have gone beyond that and said that we should also baptise 'the infants of one or both believing parents'.

The question is, Do believing parents have the right to have their faith in Christ registered in an act of baptism which includes not only themselves but their families? Should baptism, in other words, be organic, embracing not only the individual parent who believes, but his whole family?

It seems to me that the traditional argument of Presbyterians on this issue is still valid. That argument revolves around the fact that when God established His covenant with Abraham He stipulated that the sign of the *spiritual* covenant should be administered to the *physical* seed. There are two separate points involved.

First, that the sign (in Abraham's case, circumcision) was a sign of a spiritual covenant: one which held forth spiritual promises. It is sometimes argued that what was promised to Abraham was not something spiritual, but the land of Canaan. Alternatively, it is argued that what was promised in the Abrahamic covenant was worldly prosperity: political and economic privilege.

This is hard to accept. If circumcision was the sign of the land of Canaan we would have to say that Abraham never received what God promised him, because Canaan was never his. It became his descendants only four hundred years afterwards. It also seems to me that nobody with the slightest knowledge of the history of the Jewish people could ever argue that they have been in any sense the favourites of Providence: 'Under the whole heaven nothing has ever been done like which has been done to Jerusalem.' Even today they are the most hated nation on earth, surviving only under the umbrella of Western military strength. How, then, can we argue that circumcision was the sign of a covenant promising material and temporal prosperity?

In fact, the terms of the Abrahamic covenant make it plain that it was understood by Abraham himself in spiritual terms. The core promise was that God would be his God and the God of his seed (Genesis 17:4ff.). Circumcision was the sign of that promise. This is how Abraham himself understood it: it made him look for a 'city with foundations, whose architect and builder is God' (Hebrews 11:10).

This is confirmed when we read in Galatians 3:14 that we

ourselves as Christians are the beneficiaries of this very same Abrahamic covenant. We are the ones who have experienced the real fruition of its terms and promises. 'Christ,' says St. Paul, 'redeemed us from the curse of the law by becoming a curse for us' (Galatians 3:13). Why? 'That the blessing given to Abraham might come to the Gentiles through Christ Jesus.' And what was that blessing? 'That by faith we might receive the promise of the Spirit.'

The Abrahamic covenant was undeniably spiritual. It was God's irrevocable commitment to Abraham and to his seed. It was the promise of an eternal city of God. It was the promise of redemption from the curse of sin. It was the promise of the Spirit. And when the apostles saw the New Testament inheritance unfolding before their eyes they said, 'This is what God promised Abraham!' Indeed, when Jesus said, 'Go and make disciples of all nations' (Matthew 28:19), he was echoing God's promise to Abraham, 'Through your offspring all nations on earth will be blessed' (Genesis 22:18). The church is sent precisely to bring to all nations the blessing God promised them in Abraham.

Yet although it was so clearly a *spiritual* covenant, the sign was to be administered to the *physical* seed. God did not say, 'Put that sign on the spiritual seed', but, 'Put it on the physical seed: on all those born within the family of Israel.' That is why not only Jacob but also Esau was circumcised. It is not the elect who receive the sign. It is not the born-again who receive the sign. It is the physical seed.

Sometimes, within the Reformed community, the view can be heard that baptism itself, as a sign of a child's physical links with the covenant, is also a sign that our children will inevitably be saved. That is a comfort that I cannot, in God's name, extend to you at all. Esau stands there reminding us that not all the physical seed are elect or born again or saved. The mere fact of descent from covenant parents is itself no guarantee. After all, it was to one such, Nicodemus, that Jesus Himself said, '*You* must be born again.' The sovereignty of God and the imperative necessity of the new birth overshadow the sacrament of baptism just as they did circumcision. God knew that Esau was not elect. Yet He said, 'Put the sign on him' because the sign, by divine appointment, belonged to the physical seed. This is a solemn business. Even within Israel God dispenses salvation sovereignly (Romans 9:7). The circumcised and the baptised need to be born again.

We have to note, too, that it is not the sign, whether circumcision or baptism, that makes us covenant-children or that puts us in a special relationship with God. We had that special relationship before we received the sign. Indeed, the sign was put on us only because of the special relationship. We have to say, therefore, that the children of our Baptist friends are as much covenant-children as our own children. The fact of their not being baptised does not mean that they are not covenant-children. It means only that the sign of the covenant is not put on them. It was because the children of Abraham were within the covenant that the sign was put upon them. They did not become covenant-children because of the sign itself. The sign is the attestation of their special bond with the children of God. The believing parent wants the sign of the covenant not only upon himself or herself, but upon his family. But he does so not because that sign is going to put them in a different relationship with God, but because, being his children, they are already in a special relationship to God. Not only so: this physical link with the people of God immediately carries with it great privileges, and baptism is a sign of these. The children of believers are linked organically to the Word which dwells among the people of God and linked, too, to the care and prayers of the people of God.

Have things changed under the New Testament?
The principle is clear, then: the sign of the spiritual covenant was administered to the physical seed. But have things changed under the New Testament? Is there a different arrangement?

If there is, then it means that something happens here which never happens in any other connection as we move from the Old Testament to the New. Things get worse! We experience impoverishment! Under the Old Testament, parents had the privilege of hearing God say, 'Take your children, too, and put the sign on them: the sign that God's promise is to them as well. Put the sign of that promise on your child because your child is special.'

Are we to say that in the New Testament this has been revoked? Does God say, 'Not on your child now. Just on your-selves now. The child is no longer a part of it'? I cannot accept this. Surely the logic of the movement from Old Testament to New Testament is that 'the new is better'. I expect the position of the child to be better under the New Testament, not worse. I expect that God's promise will embrace the child under the New Testament at least as much as it did under the Old.

Then I check this against certain facts and I find two outstandingly important things.

I find, first of all, that the covenant is the same. It is, of course, a new administration of the covenant. But the covenant itself is the same. The great promises are the same. We are Abraham's seed. Of course, our insight is deeper. Of course, too, we have the fulness of God's Spirit. Of course, we live in the light of a completed revelation. Of course, we have a world-wide church, not simply a national church. These are significant, even magnificent, improvements. Yes! the New Testament is better. It is a new covenant. Yet it is but a new administration of the primary covenant given to Abraham. Under the Mosaic economy, that covenant was modified as to its administration, but it remained the same covenant. Now, under the New Testament, it is re-declared with great clarity. We remain under 'the blessing of Abraham'. We remain Abraham's seed. We remain beneficiaries under the Abrahamic covenant.

But isn't the New Testament so much more glorious, its terms so much more magnificent? Really? What did God say to Abraham? 'I will be your God.' What does that mean? It means that God is saying to Abraham, 'I will be for you. I will exist for you. I will exercise my God-ness for you. I will be committed to you.' There is no way that can be improved upon! There is no more glorious promise: not in Romans, not in Hebrews, not in Revelation, not in the Gospel of John, not in the Upper Room: nowhere! These words of the Abrahamic covenant have never been excelled and never will.

The covenant, then, is the same; and secondly, the church is the same. It is a remarkable thing that when Christ came He did not institute a new church, but simply grafted the Gentiles on to the old Abrahamic stock. We are the new Israel. We are the Israel of God. We are the seed of Abraham. We are the wild branches grafted into the original olive tree (Romans 11:17ff.). It is a magnificent symbol! God did not plant a separate New Testament church or a separate Gentile church. That is why, when the gospel came to the Samaritans they were not brought to perfection until the apostles came from Jerusalem, and then, in fellowship with the church in Jerusalem, they received baptism in the Spirit (Acts 8:14-17).

If, then, it is the same covenant and the same church it seems reasonable to assume that the comforting provision that God made – that when a man comes to faith he may embrace his children with himself under the sign of the covenant – would remain in place. This is precisely what we find. All the evidence we have from the New Testament points towards the continuation of the primaeval arrangement. The passages commonly adduced as arguments for infant baptism (e.g. Matthew 19:14; Mark 10:14; Luke 18:16; 1 Corinthians 7:14) merely confirm this. The children of believers continue to have the same special relationship to the covenant as their Old Testament counterparts had; and, consequently, the same right to the covenant sign.

Why do I baptise children? Is it because I believe that the infants of all believing parents are elect? No! Is it because I believe that the infants of believing parents will all one day be born again? No! Is it because I believe that one day they will all accept God for themselves? No! It is because God gave me an ordinance: Put the sign of the spiritual covenant on the physical seed. At the very beginning of this arrangement God put Ishmael and Esau there to remind us that we were not to do this on the ground that we knew theologically how the thing worked. We were to do it because God said it. In the cases of Ishmael and Esau it seemed not to work. It wasn't related to any rationale of its effectiveness. It was done (and it is still to be done) on the ground that God said, 'Put the sign of my promise not only on yourselves but also on your children.'

Which parents?

But if we say that we administer this sacrament to the infants of believers, what do we mean by 'believers'? What parents qualify for this privilege? It will prevent a good deal of confusion if we remember two facts.

First, infant baptism is given on the basis of the qualifications of the parent, not the qualifications of the child. It is given *to* the parent, and it is the parent's relationship with God that is the decisive factor. The infant is not necessarily elect or born again, but the parent who comes receives it because he or she is in a special relationship with God.

Secondly, we should not give the sacrament of baptism to a man for his child unless we would be prepared to give it to him for himself. This is the question we have to ask ourselves: If this man came as an adult wanting to be baptised, would we baptise him? I cannot baptise his infant if I would not be prepared to baptise himself. And on what grounds could I baptise him? According to Confessional theology, I can baptise him if he is a member of the visible church; that is, if he professes the true faith. I can baptise him if he is a believer; that is (again, according to Confessional theology) if he receives and rests on Christ alone for salvation.

The practical problem is that no minister or kirk session can see into the heart of a human being. We can look only at what is visible. We cannot insist on positive proof that someone is born again. What we can insist on, as overseers of the church, is a credible profession of faith: that is, a profession accompanied by some understanding of the Christian faith, a lifestyle in accordance with Christian values and public commitment to the worshipping Christian community.

Go back to the meaning of baptism. It signifies union with Christ; and, implied in that, the washing away of guilt and corruption, baptism in the Holy Spirit and a pledge of commitment to God. The question a Kirk Session has to ask is: Does this parent appearing before us understand that he is professing to be in union with Christ; to have had his guilt and corruption washed away; to have had the Holy Spirit poured out on him? Does he understand that he is pledging his commitment to God? And is the profession he is making borne out by what we see of his life and conduct? We do not need to probe minutely and inquisitorially, but we do need to say to people, 'Do you understand that you are professing to be united with Christ and to be living a lifestyle consistent with that profession?'

In the Old Testament the general principle was that the sacraments were the privilege of covenant-keepers. Within covenant-keeping there might sometimes be a great deal of spiritual mediocrity. Spiritual mediocrity, however, was one thing. Covenant repudiation was quite another. There was no circumcision and no passover for the covenant-repudiator. He was cut off from the people. In the same way, in the New Testament church there can be no infant baptism for the covenant repudiator. Baptism (and the Lord s Supper) are for those who can claim to be keeping God s covenant. Simply by coming to the sacraments they are saying, 'I am one of God's people. He is my God.'

18

Christ's Kirk

The Greek word *ekklesia* (from which we derive our English word, *ecclesiastic*) comes from two Greek words, *ek* and *kaleo*, which together would mean 'I call out'. Sometimes a whole theory of the church is built on this derivation and the church is described as 'God's called out ones'. There is no doubt, however, that the derivation had been forgotten long before the New Testament period. By that time *ekklesia* simply meant an assembly. It was applied, for example, to the political gatherings in cities like Athens, where the whole populace met to make decisions. The assembled city was called the *ekklesia*. The basic meaning of the word 'church' is, in fact, simply 'assembly'. The church is the gathered people of God. Most of the other words that the Bible uses to denote the church point in the same direction. For example, the Old Testament church was called the congregation of the Lord (*qahal Jahweh*). Hence, too, the phrase, 'the tent of meeting'; and, of course, the familiar New Testament and Jewish word, *synagogue*, which means exactly the same thing: God's people gathered together.

The simple but nonetheless important point to emerge from this is that it is not God's will for us to exist merely as individual Christians. We are meant to gather together as the people of God. There is sustained emphasis in both the Old and New Testaments on this corporate dimension of Christianity. We in the Reformed churches need to listen to this particularly carefully because the Reformation brought in a marked individualism. The conversion of the individual soul, individual converse with God in prayer and the cultivation of our own individual spirituality are all necessary emphases. But we over-reacted to the corporatism of mediaeval Christianity and now need to balance our emphasis on the individual with a due stress on the importance of the community.

One example of the way we instinctively apply individually what the Bible almost certainly intended to be applied corporately is Paul's well-known directive to work out our own salvation with fear and trembling (Philippians 2:12). It is virtually certain from the context that Paul was thinking not of the individuals at Philippi but of the corporate well-being of the congregation there. Things were being done from envy and jealousy. Paul concludes his discussion of the issue by asking them to work out their own salvation. The word *salvation* is used here in its general sense of *health* or *well-being*, reminding us of the importance of attending not simply to our own individual spiritual needs but also to the well-being of the churches and congregations of which we are a part.

Having said that, there are three major questions to ask. The first relates to the marks of the church; the second to the government of the church; and the third to the unity of the church.

The Marks of the Church

First, what are the marks of the church? The Reformation threw this question into high relief both because the Church of Rome claimed to be the one and only Holy, Catholic Church and because numerous sects arose, all claiming to be pure expressions of the idea of the church. Over against both Rome and the sects, then, the Reformers had to ask, How do we know the true church of God? What are its marks?

The full answer did not emerge overnight. Calvin indicated two great notes of the church: the preaching of the word and proper administration of the sacraments.[1] The Scottish Reformers added a third mark: discipline. It seems to me, however, that lurking in the less familiar areas of Reformed theology there was also an emphasis on two other indispensable marks of the church of God. In the Scottish tradition represented by John Knox and Andrew Melville there was a very clear stress on ministry to the poor. And in the Westminster Standards there is a clear emphasis on a fifth mark: the church is known by the fact that it worships.

The nett result of this synthesis is that the church bears five great marks.

First, *the preaching of the word*. In part this means that a true church has an orthodox creed. It is known by its official endorsement of the fundamental doctrines of the Christian faith. Note the word *fundamental*! The Second Vatican Council gave great prominence to the idea of a hierarchy of truths: the idea that some doctrines are more important than others. In fact, this is really an old Protestant distinction going back as far as John Calvin and endorsed by such Scottish theologians as William Cunningham. There are fundamental doctrines, and there are secondary doctrines. For example, the doctrine of Christ's deity is fundamental, but the doctrine of the millennium is not. The true church is known by its adherence to such fundamental doctrines: the doctrines which were set forth in the ancient ecumenical creeds and later in the great Protestant Confessions.

But the Reformers stressed that it is not the mere possession of truth which attests a living church: it is the *proclamation* of truth. Does the church preach the gospel? It is quite possible that a body of people might be very orthodox in their convictions and yet make no effort to proclaim those convictions. In fact, this familiar emphasis that the church is known by the preaching of the word means, simply, that the church is, by definition, evangelistic. If it is not evangelistic, if it has no interest in outreach, if it is not committed to Christian mission, if it is not geared to bringing God's good news to every man, then it lacks an essential mark of the church.

That is a very solemn thing, because we are inclined to imagine that so long as our creed is orthodox we measure up to this mark. We do not! We measure up to it only if we proclaim the message. There can be a heresy of silence as well as a heresy of proclamation. In the age of the Scottish Moderates, for example, you would seldom hear heresy in the pulpit, but you might go many a mile without ever hearing the truth actually preached. It is quite possible that some churches which have orthodox creeds give no emphasis at all to such fundamental doctrines as the sinfulness of man, the love of God and the wonder of atonement. It is even more possible that they do not go up to every man and say plainly, 'I have good news for you!'

The administration of the sacraments

The second mark of the church is the administration of the sacraments: baptism and the Lord's Supper. The Reformers held it to be axiomatic that we should express our faith in baptism and nourish and sustain our faith by coming to the Lord's Table. For this reason, they gave great attention to the question of the due administration of the sacraments.

The crucial issue for them, inevitably, was the Mass, which had changed the sacrament of the Lord's Supper beyond recognition, turning it into a repetition of the propitiatory sacrifice of Christ on Calvary. To make matters worse, the mediaeval church had attached to this sacrificial concept of the sacrament the further idea of transubstantiation: the literal conversion of the bread and wine into the body, blood, soul and divinity of the Lord Jesus Christ. This was expressed in the most literal terms. Every crumb of that bread was the body and the soul and the divinity of Jesus! And as a logical consequence of all this, there arose the practice of 'the adoration of the host'. To Protestants this is rather mysterious terminology because the English word 'host' has its own meaning and when we hear of the 'adoration of the host' the idea it conveys is that the congregation is adoring the priest who is the host at the Lord's Supper (the priest being, in Roman thought, the one who presides in Christ's name at the Lord's Supper). In reality, the host in the Mass represents the Latin word 'hostia' (a sacrifice), and the adoration of the host is the worship of the bread, which has ceased to be bread and is now the body, soul and divinity of Jesus Christ. It was this that led the Reformers to argue, with considerable justification, that the Mass was blasphemous: it led to the worship of what was mere bread. Today, we need to look at this position a little more cautiously, because there is no doubt that the Roman Catholic Church is highly embarrassed by its own traditional doctrine on this subject and does its best to disavow literal transubstantiation and the literal repetition of the sacrifice of Christ. These still remain, however, official dogmas of the Church, expressed in, for example, the Decrees of Trent and the Tridentine Catechism.

It was against this background that men like Calvin spoke of the sacraments being 'duly administered'; that is, stripped of all non-biblical, mediaeval accretions and enacted in biblical simplicity. It is a moot point, however, whether Calvin ever loosed himself entirely from superstition on this issue. Certainly Luther never did; and there is still a great deal of superstition on this subject.

It is worth noting at this point that the Reformers wanted the sacraments administered very frequently. Calvin's own conviction was that once a week was by no means too often and he settled for a monthly administration only to accommodate circumstances. It is a pity that we have so completely lost sight of the Reformers' attitude to the sacraments. We have made them so peripheral that it will need an enormous effort to reinstate them to their true biblical position.

The exercise of discipline
The third mark of the church was the exercise of discipline. It is true that at one level this meant that every true church of Christ was characterised by the exercise of proper control over admission to membership and over the behaviour and conduct of its members, with due provision being made for dealing with those who publicly violated the norms of Christian conduct. There can be no doubt that at the Reformation there emerged a very coherent attitude towards what are called 'church censures' (such as excommunication, and so on). But it would be a great pity to equate discipline with church censures. As in so many other instances we suffer here from the misfortune that we are using an English word which has a current connotation which differs from its original Latin meaning. The original Latin meaning of 'discipline' involved much more than church censures. Both John Knox and Andrew Melville, for example, prepared what

were called Books of Discipline. These are books, not about church censures, but about the structures and the organisation of the church. Indeed, it is a very interesting fact that men of such prophetic passion as the apostle Paul, John Calvin and John Knox were also so deeply committed to organisation. They were all fantastic organisers! It was from that concern to have an organised church that there emerged those Books of Discipline in our Scottish tradition.

What was meant by this mark was that the church must have proper biblical organisation. Things had to be done decently and in order. There were certain functionaries and officers to be appointed and certain arrangements to be made to facilitate the life and mission of the church. The church was to be known by the fact that it had a biblically derived and biblically controlled organisation. This is not the place to discuss what the details of such an organisation might be. The guiding principle of the New Testament, it seems to me, is that the church is to organise itself in such a way that it can serve the gospel with the maximum efficiency. God will have all men to be saved (1 Timothy 2:3). We please Him when we put ourselves in a position where are able to tell as many as possible, as clearly as possible, that 'there is one God and one mediator between God and men, the man Christ Jesus, who gave himself as a ransom for all men' (1 Timothy 2:5,6). Structures serve the gospel, not the gospel the structures.

Worship

Fourthly, there is the mark of worship. The church is known by the fact that it not only holds the gospel, but, in response to that gospel, meets to call on the name of the Lord (1 Corinthians 1:2). The church doesn't simply hold certain convictions about Jesus. It gathers to worship Him.

The earliest known pagan reference to the church is in an official communication from Pliny the Younger (who died around 113), the Roman governor of Bithynia, to the Roman emperor of the time, Trajan. In this letter, Pliny speaks of a sect who 'were in the habit of meeting on a certain fixed day before it was light, when they sang in alternate verses a hymn to Christ, as to a god'. The church is a doxological community. It comes together to sing hymns to Christ 'as to a god'.

Here, however, we come up against a peculiar difficulty: the New Testament never uses the language of worship for the public gatherings of the church. We read that the church met to break bread and to be taught and so on. But the specific vocabulary of worship, the Greek words for 'worship', are not used in descriptions of the church's public gatherings. We do, however, know from 1 Corinthians 12–14 that when believers met they sang psalms and hymns and engaged in prayer. Similarly, we know from Acts 2:46 that they met in each other's homes to praise God. Clearly, a good deal of praising went on.

This is an important point because there is a great danger that those of us who emphasise the primacy of preaching will squeeze the liturgical out of our church gatherings. I personally find it difficult to be patient when those conducting services reduce the praise-items, for example. Within reason, we ought to maximise participation and maximise the element of praise so as to enable people to express their joy and thanksgiving. Worship should be praise and jubilation.

Ministry to the poor
The fifth mark is concern for the poor. I have left it to the last, not because I believe it is necessarily the most important, but because it is the most neglected. In both the First and Second Books of Discipline the idea is linked very closely to the work of deacons, whose 'office and power is to receave and to distribute the haill ecclesiastical gudes unto them to whom they are appoyntit.'[2] In the First Book of Discipline, John Knox made specific provision for a ministry to the poor. 'Every several kirk,' he stipulated, 'must provide for the poor within itself; for fearful and horrible it is, that the poor, whom not only God the Father in his law, but Christ Jesus in his Evangel, and the Holy Spirit speaking by Saint Paul, hath so earnestly commended to our care, are universally

so contemned and despised.' In Melville's arrangements, one-quarter of the kirk's revenue was to be 'bestowit upon the puir members of the faithfull, and on hospitals'.

Such provision was simply a reflection of what marked the church from the beginning. We know from Acts 6, for example, that at a very early point in her history the church organised formal provision for the poor. We also know that when Paul went to discuss his Gentile mission with the apostles in Jerusalem they said to him, 'Your gospel is OK; but remember the poor': the very thing, he said, he was eager to do (Galatians 2:10). Later, we see Paul himself (and how remarkable it is!) giving time and energy to organising collections to relieve the poverty of the saints in Jerusalem (2 Corinthians 8:1-9:15).

Just, then, as a church is not a church if it does not evangelise, so a church is not a church if it has no concern for the poor. Every single congregation should have some formal provision of this kind, reaching out to the need in its own community. Tokenism is not enough. There is real need in the society around us. I am not going to give detailed formulations. I am simply laying down that the poor must be on both our consciences and our agendas and that the church must be organised, not only to evangelise, not only to worship, not only to administer the sacraments, but also to help those who are in need.

Of course, under a Welfare State that can be complicated. The very fact of such a Welfare State existing at all is often an excuse for doing nothing. But the theology is crystal clear and the Liberationists are absolutely correct: God has a bias towards the poor. Our responsibility is never merely to evangelise. We have to go about, like Jesus, doing good (Acts 10:38). That includes responding to people's temporal and material needs.

There are, then, five marks of the church. Let's try to remember them. We live in a highly mobile society and many of us (particularly young people) will one day have to think carefully about choosing a place of worship. We may find, for example, that our own denomination does not exist in a particular part of the world. How then do we decide what church to attend? There is no easy formula, but we can make a beginning by applying these criteria: Is the gospel preached? Are the sacraments duly administered? Is this church biblically organised? Does this church have real Christian praise and worship? Does this church have any concern for the poor?

According to the Westminster Confession, 'particular churches ... are more or less pure' as they conform to those marks of the church (XXV:4). This very plainly implies that there is no such thing as a pure and perfect church – 'The purest churches under heaven are subject both to mixture and error' (XXV:5). But the degree of purity of particular churches is indicated by the degree of conformity they show to those five marks. There is a difference between a true church and a pure church. We are true churches if we possess those five marks in embryo. We are pure churches in proportion as we measure up to those marks more or less fully.

The government of the church

What about the government of the church? Scottish theology has distinguished itself by the attention it has given to this particular question. I can best access it by introducing you briefly to the three main forms of church government.

First, *episcopacy*: that is, government by monarchical bishops. These bishops are deemed to be a superior class to elders (being their overseers and superintendents) and to have some kind of territorial sovereignty. They are bishops of a given geographical area, sometimes of very large extent. In essence, this position is found in Roman Catholicism and also in Anglicanism and in various mixtures in some of the Reformed churches of Eastern Europe (which, though Calvinist in derivation, happen to have bishops).

All this was anathema, of course, to Scottish churchmen from Andrew Melville downwards and they attacked it in terms which were often unrestrained. Today, we have to say the same thing in more moderate and courteous tones. But it is one of the curiosities of the modern situation that ecumenical discussion, however uncertain it may be on matters of fundamental doctrine, is absolutely assured that any resultant church will have to be episcopal. That is quite remarkable because there is virtually unanimity among scholars of all shades of opinion – Presbyterian, Anglican and even Roman Catholic – that we do not find monarchical bishops in the New Testament. One of the most important studies of the meaning of the Greek word *episkopos* [3] was by the great Anglican bishop, J. B. Lightfoot of Durham. Lightfoot, without peer as a New Testament scholar, showed beyond the possibility of challenge that in the New Testament *bishops* and *elders* were equal and synonymous. Episcopacy is based on tradition, not on the New Testament. It so happens that in the second century monarchical episcopacy (or bishops who were bosses!) did emerge. In that sense bishops are of great antiquity and if antiquity is your norm then you must have bishops. But if the New Testament is your norm then you cannot impose bishops on the church because the New Testament had no bishops in the monarchical sense.

That does not mean that Presbyterians have no bishops. All our elders are bishops. We also have something more subtle than that: the episcopacy of presbytery. Presbyteries have all the functions of bishops. For example, they can direct a minister to leave a congregation and undertake outreach elsewhere. As it happens, presbyteries today seldom perform these episcopal functions, but they certainly have the power.

Secondly, there is what is called *Independency* or *Congregationalism*. This means that each local congregation is seen as an autonomous unit, independent of all other units and governed by local office bearers. At the moment, this is undergoing some modification. Historically, independent churches in Britain did not have elders. The independents who were members of the Westminster Assembly, for example, were profoundly averse to the idea that the church should have ruling elders distinct from teaching elders. More recently, however, independency in England has been trying to incorporate elders into its own historic structures, sometimes with unhappy results.

Independency means that the local church answers to nobody

èlse: not to presbytery, not to synod, not to general assembly. It is a self-contained entity with a pastor who preaches and deacons who lead and govern. But even this needs qualification, since it is also a feature of independency that power lies with the local Church Meeting. Every member of the congregation has a right to attend such a meeting and to have a say in all its decisions. It follows from this that in independency everyone admitted into membership of the church must subscribe to the constitution. It is as if Presbyterians were to require every new communicant to sign our Confession of Faith. We don't, of course, because in presbyterian polity the members do not govern the church and therefore don't need to be sworn to the whole range of Confessional doctrine.

Which brings us to *Presbyterianism*: the option to which, obviously, I am personally biased. I believe that the New Testament lays down very few principles of church government, stressing, by and large, the merit of flexibility and adjustment to varying circumstances. Structures exist for the gospel, not the gospel for structures. Any structure that helps us preach the gospel is healthy and acceptable.

The New Testament does, however, lay down three fundamental principles. One is the parity of elders and bishops. All elders, as far as authority goes, are equal. In the New Testament the word *elder* and the word *bishop* mean exactly the same thing; all elders are on the same plane and elders/bishops function together in the local churches as a collegiate oversight in which none is boss and none is dictator. None is *the* elder or the *senior* elder or any other combination of rank-orientated words. There is parity among all elders. This carries with it the idea that so far as pastoral oversight is concerned the minister, too, is on a par with elders (although as preacher and teacher he has, of course, his own special gift and special calling).

The second fundamental principle of New Testament church organisation is that in every church there should be a *plurality of elders*. At Ephesus, for example, Paul called together the elders of the church (Acts 20:17). He also defined their function: they are overseers (Acts 20:28). They are leaders, not delegates or shop stewards. Their responsibility is not to find out what the congregation want and simply give it to them. They have to work out for themselves collegiately what is best for the congregation and to lead them towards it. This responsibility never devolves upon one man. It falls on the whole body of elders. Every church needs more than one bishop.

The third essential principle is *connectionalism*. I mean by that that Presbyterianism (presuming upon New Testament warrant) takes the view that all churches are connected and therefore cannot exist as autonomous entities. This is why local churches are organised in a presbytery, presbyteries are organised in a synod, synods are organised in a national assembly and (in theory), all national assemblies are organised in an Ecumenical Synod embracing all the churches.

Let me go back a little to what I said about Independency. Independents suspect that in presbyterian polity individual congregations have little liberty. Assembly committees, they say, are always meddling in the affairs of local churches. The presbyterian polity of Scotland, however, has firmly emphasised the autonomy of local churches. In fact, only on rare occasions would presbyteries, synods or assemblies feel warranted in interfering in the internal affairs of a particular church. It will do so only by invitation; and only when a crisis warrants it.

Connectionalism, then, does not detract from the independence of the local church. What it means is that local churches can co-operate. They can pool their resources. The strong can help the weak. For example, in the Free Church of Scotland our Sustentation Fund assumes that we can place a minister in every corner of Scotland provided the big congregations are willing to remit to a central fund as much as they can afford. Out of that fund we can pay a stipend for a man in a small congregation which could not possibly support a minister. Without some such connectionalist arrangement it is extremely difficult to provide full-time ministries in rural areas. The point of connectionalism is not that it allows churches to meddle in each other's affairs, but that it facilitates (and indeed demands) cooperation over a wide range of activities from church extension to foreign missions and theological education.

That is its pragmatic merit. The theological basis for connectionalism is that in the New Testament local churches clearly acted together. All the churches at both Jerusalem and Ephesus, for example, were one. Similarly, the Christians in Judea, Galilee and Samaria are seen as constituting not an aggregate of *churches*, but one church (Acts 9:31). More fundamentally, Christ has but one body and all its members must act in coordination and harmony (Ephesians 4:1-16). Schism between churches is as unthinkable as schism between individual Christians.

Let me come back again to my guiding principle: the structures exist for the gospel, just as Jesus said that the Sabbath exists for man, not man for the Sabbath (Mark 2:27). It is a sad thing when canon law gets in the way of evangelism. Sometimes we have to accommodate, yielding to circumstances. When, in 1647, the fathers of the Church of Scotland adopted the Westminster Confession of Faith they had reservations about a statement to the effect that the civil magistrate has power to call synods (XXIII. 2). That, said the General Assembly, can refer only to 'kirks not settled'. In other words, in times of unsettledness we have to adapt to suit the particular situation. That is enormously important. Within the fundamental principles there is abundant scope for flexibility and adaptability.

The unity of the church

I am going to say just a word on the unity of the church. This is an area where evangelical thinking has been tragically weak. Indeed, the evangelical mentality today is often more concerned to find grounds for separation than grounds for unity. We even seem to regard unity and separation as symmetrical, as if there were a New Testament doctrine of separation coordinate with its doctrine of unity.

My position on this is quite simple: we don't need justification for union and cooperation. It is obvious – it is indeed a first principle of the New Testament – that Christians co-operate. It is our separation and disavowal of each other that requires explanation: urgent explanation. We have been very cavalier in our reaction to this thing we call 'the Ecumenical Movement'. There are people who are dismissed as 'ecumenicals': as if it were a bad thing to be concerned for the unity of God's church!

The basis of Christian unity is the new birth. All who are members of God's family are one with every other member of God's family. If we have God for our Father we have every other Christian in the world for our brother and sister. That really is a remarkable and (to me) a thrilling fact. It doesn't matter what their denominational affiliation may be or what their theological peculiarities may be. If they are in Christ, if they are born again, they are my sisters and my brothers.

Of course, you can say, 'Ah, but if they're heretics they're not born again!' That is as may be. But if they are born again they are my brothers and my sisters, I am one with them and I must therefore express my oneness with them in every way possible. The model God has given us for the expression of this unity is His own unity as the Triune God: 'that they may be one as we are one' (John 17:11). That is really very humbling, in some ways even devastating: all the Christians in the world should be as united as the three Persons of the eternal Trinity! You'll never hear God the Father and God the Son quarrelling. You'll never hear them miscalling each other or using abusive language about each other. You'll never find them discouraging each other. They are One. They love each other. They share with each other. They co-operate. They live in and through each other

The churches of God ought to present that same picture: at two levels.

First, at the level of the local church (which, as far as the New Testament is concerned, is the basic ecclesiastical unit). Within the local congregation relations between the various members should be reflections of the relations between God the Father, God the Son and God the Holy Spirit.

Secondly, the Trinitarian model applies to relations between churches and denominations. Christian churches, distinct from each other as God the Father is distinct from God the Son, are yet one and should love, share, comfort, help and co-operate with each other. That is not some peripheral ideal. That is an absolutely fundamental and unequivocal New Testament imperative. What is a heretic? An Arminian? A Modernist? No! In the New Testament a heretic is a divisive man. He is a man who causes divisions; who miscalls other Christians; who miscalls other Churches; who is factious. That's what a heretic is. Of course, there is a link between our modern use of the word and the New Testament use. The great trouble with false doctrine is precisely that it divides churches. That is its evil. Dividing the church is evil. Fragmenting, fomenting discord, behaving in a way that shows disregard for the peace and harmony of the church or of an individual congregation or of inter-church relations is a heinous sin.

Today, we are totally unrealistic about this whole problem. There are many Christians in this land, far more than there are Marxists or secularists or Muslims, and yet because of our fragmentation we are virtually impotent and powerless! We really have to abandon our age-old habits of majoring on the minor and firing our salvos at brethren rather than at the enemy. If we're not careful we could spend our whole lives fighting with those who argue that the Authorised Version is the only reliable version of God's word, or with those who maintain that the only acceptable form of worship is unaccompanied psalm-singing, or with Pentecostals, Arminians and other septs of the Protestant churches. Christendom is collapsing round our ears! We have to decide which battles we are going to fight, not waste our energies fighting members of our own family: not even those family members who infuriate us and drive us to distraction. After all, there is a spiritual war going on! During the Second World War even the Labour Party and the Tory Party stopped fighting each other! We are at war. We have to stop fighting each other and fight the enemy outside.

That's the great pragmatic importance of the unity of the church and it's something to which we must be keenly sensitive. Let's encourage the maximum possible interaction and co-operation between local churches and between all the Christian denominations in this land and further afield.

References
1. John Calvin, *Institutes of the Christian Religion*, Book IV, Chapter 1, 7-29. The most reliable translation is still that of Henry Beveridge.
2. *The Second Book of Discipline*, VIII. 3. Cf. Knox's *Form and Order for the Election of Superintendents, Elders and Deacons:* 'some to be Deacons for the collection of alms to be distributed to the poor of their own body.'
3. J. B. Lightfoot's essay, 'The Christian Ministry' in his *St. Paul's Epistle to the Philippians*, London: Macmillan, 3rd. edition, 1873, pp. 179-267.

19

The Lord's Supper

I want to begin this chapter on the Lord's Supper by making three general points.

First, the New Testament contains remarkably few references to the Lord's Supper. Some churches (those of more priestly inclination) place it at the very centre of their life and liturgy, and convey the impression that this sacrament is the be-all and end-all of Christianity. It is a very full answer to that practice that in the New Testament it is referred to so very infrequently. We have the Gospel accounts of its institution (in Matthew, Mark and Luke). We have some references in Acts to the breaking of bread, and in First Corinthians one or two references from the pen of Paul. These exhaust the New Testament references. Some detect allusions in other passages, but these are only allusions.

All this reminds us that, though the Supper is not to be marginalised, it certainly is not what lies at the heart of Christian life and discipleship. It has its own importance, but the preaching of the word is always more important than any sacrament. I intend no dishonour at all to the Lord's Supper, but I do want to assert this corrective to a widely prevalent sacramentalism.

Secondly, it is remarkable how anxious is the Apostle Paul to indicate the precise dating of the institution of the Supper. He tells us that it happened on 'the same night in which he [the Lord] was betrayed' (1 Corinthians 11:23). It is a tribute to Jesus' pastoral concern that on this night when so many other claims pressed upon His attention – this night when He had His own pressing personal problems – He was so concerned for His church that for its benefit He set up this 'comfortable ordinance'. Had we been facing what He faced on the following day we would have been immersed in our own problems. By contrast,

His heart was so sharply focused on the needs of His people that for their sakes He calmly attended the Passover meal and, with great dignity, instituted this sacrament for the benefit of the church.

Thirdly, St. Paul claims that his teaching on this subject came directly from the risen Lord Himself (1 Corinthians 11:23). This is all the more important in that First Corinthians is earlier than all our Gospels and therefore contains the earliest canonical account of the institution of the Supper. Paul uses a very interesting form of words in introducing the matter: 'I received from the Lord what I also passed on to you.' There is a kind of circularity here which is very instructive for our whole Christian lives. The believer stands in the middle of a process of transmission. The Apostle 'received' and the Apostle 'transmitted', and that is symbolic of all Christian life and witness. We receive testimony: we all owe so much to others. But we also pass on the testimony. It comes to us, but it doesn't stop with us. We have to transmit what we receive.

But the really important thing here is that Paul indicates that what he received he received from the Lord Himself. The natural meaning of these words is that his teaching on this subject had come to him by direct revelation from Christ. Paul was not himself present with the eleven disciples at the original Supper. Nevertheless, his account, he says, was not derived from any other apostle, but from the Lord Himself. It goes back, as far as Paul is concerned, to a dominical revelation: a word given to him by the risen Saviour.

The nature of the Lord's Supper

But what is the nature of the Lord's Supper? The best way to approach this is to look at some of the words that have been used to describe it.

The first of these is the word 'sacrament' itself. I am sure you have all heard this word used in explanation of the Lord's Supper and you have been told that it comes from a Latin word, *sacramentum,* which meant the oath taken by a Roman soldier.

It is therefore suggested that the Lord's Supper was the taking of an oath to Christ and an entering into an obligation of loyalty to Him at a personal level. Now that, of course, is not untrue. But the word *sacramentum* is a Latin word, not a biblical word, and therefore it cannot be used for theological purposes because it is not something sanctioned by revelation itself.

But there is a further, more serious difficulty: the word *sacramentum* entered Christian vocabulary in dubious circumstances. The Latin Vulgate used it to translate the New Testament word *mystery*. For example, when Paul discusses marriage in Ephesians 5:32, he says, 'This is a great mystery': a great *musterion*. The Vulgate rendering is that marriage is a great *sacramentum*. One result of this is that in subsequent Catholic thought marriage came to be seen as a sacrament. But the even more serious result was that the word 'sacrament' came to be identified with the word *mystery*. People began to speak of the 'mystery of the Lord's Supper'. It was a short distance from that to actually mystifying the Lord's Supper, something which, I am afraid, has often happened in Christian history. Even such an eminent Scottish theologian as Robert Bruce of Edinburgh entitled his famous sermons on this subject, *The Mystery of the Lord's Supper*.

It is very important to shake off this whole notion of mystery and of mystification. There were in New Testament times (or shortly afterwards) what were called 'mystery religions'. In some ways they were like Masonic Lodges. They had mysterious initiation rites and it is important for us to distance ourselves as far as we can from such a view of Christianity. In fact, the word *sacrament* has very limited value in helping us understand the Lord's Supper. It is a Roman, not a Christian, word; and because it was used (quite wrongly) to translate the Greek word *musterion* it now has unavoidable connotations of mystification.

The second word which is often used of the Lord's Supper is *eucharist*. This term has been more common in Episcopal and Catholic circles than among Presbyterians. But it is utterly biblical. Its use in connection with the Lord's Supper goes back to the fact that on the night of His betrayal Jesus 'took bread and, giving thanks (*eucharistesas),* broke it' (1 Corinthians 11:24). This rite of thanksgiving has become central to the Sacrament in virtually all Christian traditions. The Supper becomes an occasion for saying, 'Thank You, Lord, for Jesus. Thank You for the broken body, for the incarnation and for the death of Christ on the cross of Calvary.' But it is important to widen the scope of the thanksgiving to embrace not only the unique gift of Christ, but all of God's benefits. The bread symbolises the daily bread God gives us and, within that, all those ways in which God supplies our needs.

Thirdly, the Lord's Supper is a *proclamation*: 'You proclaim the Lord's death until he comes' (1 Corinthians 11:26). In some ways, of course, this proclamation takes place through the visible signs: the bread and the wine, the sacramental actions and the sacramental words. Through all of these there is a proclamation. The bread, for example, is broken. In Presbyterian liturgy (if it is administered carefully) there has been a great emphasis on the breaking of bread as a specific point in the ritual. I personally always try to observe that particular emphasis, pausing and quite deliberately breaking the bread, because that is part of our historical tradition. My only difficulty is that I am not entirely convinced as to its propriety because in Jewish practice the breaking of bread was itself part of the act of thanksgiving. It was, in fact, the Jewish grace. The head of the household said the grace by breaking bread, or broke bread as he said grace. From this point of view the breaking of bread was historically a part of the act of eucharist rather than a pointer to the sacrificial significance of the broken body of Jesus.

But there can be no doubt, taking the overall symbolism, that the focus does fall very much on the sacrifice of Christ: 'This is my body' (Matthew 26:26; Mark 14:22; Luke 22:19); 'This is my body, which is for you' (1 Corinthians 11:24, NIV): 'This is my blood of the [new] covenant, which is poured out for many for the forgiveness of sins' (Matthew 26:28, NIV). All such language is pointing to the sacrifice of Jesus, and when He says, 'Take, eat:

this is my body' (Mark 14:22), what He is saying to us is, 'The body is broken. It's there! The crucified Christ is there for you, but you get no benefit unless you take it and eat!' The sacrament is saying both that Christ has given Himself for us and that we must take Him for ourselves. God is standing there at the Table saying to us very directly, 'Take, eat.'

But, however eloquent the symbolism, there is good reason to believe that what Paul is really pointing to is that at the Sacrament as celebrated in the early church there was a narrative given of the Passion of Jesus. It is not simply that there was a symbolic proclamation of the death of Christ. It was more explicit than that. As they sat at the Supper the story of the cross was narrated, from oral recollection in the first instance, but later from the various written accounts which gradually appeared. Isn't this deeply suggestive? I have often wished that as we sat at the Table we had someone read the gospel story to us, or Isaiah's account of the Suffering Servant (Isaiah 53). The view is sometimes expressed that in the Presbyterian liturgy there is too much talking at the Lord's Table and that we ought to receive it in silence. There is some plausibility in that if you attach the main importance to the elements themselves. The impression conveyed by Paul, however, is that as they sat at the Supper there was a proclamation going on. Similarly, if we go back again to the scene in the Upper Room on that Passover night, we see from John's Gospel that Jesus was delivering some of His greatest discourses at that very moment. Of course, we don't know exactly at what point in the evening the Last Supper took place. Some of the discourse obviously occurred after they left the Upper Room, but, equally obviously, some of it took place while they sat at the Table. I am not convinced, then, of the merit of receiving the Sacrament in silence. It certainly cannot be advocated dogmatically.

So then, the Lord's Supper is a sacrament, the Lord's Supper is a eucharist and the Lord's Supper is a proclamation. But it is also a *commemoration.* 'Do this in remembrance of me' (1 Corinthians 11:24). It takes us back to the foundation-events of redemption. It is a reminder that Jesus Christ, God's Son, came into this world of material bread: this three-dimensional world. He came into space-time history. He was there, that night, doing these things and saying these things; and the following day, on the cross, in that same material world of time and space, He literally gave Himself for us. The Lord's Supper is there to make sure we never forget.

Again, the Supper is a *communion* (1 Corinthians 10:16). It is a communion in the body and the blood of the Lord Jesus Christ. Like many other words in this area, the word for 'communion' requires to be demystified. It comes from the Greek word for 'common' and means 'having things in common' or simply 'sharing'. At the Communion the Christians shared the bread, they shared the cup and they shared Christ. They had them in common.

The best way to see this is to go back to Melancthon's principle that 'to know Christ is to know Him in His benefits'. Communion in the body of Christ means that together we share in the benefits which have been secured to us by the whole life and ministry of Jesus, and specifically by the breaking of His body and the shedding of His blood.

There is a very interesting liturgical point here. In many traditions each individual believer receives the bread or the wafer from a clergyman: a minister, a priest, or sometimes an elder. This requires more thought than we commonly give to it. We should seek a form of celebration which provides that each believer receives the bread from his companion and in turn passes it on to his companion, thus maintaining the circularity of giving and receiving. Otherwise we are encouraging priestcraft and superstition. The best thing is to keep the involvement of the clergy to a minimum.

But the Lord's Supper is, again, precisely that: a *supper*. It is a means of grace. Indeed, that is its primary purpose. People came to a supper to be fed. Unfortunately, this is the area where Reformed thought has been most bound by the legacy of pre-Reformation thought. We have turned the Lord's Supper into an

ordeal and given it a crisis-ridden existential significance. I have
often been struck at Scottish Highland Communion Services by
the note of urgency that comes in on Saturday mornings, when
there is a deliberate attempt to motivate people to come to the
Lord's Table. It is very similar to evangelistic urgency, as if
coming to the Supper were parallel to coming to Christ. I have
heard solemn warnings about letting the opportunity pass and I
have heard sentimental stories about people who were refused
admission and died before the next Communion Season, as if this
were something of enormous spiritual significance. Nowhere in
the New Testament could you find a text for such a sermon, for
the simple reason that the New Testament church never saw the
Lord's Supper in that light. Coming to Communion wasn't an
ordeal or a crisis. It was the most natural thing in the world.
People came to be fed. They came to get the benefits of Christ.
They came because they hungered and thirsted after righteousness.

If we ask, 'What, more precisely, do we get at the Lord's
Table?' the best analysis I know is given indirectly in the Shorter
Catechism, in reply to the question, 'What are the benefits which
in this life do accompany or flow from justification, adoption,
and sanctification?' (Question 36). The answer is: 'Assurance of
God's love, peace of conscience, joy in the Holy Ghost, increase
[or growth] of grace, and perseverance therein to the end.' That's
an excellent summary of the feast awaiting us at the Lord's
Supper!

I don't quite know if I should warn against coming to the
Lord's Supper expecting to be filled with a warm glow of
religious feeling. I'm not at all opposed to what Edwards called
'religious affections', especially in an age of rampant moderatism,
when there is little enthusiasm in religion. But many folk come
to the Table expecting a great wave of emotion, especially at the
moment of eating the bread and drinking the wine. When they
don't get that, they're hugely disappointed. But we're not there
to get great waves of emotion! We're there to get assurance of
God's love, peace of conscience, joy in the Holy Spirit and
growth in grace.

We can put it again in terms of another antithesis. We speak, often, of people 'professing'. That would make no sense in the New Testament context because in that context there were no spectators. There was simply the gathered church. The Lord's Supper was never seen as a profession. Of course, in the New Testament church profession was important, but you confessed Christ in the world, during the week. That was where you let people know where you stood. The Lord's Supper had different purposes. It was a spiritual oasis. It was a time of spiritual relaxation. It was a spiritual feast. You came to the Lord's Table to get refreshment for your soul.

Put it this way: What is the qualification for coming to a supper? Hunger! Appetite! You want the things on the table! If I ask, 'Am I qualified for the Lord's Table?' then I'm really asking, 'Do I want what's provided in this feast? Do I want the blessings and benefits of Christ?'

I want to make one last point here, a very elementary but very important one. The Lord's Supper is an *ordinance*. In our Gaelic communities that is the most frequently used word: *na h-orduighean*, 'the ordinances'. That was also prevalent in some English-speaking parts of Scotland at one time. I want to take from that just one simple fact, namely, that this is not something optional. It is a divine ordinance. I am often amazed at people's attitude to this. They view the preaching of the Word as something they must attend, and the Lord's Day as something they must observe, because these are both *ordinances*. But they have a completely different view of the Lord's Supper. They regard it as discretionary: as if it weren't an *ordinance*. Much is made of the sin of what is called 'unworthy communicating', but little is said of the sin of not communicating at all. That really is a glaring act of defiance on the part of a Christian.

The best motive for coming to the Lord's Table is simple obedience. We come because Christ told us to *do this*. We have no option, and where there is faith it will hear Christ's clear directive. Preachers have no right to make Christians feel guilty about coming to the Table. They should feel guilty about *not* coming. Thankfully things have changed a good deal in this respect, but there is still a lingering suspicion in some quarters that it is commendable that people should stay away and that 'coming forward' is a great spiritual climax and a great personal crisis. I find none of this in the New Testament. There, it was the most natural thing in the world that a Christian should come to the Lord's Table.

Unworthy participating

Yet St. Paul does raise the question of unworthy participation. We can come to the Supper in such a way that we incur guilt, and guilt of the gravest kind: not that we have offended against some human ordinance, but that we have offended against the body and blood of the Lord (1 Corinthians 11:27f.).

The whole argument here hinges on this: What is meant by 'in an unworthy manner'? It is not a poor, trembling soul fearing that she may be a hypocrite. The nature of the offence is defined by the context. The abuses at Corinth were horrific. The sacrament had become a virtual orgy. There was drunkenness, gluttony and snobbery and it was all happening around the Lord's Table. It was that level of abuse that distressed Paul.

But if we want an abiding theological definition of the phrase 'in an unworthy manner' we have to link it to what we have already seen with regard to the nature of the Lord's Supper. To come in an unworthy manner is to come in a way that is not controlled by the nature of the Supper: in a way that disregards the purposes it was meant to serve. That was Paul's basic complaint. He speaks of *this* bread and *this* cup. The Lord's Supper is not just any feast. It's not a party. It's not an orgy. What then is it? It is a eucharist. It's a proclamation. It's a commemoration. It's a supper. It's an ordinance, You come 'worthily' if in your coming you are controlled by these things.

To be more precise: Paul is asking, Are we coming to give thanks for His Son? Are we coming to commemorate His Son? Are we coming to share His Son? Are we coming because we are hungering and thirsting? Are we coming because Christ commands us? It is a question of motivation, and that motivation must arise from what the Supper is. That's the point!

Take just one of these aspects: thanksgiving. The Supper is a eucharist. To come in an unworthy manner is to come in a way that has nothing to do with eucharist, that is not in the least concerned to give thanks to God and that completely disregards thanksgiving. But if we come with thankfulness and come because the memory of Christ is precious to us and come because God commands us and come saying, 'Well, I don't deserve to come, but God doesn't leave that up to me. He commands me to come' – then we are coming in an appropriate manner. It's appropriate because it's regulated by the nature of the sacrament itself.

Self-examination

It is precisely because this is so important that Paul stresses the duty of self-examination: 'A man ought to examine himself before he eats of the bread and drinks of the cup' (1 Corinthians 11:28). We must do it every time, not just the first time, because the danger is ever-present. We have to ask ourselves, Am I coming to the Table in a way that is controlled by the nature of the Table itself? Am I coming for the right reasons and with the right motives? And how precise this pastor, Paul, is! 'Let a man examine *himself.*' Not other people! It is not a place for censoriousness. We examine ourselves every time we come, lest we eat and drink judgment to *ourselves* (1 Corinthians 11:29). Unfortunately, in the Authorised Version the word used is 'damnation'. That is not because the Authorised Version men were mistaken. It is because the word 'damnation' has changed its meaning since 1611. The Shorter Catechism (written about 1644) has the word 'judgment' (Answer 97). That is the correct translation. There is no place in the Bible for the notion that coming to the Lord's Table unworthily or inappropriately is *the* sin or the unpardonable sin. It will indeed bring judgment, but not final judgment. If it did, who could stand? None of us!

And so we examine ourselves, knowing that if we come inappropriately we expose ourselves to God's chastisement. It would help us to understand the whole thrust of the Apostle's thought here if we remembered one simple fact: Paul is writing to Christians. The idea of unbelievers at the Table is simply not on his horizon. He is not saying that if we are converted we are all right and have nothing to fear. That is not Paul's teaching. It is the converted Paul is interested in. He is not saying, 'Examine yourselves to see if you are converted.' That is an appropriate enough question in some contexts. But here what we have is a word to the 'saints' in Corinth. He wants them to examine themselves, not to see if they are saints, but to see if they have a correct understanding of the Lord's Supper and a proper attitude towards it.

In other words, as far as Paul is concerned here, only Christians can come to the Lord's Table inappropriately (of course, it is also inappropriate for unbelievers to come, but what he is interested in here is Christians who forget what the Lord's Supper is all about). That is not something we can wriggle out of. Those who, for example, come to the Lord's Table believing that it is a Mass in which Christ is physically present have a wrong view of the Supper, as did those Corinthians who came as if they were going to a party. But what about those who come thinking it is some great ordeal, some test, some act of heroism? Is that also not inappropriate? Here is a spiritual feast prepared for us by our Heavenly Father; and we are coming to it with fear and trembling!

It is as Christians that we are to examine ourselves. If we come inappropriately we will be judged. It doesn't mean that we will go to hell or that we will be damned. But if we are wrong in our approach to the Lord's Supper God will judge us. Conceivably, a Christian may say, 'Oh! That's OK. I don't go to the Lord's Supper. I'm safe enough!' But that itself is wrong. He is wrong if he does not come. His whole discernment is wrong and that exposes him to this chastening. We have to say that! Those who guiltily and wrongly absent themselves from the Lord's Supper are as much at risk of God's judgment as those who come with a false understanding and with false practices and attitudes. We must all examine ourselves.

People sometimes say that a very special solemnity attaches to the sacrament because there is no comparable warning about damnation if we listen to the word 'unworthily'. I can well recall when it was a mandatory part of every Highland Communion Service that the preacher should say, 'We now come to the most solemn part of the service.' Then one or two men began to protest that the preaching of the Word was equally solemn. Quite rightly so, because there is at least one extremely solemn warning in connection with the preaching of the Word: 'How shall we escape, if we neglect so great salvation; which at the first began to be spoken by the Lord' (Hebrews 2:3). It is as solemn to sit unresponsively under the Word of God as to sit inappropriately at the Lord's Table. Notice, once more, the context: 'How shall *we* escape – we Christians?' The whole context is about Christians; Christians neglecting their own salvation; Christians not putting their hearts into their salvation. How shall they escape if they neglect it? They will experience condign judgment: not damnation in the sense of going to hell, but divine chastisement. Clearly, listening to preaching in a negligent way is as risky as coming to the Lord's Table 'unworthily'.

The *real* presence

Throughout history, discussion of the Lord's Supper has been complicated, if not indeed be-devilled, by the question of the presence of Christ in the sacrament. People sometimes refer to it as the 'sacramental presence'. They also speak of the 'real presence', and that is a useful place to enter the discussion, because the 'real presence' is a highly specific concept. It does not mean 'real' in our sense of 'genuine', but 'real' in the highly technical sense of 'the presence of the thing itself'. The 'reality' (from the Latin *res*, a thing) is the *thing*; and the *thing* is the body of Christ. The precise meaning of the phrase 'the real presence' is the presence of the thing, namely, the body of Jesus. Many branches of the church hold that at the Lord's Supper this is exactly what happens. This is the mystery; the *sacramentum*. The *thing*, the body of Christ, is literally present.

This is an idea with which I find it exceedingly difficult to be patient because it is utterly incomprehensible how we ever got from the New Testament to this. But somehow we did get to it and even the most Reformed of churches have never quite shaken it off.

Let's look briefly at the history of the discussion. According to the Roman Catholic idea of transubstantiation, the bread and wine are literally changed into the 'thing'. The bread becomes the body of Jesus and the wine becomes the blood of Jesus. The Counter Reformation asserted that doctrine with the utmost vehemence and with total lack of ambiguity, going to the crassest lengths and laying down that every crumb of the bread is the body, soul and divinity of Christ; and every drop of the wine is the body, soul and divinity of Christ. (This is why the laity were not allowed to take the Cup. They might spill it, and thus spill the body, soul and divinity of Christ.) There was no limit to this. In the sacrament Christ was chewed because the body, the 'thing', was there in the most literal sense.

To any ordinary mind, not conditioned by philosophical assumptions, all this is fairly absurd, but that is the Catholic doctrine and that is why the Reformers reacted so strongly and controverted it so vigorously. We must maintain this debate unabated. We must be aware of two things, however: first, that very few Roman Catholic laity know what the Church teaches on this subject; and, secondly, that modern Catholic theologians are often anxious to escape from the strait-jacket in which they were tied by the Council of Trent. But the Church's official position is utterly unambiguous. The bread and wine become the literal body, blood, soul and divinity of Jesus.

Then there is the Lutheran position, conveniently labelled as 'consubstantiation'. It is at least as mysterious and unintelligible as the Catholic doctrine. It lays down that the bread remains bread (whereas in Catholicism the bread is changed), but alongside of it there is the body of Christ, which is present 'in, with and under' the bread. In other words, in Catholicism when you eat the bread you eat one thing, the body of Christ. In Lutheranism you eat two things, the bread *and* the body. They are both there: *con*substantiation, two substances side by side.

Thirdly, there is the position of John Calvin. Calvin never managed to shake off the legacy of Rome and Luther on this particular issue. William Cunningham, in his essay, *Zwingle and the Doctrine of the Sacraments*[1] (probably the best treatment of the Lord's Supper in the English language), is very critical of Calvin's position on this matter. In Cunningham's view, Calvin is as unintelligible as Luther. The problem was that Calvin had a tremendous regard for Luther and was extremely reluctant to go against him. He was also mentally conditioned by medievalism and simply could not shake off the idea that somehow the 'thing', the body of Christ, was present in the sacrament. Just as the sun's rays come from the sun to earth, wrote Calvin, so something emanated from the body of Christ in heaven down to the Lord's Table. If you asked, 'How is it possible? How can influences emanate from the Body in heaven to earth?' Calvin said simply, 'The Holy Spirit can do anything!' What was this but an attempt to put the best possible face on an absurdity? But it explains why even Reformed theologians like Robert Bruce continued to speak of the mystery of the Lord's Supper. It was a real mystery! There is nothing more mysterious than bread being made into the body of the Son of God or bread being accompanied by the body of the Son of God or bread being the occasion for spiritual rays to emanate from heaven to earth. All that is very mysterious. But I doubt very much if it's biblical.

There remains a fourth point of view: that of Zwingli. Everybody has some idea that there is a heresy called Zwinglianism, according to which the sacraments are only naked and bare signs. It is not at all certain that Zwingli set forth any such teaching. Nor is it at all clear what we mean when we deny that they are only naked and bare signs. To some people, at least, they are very naked and very bare.

Zwingli argued two things. First, that the physical, resurrection body of Christ is not present. This element of Zwingli's teaching is echoed in the Shorter Catechism: we do not partake of His body and blood 'after a corporal and carnal manner' (Answer 96). The body is not there. The flesh, the *caro,* of Christ is not there. That is the most important single negative with regard to the Lord's Supper. There is no sense in which the flesh, the body, of Christ is at the Lord's Table. It remains, Zwingli insisted, at the right hand of the Majesty on high (Hebrews 1:3).

But Zwingli argued, secondly, that Christ is at the Lord's Table. His body is not: but He is. He is there in the hearts of His people. He is there by His Holy Spirit. He is there not to be seen and touched and handled, but to be received by faith. This is no mere metaphorical presence. It is a genuine presence, 'real' not in the sense of the body being present, but in the sense of Christ being personally present. He is present at the Lord's Table as He is present wherever two or three gather in His name (Matthew 18:20). He is present as He is present in the prayer-meeting. He is present as He is present in the preaching of the Word. He is present as He was present to the saints of the Old Testament. There is no peculiar sacramental presence. We cannot teach that tonight we have the prayer-meeting presence and tomorrow we have the preaching presence and next month we have the sacramental presence, as if somehow these were gradations on some kind of scale. The person, Christ, is present wherever His people gather, wherever His Word is preached, wherever His name is invoked in prayer. He is present in our hearts, present with His grace, present with His help in time of need, and present in His benefits.

Have I taken all the mystique out of it? Have I made it all too logical? God forbid! I am left with my own mystery: the mystery of the personal, spiritual presence of the Lord Jesus Christ in the hearts of His people and in the gatherings of His church. What I am questioning is a specific mystical presence peculiar to the sacrament of the Lord's Supper. In my view, the mystery is the same here as it is in the prayer-meeting, in the preaching and in Christian fellowship. Christ lives in us.

Practice

Finally, a brief look at two questions of New Testament practice.

First, the issue of frequency. In the early days of the New Testament the Lord's Supper was administered not only every Lord's Day, but virtually every day (Acts 2:46). In Scotland it came to be observed much less frequently. But this was never a matter of principle. It was a matter of circumstances. In the sixteenth century there simply were not enough ministers to administer the sacrament as often as John Knox wanted and this set an unfortunate precedent. Of course we should have it more frequently: much more frequently. But that is up to the local kirk session. The difficulty that would pose for the smaller Presbyterian churches is that our 'Communion Seasons' would have to be much less elaborate. But the difficulties there are emotional, not theological. To many, it just would not feel right! But there is no biblical necessity for preparatory services (although I certainly think we should have high days on the church's calendar. Human nature need feasts and festivals and the old Scottish practice provided these).

Secondly, I would love to experiment with the Lord's Supper in a genuinely biblical setting. If I understand it correctly, the Last Supper began with the eucharist (the breaking of bread) and ended with the cup (the cup of blessing). In between there was the Upper Room discourse. I have this dream that some day I will see the Lord's Supper administered in that kind of framework: the service beginning with the breaking of the bread, then the preaching and the singing; and, at the end, the cup. I think that would approximate much more closely to the biblical pattern and I would love to see it as the norm for all Sunday-morning worship. But I suppose it will remain a dream.

Reference
1. William Cunningham, *The Reformers and the Theology of the Reformation*, Edinburgh: 1866, pp. 212-291.

20

The Last Days

Hope is central to Christian discipleship. We often present our faith in very pessimistic colours, emphasising the more sombre aspects of our religion, but, in essence, Christianity is good news. The Apostle Peter sums up the position when he urges believers to be prepared to give a reason for their hope (1 Peter 3:15). We live in a world that is marked by despondency, often conscious of its own futility and vanity and often terrified by the course of history. The church stands in the midst of this darkness as the sole bearer of light and hope. All our witness to God's holiness, to God's judgment and to the solemnity of human existence is but preparatory to the proclamation of this hope.

The Last Days
There is much misunderstanding of the term 'the last days'. As we reflect on our tumultuous era with its unprecedented violence, its great global wars, the collapse of great empires, the incidence of famine, earthquake and catastrophe, we often hear it said that we are living in the last days. It is assumed that such an expression means that we are living close to the end of history and to the second advent of Christ. In the New Testament, however, the phrase 'the last days' refers to our present era. In fact, the last days began with the advent of Christ and continue until the *parousia*, His second coming. In Acts 2, the Apostle Peter uses the words of the prophet Joel to explain the phenomena of Pentecost: 'In the last days, God says, I will pour out my Spirit on all people' (verse 17), and he tells them that this is being fulfilled before their very eyes. The last days are upon them.

The writer to the Hebrews reflects the same point of view when he says that in these last days God has spoken to us by His

Son (Hebrews 1:2). The last days were inaugurated in the mission of Jesus. The Apostle John, too, speaks in similar terms: 'Little children, it is the last time' (1 John 2:18). We are living in the last great era of human history.

That is the biblical view of time. Before Christ, we had the days of the Fathers. Since Christ, we have 'the last days': the Age of Fulfilment. The whole of Jewish and Gentile history before Bethlehem was preparatory; then there came 'the fullness of time', when God sent forth his Son (Galatians 4:4); and all that comes after that is simply the outworking of what was implicit in that great event.

In other words, the coming of Christ is the centre of history: the midpoint of time. It inaugurates the Age of Messiah and therefore marks the fulcrum on which the whole of history turns.

This is of enormous significance for our understanding of Christian mission. We have not been asked by God to evangelise the world in the days of the Fathers. We have been given this commission in the age of the Messiah. What, then, are the marks of the last days?

Satan is bound

The first is that Satan is bound. That may sound very strange because there is so much Satanic activity. The Devil still exercises all his wiles. The 'roaring lion' still prowls (1 Peter 5:8). But the New Testament consistently defines the cross in terms of the victory of Jesus Christ over all the forces of darkness. By that cross He made a show of principalities and powers and put them to an open shame (Colossians 2:15). By death He destroyed 'him that had the power of death, that is, the devil' (Hebrews 2:14). The serpent is bound with a great chain (Revelation 20:1-2). The Devil is a conquered adversary.

If we ask, 'In what respect is Satan bound?', the most important part of the answer is given in Revelation 20: he is bound in the sense that he deceives the nations no more (verse 3). The word for 'nations' is, more precisely, 'Gentiles'. Before Christ, Satan had complete dominion over the Gentile world.

Every nation but Israel lay 'in darkness and in the shadow of death' (Psalm 107:10). Before the cross, even Christ Himself forbade the disciples to evangelise the Gentiles: 'Go rather to the lost sheep of the house of Israel' (Matthew 10:6). Up to the moment of Pentecost Satan held the Gentiles enthralled. They were in moral and spiritual bondage: in total spiritual darkness.

But now all that has completely changed. Whatever the power and influence of Satan over modern civilisation, the kingdom of Christ has made great inroads into the world community. Whole continents which once lay in darkness and in the shadow of death have received the light of the gospel. It shines in Europe, in North and South America and in large areas of Africa and Asia. It influences millions upon millions of human lives; and it does so because Satan is bound and no longer holds the Gentiles in thrall. They have become the inheritance of Christ: 'Ask of me and I will make the nations your inheritance' (Psalm 2:8). That is one of the great impulses to world mission. The Gentiles belong to Christ by right.

Jesus reigns

Secondly, in these last days Jesus, the Messiah, reigns. He sits in the midst of the throne (Revelation 5:6). He has all authority in heaven and in earth (Matthew 28:18). He has power over all flesh (John 17:2). This reign is no mere future hope. It is a great present reality. 'Your God reigns!' (Isaiah 52:7). God's sovereignty is upon the shoulders of Jesus (Isaiah 9:6). Of course, God always reigned. He was King, even under the Old Testament. But now God the Son reigns in our human nature, 'touched with the feeling of our infirmities' (Hebrews 4:15). And He reigns to carry out the specific policy of giving 'eternal life to all those you have given him' (John 17:2). The unlimited resources of Messiah are pledged to the furtherance of the gospel.

Christians often convey the impression that the gospel is a poor, puny, little thing, under-resourced and starved of means. They forget that the Saviour has all authority and that He is head over all things for the church (Ephesians 1:22). That means, in the most practical terms, that He can move heaven and earth for the sake of the gospel. There, again, is one of the great impulses to Christian mission. Our responsibility is only to bring the gospel wherever Jesus reigns; to go to every land in the empire of Christ. There is no place where He is not Lord. Our task is to ask every knee to bow and every tongue to confess Him.

The outpoured Spirit

Thirdly, the last days are days of the outpoured Spirit. Peter, again, makes this clear: 'In the last days, God says, I will pour out my Spirit on all people' (Acts 2:17). During the Old Testament, the Spirit had been confined to Israel. Now, in the last days, the Spirit is poured out on every single believer: not only on Jews, but equally on Gentiles. This is the fulfilment of Jesus' promise: 'You will receive power when the Holy Spirit comes on you; and you will be My witnesses' (Acts 1:8).

It is power, specifically, to witness. The Spirit is given to enable us to understand what God has done in Jesus Christ and to enable us to face the hazards of Christian witness. He gives wisdom, courage and boldness so that we know what to say when questioned about our faith (Mark 13:11).

The New Testament evangelists, says the Apostle Peter, preached the gospel with the Holy Spirit sent from heaven (1 Peter 1:12). Here again we see the link between the features of the last days and the responsibility of Christian mission. God gave the church an apparently impossible assignment: 'Go to all the Gentiles! Go to every creature!' (Matthew 28:19; Mark 16:15). The church might easily have said, 'These people are dead in sin. They hate You. They've slain Your Son. They hate Your gospel. There's no point in sending us!' But, in these last days, we evangelise *in the Spirit*. The gospel cannot be disjoined from this divine power. Where it is disjoined – where the gospel is unacknowledged from on high – there is an unendurable anomaly, and we must plead with God for the restoration of normal service.

God will perform miracles

The fourth sign of the last days is that God will perform miracles. 'Anyone who has faith in me ... will do even greater things than these' (John 14:12). Literally, that means that the followers of Christ would perform greater miracles than He Himself ever performed. If we think of miracles only in terms of healings and exorcisms and controlling the elements, then of course we haven't surpassed Christ. But if we think of the miracle of evangelism and of spiritual renewal by the power of the gospel, then Christ's followers have seen far greater things than Jesus Himself ever saw. Three thousand converts at Pentecost in one sermon! George Whitefield proclaiming the gospel to audiences of twenty thousand, and thousands converted! The gospel in modern times has, in an instant, almost total global exposure through mass communication. Let us rejoice that all things are ours (1 Corinthians 3:21). Let us claim the miracles of the last days, the wonder of the eruptions of grace in the lives of countless individuals and the salvation of whole communities. That is what God has led us to expect.

Today, then, the church exists in extraordinary times, under extraordinary obligations and possessed of extraordinary resources. God has nothing new to give us. There is no new factor ever again to be introduced into human history. It is all there already. All God will ever give us is already ours. He has sent His Son, He has bound Satan, He has enthroned His Son, He has poured out His Spirit, He has given us the commission and the promises. There will be nothing more to the end of time.

What about the future?

Does that mean that we simply rest satisfied with our present? Is there no specific futurism in the New Testament? One school, the school of *realised eschatology,* stresses that God's promises have already been fulfilled. That is true, but it is not the whole truth. The *futurist school* (advocates of what is sometimes called *consistent eschatology)* on the other hand, tends to minimise the importance of what has been fulfilled and conveys the impression that it all lies in the future. In this, too, there is a grain of truth. What we have to do is to join together the truth contained in both realised and futurist eschatology. The result is what we may call *inaugurated eschatology*. The Last Time has been established and set in motion, but it has not yet been consummated. We live in this age of the inaugurated End.

Oscar Cullmann has described the situation in terms of D-day and V (Victory)-day. On D-day Allied forces landed on the beaches of Normandy and established a hold which led eventually to the overthrow of the whole Nazi empire. In other words, D-day was decisive. Once that beach-head was established the war was effectively won. Yet D-day was not V-day. It took many months of bitter fighting and many casualties, involving no doubt moments of uncertainty and even of despair for the Allies, before the victory was finally won.

That is what we mean by inaugurated eschatology. God has had his D-day. He has landed the forces of grace on the beaches of human history. The victory is assured, the outcome is certain, but the final victory is not yet won. The End has been inaugurated, but not yet consummated. God's great promises have been to a large extent realised. Yet there is still an unfulfilled future. The great promises of the second advent and the resurrection, the sombre reality of hell and the glorious reality of heaven all remain to be fulfilled in the future.

What sort of future is it to be?

First, it will be *cataclysmic*. The final phase of the kingdom of God will not be established by gradual and imperceptible evolution from the present or by factors already operating in the world, but by a fresh, unprecedented intrusion of the glory of God. It is the eruptive might of God that will one day raise the dead and create a new heaven and a new earth. The voice that spoke at the beginning and said, 'Let there be light' (Genesis 1:3) will speak once again and the heavens will disappear with a great roar and the elements will melt with fervent heat (2 Peter 3:10,12). It will happen not because the elements carry in themselves any potential for transformation, but because of 'a flash of the will that can'. Our future rests on this one, great fact: what He has promised He is able to perform (Romans 4:21).

Again, it is a future of *unqualified optimism*. God has given an assurance that right and love and grace will triumph and that one day all the evil that has ever been will be banished to Hell, that cesspool outside the universe. That is the foundation for the infinite optimism of the church. The triumph of right is guaranteed by the cross and resurrection of Christ.

But the Christian hope also represents an *eschatology of consolation*. As C. S. Lewis once said in the depths of bereavement, 'Reality, looked at steadily, is unbearable.'[1] There is no earthly comfort. That's why we need to look beyond reality, beyond earthly comfort, to that moment when God will wipe away all the tears from our eyes (Revelation 7:17). It is quite wrong for the Christian to banish the consolations of God and try to live without hope, without the prospect of heaven and without the assurance that God will one day wipe away the tears. Christ Himself endured because of 'the joy set before Him' (Hebrews 12:2) and in the shadow of the cross He found His consolation in turning to God and asking Him, 'Father ... glorify Your Son, that Your Son may glorify You' (John 17:1).

I wouldn't want to complain about the way it has been. Goodness and mercy have followed me all the days of my life. But I would not live always. There is no earthly comfort. Instead, we set our hope fully on the grace to be given to us at the revelation of Jesus Christ (1 Peter 1:13).

Reference
1. C.S. Lewis, *A Grief Observed*, London: Faber, 1966, p. 25.

21

The Second Coming

The Bible never actually describes the Second Advent of Christ as 'the Second Coming'. Instead it uses three other highly descriptive words.

First, it refers to it as the *parousia*. This Greek word means 'presence' or 'arrival', and is best understood in this connection as referring to a royal visit. The church lives in expectation of a royal visit on the part of its living and risen Saviour.

Secondly, the Bible uses the word *apocalypse*: literally, an unveiling of Jesus. At the moment, the dominion and sovereignty of Christ are veiled. One day that veil will be drawn aside and the whole world will see the reality of His sovereign dominion.

Thirdly, the return of Christ is referred to as an *epiphany*. The church is expecting the glorious *appearing* of her great God and Saviour, Jesus Christ (Titus 2:13). This is very similar to the concept of apocalypse, but whereas *apocalypsis* means drawing aside the veil, *epiphany* is unmistakable manifestation. Once again, the idea is that at present the glory of God in the face of Jesus is not visible to us, but one day we shall see Him clearly in all His divine splendour.

Features of the second advent

What, then, are to be the leading features of the Second Advent of Christ?

First, it is going to be *personal*. It will result in the personal presence on earth of the Lord Jesus Christ. It is not going to be simply the presence of His memory or of His power or of His Spirit. It is going to be His real, personal presence in this world. The Bible does not tell us by what kind of process this becomes possible or what kind of journey it involves. All it says is that just as Christ was once really present in this world in His incarnate state, so one day that presence will again be a physical reality.

Secondly, it is going to be a return of Christ *in glory*. The first advent was a real presence, but it was a presence in lowliness and humiliation. He came in obscurity. He came in hiddenness, in anonymity: *incognito*. He came into poverty, homelessness, oppression, lowliness and weakness. He came into pain, shame, dishonour, rejection, death and the cross. He came in *kenosis*, as the great Nobody: the one who looked simply like a servant. He came 'in the likeness of men' (Philippians 2:7).

But when He returns He will return in the glory of the blessed God (Titus 2:13). He will look like what He is. He will look like the world's Saviour. He will look like God. He will come with the *doxa*, with the form, the splendour, the majesty, of God Himself. He will come in all the paraphernalia of deity. He will come in the form that He had for a moment on the Mount of Transfiguration (Matthew 17; Mark 9; Luke 9) . He will come in the kind of glory with which Yahweh came to Mount Sinai in the days of Moses (Exodus 19). He will come in the splendour with which Isaiah saw him in Isaiah 6. He will come with all the accoutrements of deity. He will come 'in the clouds of heaven'; He will come with the holy angels. He will come with His glorified church. He will come with the voice of the trumpet that awakes the dead (Matthew 24:30-31; 1 Thessalonians 4:16). He will come to the accompaniment of events such as never were seen since the first dawn of creation: the resurrection of the dead, the great judgment and the re-formation of heaven and earth.

Thirdly, it is going to be a *single* Second Advent. That may sound a strange thing to say. Who could possibly imagine that there would be two second advents? Yet that idea is widely prevalent among Christians today. It is, for example, a fundamental tenet of Dispensationalism. There is, we are told, a *parousia* of Christ before the Tribulation to take away His saints (in case they suffer). Then after the seven years of the Tribulation, there is a *revelation* of Christ, when He comes back again with His saints to establish His millennial kingdom. This form of teaching is sometimes called a system of double *pre*'s: there is a *pre*-Tribulation advent and there is a *pre*-millenial advent. Christ comes first *for* His saints and then He comes *with* His saints.

This idea seems to have been first proposed in a meeting in Edward Irving's church in London in the early nineteenth century. It was taken up by J. N. Darby, who took it into the infant Brethren movement, thereby causing a split. More importantly, the Scofield Reference Bible took up the idea, and the widespread use of this Bible by American fundamentalists means that most evangelicals in the world today hold this view of separate pre-tribulation and post-tribulation advents of Christ. One result of this is that the horizon of Christian hope is no longer the end of the world but the 'Rapture', when Christ comes for His saints.

One response to this is that it is a very modern idea, dating only from the nineteenth century. Another is that it is obvious from the New Testament that the church goes through the tribulation, whatever that tribulation is: 'These are they who have come out of the great tribulation' (Revelation 7:14) and, 'for the elect's sake God has shortened these days' (Mark 13:20). Yet another is that a careful comparison of New Testament passages shows that it does not distinguish the *parousia* on the one hand from the *apocalypsis* and *epiphaneia* on the other. The three words are applied equally to the same event, the last and consummatory advent of the Lord Jesus Christ.

Time of the second advent
There has been much discussion of the actual time of the Second Advent. When is the Lord going to return? The New Testament has three distinctive strands of teaching on this.

First, *only God knows*. We find this in the famous confession of ignorance on the part of the Jesus Himself: 'No-one knows about that day or hour, not even the angels in heaven, nor the Son, but only the Father' (Matthew 24:36; Mark 13:32). This is something the Mediator does not know; and since the church can know only what He knows, the church can never know this.

Isn't there something hugely instructive in Christ confessing that He doesn't know? Sadly, many Christians have pretended to know. There have been people in all ages who have said that Christ is coming at such and such a time. There are many today who believe that He is coming in our lifetime. Whenever a man says that, he is claiming to know something that even the Mediator did not know. Whoever, therefore, is the source of these guesses, it cannot be Christ.

The second strand is that Christ may come *at any time*. He will come 'like a thief in the night' (1 Thessalonians 5:2). He will come suddenly, without warning, when least expected and when men are least prepared for it. People will be spinning and reaping and sowing; they will be grinding corn and baking bread; they will be asleep in bed, and the Lord will come (Matthew 24:40-41; Luke 17:34-36). We are to remain in a state of constant alertness because at any moment Jesus may be here.

It's said that John Wesley was once asked what he would do if he were told that Jesus was to return this evening. His answer was, 'I should continue to do exactly what I am doing.' He was ready. Are we ready? What changes, what re-adjustments, would we need to make if we knew the Lord would be here tonight?

Thirdly, there is a vein of New Testament teaching which seems at first sight to go against this second point: the Lord will not return until certain great signs have been fulfilled. There are four signs to note.

First, the gospel must first be proclaimed worldwide (Matthew 24:14; Mark 13:10); secondly, there will one day be a Great Tribulation; thirdly, there will come a great falling away, a great apostasy (2 Thessalonians 2:3; 1 Timothy 4:1); and, fourthly, the Man of Sin will be revealed (2 Thessalonians 2:3). How can we say that Christ may come at any moment if we are also saying that He will not come until these signs have been fulfilled?

There are no straightforward answers to that, but it is highly possible that all these signs have already been fulfilled: fulfilled even before the close of the New Testament age itself. Take the fact, for example, of the gospel being preached to the whole world. We are inclined to assume that that means literal penetration of every people-group on earth by the Christian message. Supposing that to be true, there never has been such missionary effort as there has been in the last 150 years, and almost every corner of the globe has been reached with the gospel.

But it is possible that what the New Testament really meant was that Christ would not come until the gospel had been established among 'the Gentiles'. To us, the gospel moving beyond its Jewish confines into the Gentile community seems but a little step. But to early New Testament believers it was almost inconceivable that the kingdom of God would be opened to the whole Gentile community. Indeed, that caused huge problems in the early church. Yet, so very quickly, the gospel went to Samaria, to Europe, to every corner of the Roman Empire and to all the great cities of the world: to Antioch, Philippi, Athens, Corinth and Rome. By the time Paul was martyred, some thirty years after the death of Christ, the gospel was established immovably in the western world. From the standpoint of the Old Testament that was utterly revolutionary. From our standpoint, the first sign of the imminence of the Advent has already been fulfilled: the gospel has gone to all nations.

In the same way, it is doubtful if the Tribulation refers to any one single episode in Christian history. More likely, it embraces the whole period of the church's existence. We live in 'the sufferings of this present time' (Romans 8:18), when 'all who live godly in Christ Jesus will suffer persecution' (2 Timothy 3:12). Yet this persecution did not begin with real intensity immediately after Pentecost. There was a brief breathing-space, during which the church was highly esteemed in Jerusalem (Acts 2:47) and Paul could speak in glowing terms of the imperial power (Romans 13:1-7). But shortly afterwards, the 'crushing' began and there were three terrible centuries for the church. In many ways that has been the pattern ever since. In every age of the church, God's children, somewhere, have been in that same crucible of persecution. Once it was the turn of Scotland. In our own day it has been the turn of Uganda, Eastern Europe, China, Manchuria and Iran.

The same is true of the Great Apostasy. Paul told the Church at Thessalonica that the end would not come until there had been this great 'falling away' (2 Thessalonians 2:3). It is not clear whether this refers to a Jewish or to a Christian apostasy. Certainly there was a Jewish rejection of the Messiah during the lifetime of Peter and Paul. The later New Testament documents also bear out very clearly that by the close of the apostolic age there had been a very significant falling away within the Christian church itself. For example, the original Church in Ephesus was a glorious church. It was to it that Paul sent that incomparable document, the 'Epistle to the Ephesians'. What great Christians they were! What minds they must have had! Had they understood that great teaching, as Paul in the first chapter soars like an eagle, expounding 'every spiritual blessing in the heavenlies in Christ Jesus'? Had their children listened to Ephesians 6 read in the congregation? But it is to this very church that the Lord says so sadly in Revelation 2:4: 'Yet I hold this against you: You have forsaken your first love.' Had the apostasy not already come?

The same is true, too, of the revelation of the Man of Sin. It is quite evident that the Principle of Lawlessness which was in some special way manifested in this Man of Sin was already at work during the New Testament period. In 2 Thessalonians (2:1-12) Paul seems to have in mind some specific personality, but it is a very obscure passage; and one to which, unfortunately, we seem to lack the key. 'Don't you remember,' he says, 'that when I was with you I used to tell you these things?' (verse 5). We don't have that essential background information and that makes it hazardous to be confident who the Man of Sin was. There have been some very eminent theologians who held that it was the Roman emperor (the institution itself or a particular emperor). The Reformers were sure it was the Pope. Others have been equally confident it was Mohammed or one of the great leaders of world Communism.

But according to the clearest indication we have, this sign, too, was already fulfilled before the close of the New Testament. John, the last of the apostles, clearly indicates that in his own day the Antichrist was already active. He even says that 'even now many antichrists have come' (1 John 2:18). More specifically, he identifies the Antichrist with those heretics (the Docetists) who were denying that Christ had come in the flesh. Such a man, he says, is the Antichrist (1 John 2:22).

There is nothing, then, in these signs by themselves to rule out the possibility that Christ may come at any moment. All the signs that have to be fulfilled before He comes can be said to have been fulfilled already.

The conversion of Israel

Except, possibly, one: the promise that one day the Jews will be brought back to Christ. There have been many distinguished Christian scholars, from the earliest ages through the Reformation and down to the present day, who have believed that in Romans 9–11 the Apostle Paul teaches that one day ethnic Israel, the physical seed of Abraham, will be re-grafted into the olive tree (Romans 11:17, 23) and brought to faith in the Messiah.

At the moment, I see no reason to abandon that interpretation. The context clearly indicates that the constituency in question is not the spiritual, but the ethnic, Israel. 'Brothers,' says Paul, 'my heart's desire and prayer to God for the Israelites is that they may be saved' (Romans 10:1) and he says, 'I could wish that I myself were cursed and cut off from Christ for the sake of my brothers, those of my own race' (Romans 9:3). This doesn't mean that every single Jew living at some point in time is going to be saved. It means that just as today Israel is collectively separate from Christ (although there are many Jewish Christians), one day the proportions will be reversed. Israel collectively will be Christian while a minority will remain unbelieving. That seems to be God's promise. He also promises that through this conversion of Israel there will come to the church an experience which Paul describes in Romans 11:15 as 'life from the dead': an in-rush of spiritual power such as the church has never known.

Now I have a problem. If that is the correct interpretation of Romans 9–11, I would have to say that Christ will not return until the Jews are converted. I then have to live with this tension between the New Testament teaching that the Lord may come at any time and the teaching that the end will not occur until the Jews have been brought back to Christ. It is possible, of course, that I am wrong in my interpretation of the passages which seem to say that He may come at any moment. It is even more possible that I am wrong in my view of Romans 9–11. After all, the church has often been wrong in its interpretation of prophecy and I know that I must hold this view of Romans 9–11 with a loose grip. I can't assert it dogmatically, because only the fulfilment can really interpret the prophecy.

So much for the question of the time of the second advent. God alone knows; it may happen at any time; it will not happen until certain signs have been fulfilled; most of these have been fulfilled already. There is one more strand to add: the Lord will come *at the end*. The Second Advent is the terminus, the point at which everything is completed and consummated. That means that the Second Advent is simultaneous with the resurrection of the dead, the final judgment and the regeneration of heaven and earth. It is the day beyond which there is no other day: nothing but glory. It is the absolute End.

The millennium

The question of the millennium fascinates many Christians. At some point in the future will there be a period, whether a literal thousand years or not, of special glory, prosperity, power and blessing for the church on earth? There have been three views on this issue.

First, there is the *pre-millenial* view that Christ will come *before* the millennium to establish a personal reign on earth. There two varieties of this: the Classic Pre-Millenial view and the Dispensational view. Both involve the idea that when Christ comes He will raise the blessed dead and they will reign on earth with Him for a thousand years. The Jewish theocracy will be re-established, the whole world will be governed from Jerusalem and there will be a universal peace.

This interpretation is intensely literalistic. It implies that during this millennium the resurrected dead will live on this earth reigning with Christ and at the same time mingling not only with recently converted Christians, but even with unbelievers. Yet, incongruous though it sounds, this view has been held by some men whose praise is in all the Reformed churches, not least in Scotland. Robert Murray McCheyne, Andrew Bonar, Horatius Bonar and John Milne were all pre-millennialists, holding views on this matter which were very similar to those of the Plymouth Brethren and J. N. Darby. They never accepted the idea of the pre-Tribulation Rapture (that, in fact, was later than McCheyne), but their piety was sharply focused on a pre-millennial advent

Then there is the *post-millennial* view that Christ will not come until the world and the church have experienced a kind of golden age of spiritual prosperity. From this point of view, the advent is post-millennial. There is a real problem here with terminology because the post-millennial millennium is a completely different kind of millennium from the pre-millennial millennium. In the latter, there is an earthly reign involving physical, economic and political prosperity. Post-millennialists, on the other hand, think of the millennium only as a period of unprecedented spiritual revival. This was the view of men like Jonathan Edwards, who longed for the gospel to spread to every continent on earth and wrote to friends urging them join him in a great 'concert of prayer' for worldwide revival.[1] Such a 'Latter-day Glory' would come not as the result of the intrusion of new factors (such as the Advent) into human history, but by God's blessing the means of grace already given. It was closely linked to the idea of the conversion of Israel and the resulting 'life from the dead' which would come to the church.

Thirdly, there is the *a-millennial* view, according to which there is no millennium. Things will simply continue as they are, and as they have always been, until the Lord comes again. This takes a very pessimistic view of Christian and world history. In fact, those who hold it tend to believe that the world will get worse and worse so that when Christ comes He will not 'find faith on the earth' (Luke 18:8). Paradoxically, this view is the one that dominates the Reformed churches in North America today, but it is to a large extent a reaction against the more shallow forms of pre-millennial thinking

I don't think it would be helpful for me to pronounce on these issues. Our Confession of Faith has no position on the millennium and that leaves us total liberty of conscience on this particular issue. I have great sympathy with both the post-millennial position and the a-millennial position. On the other hand, I have great difficulty with the pre-millennial point of view.

There are many reasons for that, but I shall just mention one: it reduces the Second Advent of Christ to just a transitional point on the line of history. Christ comes, and then history goes on for at least a thousand years. In the New Testament, by contrast, the Second Advent is definitive. It is the Day of the Lord; the great *denouement*; the day when the elements will melt with fervent heat and the heavens shall be dissolved (2 Peter 3:10). It is a curious fact that pre-millennial belief, which by its own estimation makes so much of the Second Advent, in actual practice reduces its significance, shrinking it to only a transitional point. At the same time, I wish the Free Church of Scotland had adhered more durably to the piety of men like McCheyne and the Bonars.

The word *millennium* occurs only once in the New Testament (in Revelation 20) and it is a great pity that on that one reference we should build such a beguiling concept. I might best describe my own position by saying that I am an a-millennialist who believes in the conversion of Israel. I believe (tentatively) that one day God will bring His ancient people into the Christian fold. If I am correct in that, I must also believe that that conversion will be like life from the dead to the church, bringing a level of spirituality and effectiveness such as it has never known before.

To that extent, and to that extent alone, I am a millennialist.

Reference
1. See in particular Jonathan Edwards' *Humble Attempt to Promote Explicit Agreement.* The full title was, *An Humble Attempt to Promote Explicit Agreement and Visible Union of God's People in Extraordinary Prayer for the Revival of Religion and the Advancement of Christ's Kingdom on Earth, pursuant to Scripture-Promises and Prophecies concerning the last Time.* It was first published in 1747.

22

The Resurrection

The resurrection is a distinctive Christian doctrine. Most civilizations have held the view that the soul is immortal but the idea that the body will also share in the post-death systems is unique to the Christian faith. That is one of the many reminders to us in the Bible of the importance of the human body. Ancient religions and philosophers despised the body but in the Jehovahism of Christianity it has a very honourable role. It was made directly by God Himself. He formed and fashioned it lovingly away back in Genesis 2. It was also taken by the Son of God into His own Person in the glory of the incarnation when 'the Word became flesh' (John 1:14) and that act brought deity and materiality into the closest imaginable union. The same emphasis is made by the resurrection: it reminds us once again that the body is central to God's purpose of redemption.

These emphases underlie the concern of Christian ethics with the human body; the concern to protect it, to honour it, to consecrate it to God and to His service. 'Present your bodies a living sacrifice, holy, acceptable to God, which is your reasonable service' (Romans 12:1). That means we must take constant regard to our own physicalness in all that we do. We have no right to abuse or pamper or despise our bodies; we must keep our bodies at the maximum peak of efficiency because in and through these bodies we have to serve God. Even those whose work is least obviously physical rely on their physical organ, the brain, to do the work to which God has called them. So this doctrine is simply one of many ways in which God's Word emphasises for us the importance of the body and beyond that, the importance of matter in general.

The doctrine is almost entirely a New Testament doctrine; it appears only minimally in the Old Testament. I make this point not only to acknowledge a fact in theology but also to underline the humanity and progressiveness of the revelation that God has given to us. God has in the Bible taught the church as the church was able to bear: line upon line, belief upon belief, doctrine upon doctrine. Not all the doctrines appear in the Book of Genesis. The whole is not revealed at once. God is a superb educator. He reveals first of all the most basic Christian doctrines: His own existence, His own unity and personality, His holiness and so on, and it is only very infrequently and very faintly that we find this doctrine of the resurrection of the body in the Old Testament. It is there, for example in Daniel 12, but it is not there frequently and not at all in the earlier parts of the Bible.

Augustine laid down a very important principle in this connection when he said that what is patent in the New Testament is latent in the Old Testament. That is true of the resurrection of the body: it is not patent or obvious in the Old Testament but it is a doctrine that lies there hidden. Again, Augustine said that the Old Testament is an unlit room fully furnished. In other words, all the great principles and doctrines are in the Old Testament, in this fully furnished room; but there is no light and so the doctrines were not obvious to Old Testament saints and believers. When gospel light comes it puts nothing there that was not there before, but it shows up what was there but had not been seen before. For example, Job says with confidence that his Redeemer is alive and that one day in his flesh (or, from his flesh) he will see God (Job 19:25-26). We can be fairly confident that no Old Testament saint deduced from that language the resurrection of the body; but we can be equally confident that in the light of the New Testament, in the light of Christ, in the light of the empty tomb we have every right to see the resurrection in those great words of Job. The doctrine was always there but it is only seen with the light of the New Testament.

The nature of the resurrection body

What, we may ask, is the nature of the resurrection body? It is not a speculative or a useless question because the criterion of what is useless and speculative is that there is no teaching on it in scripture; and there is some clear teaching in the Bible with regard to the resurrection body. For example, we read in Philippians 3:21 that the Lord Jesus Christ 'will transform our lowly bodies so that they will be like his glorious body'.

It is not entirely clear what the Lord's glorious body was like. We may think immediately of His post-resurrection appearances: to Mary in the garden on the first Easter morning; to the two on the road to Emmaus; to the disciples and Thomas; but the body with which He was seen on these and other occasions has, in my view, undergone serious transformation or transfiguration. When Mary saw Him she thought He was the gardener (John 20:15): He looked so very ordinary. But not for a moment did Saul of Tarsus on the Damascus road imagine that what he saw was a gardener. All the paraphernalia of divine majesty was there. Again, the One John describes in Revelation 1, who is 'like a son of man', is a splendid and glorious figure.

The position appears to be that the risen Christ and His various appearances assumed different forms. We are told explicitly that He appeared to some of the disciples 'in another form', another *morphe*, looking different (Mark 16:12). Besides that, we know that the Lord underwent not only the experience of the resurrection but also the ascension to 'the right hand of the Majesty on high' (Hebrews 1:3), and His post-ascension appearances are quite different to the pre-ascension appearances. So, when Paul speaks of our one day having a body like the glorious body of Christ he is speaking not of the resurrection but of the ascension body of Jesus: the kind of body that Saul saw on the road to Damascus; the glory that John saw on Patmos; and perhaps most significantly, what Peter and James and John saw on the Mount of Transfiguration. Brilliant, brilliant light. God is light (1 John 1:5). Light is the primal basic form of energy and the resurrection body is described so often in terms of light: bodies so luminous, so splendid, so light-bearing, so majestic that in them the glory of God Himself is seen.

The fact that the Lord's post-resurrection body appeared to be able to move with great rapidity, to appear and disappear at will, is perhaps a further hint of the nature of our resurrection body; but it is probably not possible to understand the resurrection body without understanding the new heavens and the new earth. That body will have different physical properties because the world itself will probably have different properties from those that we know at the present moment. It is possible, in fact, that when God gives us the new universe it will be multi-dimensional and our bodies will behave in it in ways that today we cannot even begin to imagine.

We turn from that to 1 Corinthians 15:35: 'How are the dead raised? With what kind of body will they come?' In answering the question, Paul asks us to consider the relationship between the seed that is sown and the standing corn: the ultimate product is so unlike the original seminal entity and yet, he says, there is the closest possible organic connection. It is the same organism in a different form. It is the developed, germinated seed and Paul is saying that the resurrection body has the same continuity with our current bodies as the standing corn has with the seed. There is organic continuity: it is the same body and yet the two entities are very different. The resurrection body may be as different from the body we bury or cremate as the standing corn is from the seed corn.

There are parallels from other areas of the Christian life. A converted person is the same person before and after conversion and yet he is so different, especially if the conversion to Christ was from being a drunkard, an addict or a derelict. He is the same person; there is continuity and yet he is so different that Paul can say, 'I live; yet not I' (Galatians 2:20).

We think also of God's promises with regard to a new universe. There will be 'a new heaven and a new earth' (Revelation 21:1). The universe is to be transfigured. It puts on another *morphe*, another form. It looks different to us in many different qualities and yet it remains the same.

The Bible further describes the glorious resurrection body as having four distinctive qualities (1 Corinthians 15:42-44).

First, it is *imperishable*. The universe in which our present human bodies live is itself perishable. It is subject to the law of entropy and our bodies, as part of the cosmic energy system, run down: they are liable to disease, to weariness, to the whole process of senescence. The broad principle here is that in the world to come there is no entropy. In all probability the body will continue to develop positively and will maybe do so infinitely; not in its quantity but in its competence. Here, there is often tension between spirit and body; our minds may still be active but we know the frustration of our bodies not being able to produce. The new body will not know corruption; it will, of course, never be independent of God, who is Himself the source of all energy, but in its dependence it will be imperishable.

Secondly, it will be *glorious*. The Hebrew uses the same word for 'glory' and 'weight' and indeed the Apostle makes a play on that fact in 2 Corinthians 4:17 when he speaks of our bearing eventually 'a far more exceeding and eternal weight of glory'. He is saying that our current bodies cannot bear the weight of glory but one day we will have bodies which will be able to sustain that glory. The clue to the meaning here is the reference to the Lord Himself, of whom it is said that we see 'the glory of God in the face of Jesus Christ' (2 Corinthians 4:6). The remarkable thing is that that was not said of the Lord's resurrection body but of His earthly body, and that surely gives us the confidence to say that since we are going to have bodies like the body of the glory of Jesus then they will be bodies in the faces of which the glory of God is going to be seen.

We find another clue in the fact that in scripture the word 'glory' and the word 'image' are closely related. And the glory of these bodies is going to be the image of God. Our faces will image forth God. We were created in the image of God. That image has been marred and disfigured by the Fall but it is restored in Jesus Christ and it is going to be restored not simply in the realm of the spirit but also in the realm of the physical. We will have glorious bodies, bodies reflecting the glory of God whose image we bear and bodies which are appropriate to the mandates given to us as divine image bearers.

Thirdly, it is *powerful*. 'It is sown in weakness'. We have mental images of this. We have seen what we think is the peace of the dead but it is the peace of inertia and immobility. The dead body responds to no stimulus; it is not able to initiate or to effect anything. But God is standing over it and saying, 'I will raise it in such power and such prowess as it has never had before. I will give it the power of the body of the glory of Jesus.' The body is going to have more energy, more physical capability, more stamina, more athleticism, more speed, more co-ordination, more durability than it ever, ever had because we're not going to need the body less, we're going to need it more and use it more. The resurrection is a protest against the hyper-spirituality that says only the spiritual matters: it says emphatically that the physical matters. Heaven is to be a physical universe; the saints are to have physical bodies. They are not going to find themselves in a heaven that is simply a theological college or even a prayer-meeting any more than man in his primitive perfection found himself not in a university but in a garden.

Fourthly, it is a *spiritual* body. In the New Testament the word is always used of the Holy Spirit – the spiritual man is a man led by the Spirit of God. A spiritual mind is a mind dominated by the Spirit of God. If we think of spiritual things we think of the things of the Spirit. Spiritual gifts are gifts of the Holy Spirit and a spiritual body is a Holy Spirit body. Now the body is by definition material. There cannot be such a thing as a non-material body. We must guard all the time against this aversion to the material and to the physical. We must concede at once that the Bible also says, 'flesh and blood cannot inherit the kingdom of God' (1 Corinthians 15:50). That means that we must further concede that this material body is not a flesh and blood body; but to say that it is not flesh and blood is not to say that it is immaterial. This is an imperishable, glorious, powerful, material body which is spiritual; that is, it is a fit organ for the purposes of the Holy Spirit. When the Lord said to his disciples in Gethsemane, 'The spirit is willing, but the body is weak' (Mark 14:38), he was saying that their spirituality was hampered by their physical condition. That will never happen in glory. Here, our bodies become exhausted and our spirits are dragged down. Our physical disorders have a detrimental effect on our emotional, affective and devotional lives. A spiritual body is one that is fully amenable to the Holy Spirit, which offers Him no resistance whatever and is in complete accord with His purposes.

How will the change come about?

The second question we may ask is: How will the change come about? A corpse cannot remotely be said to carry the potential of its own re-emergence from the grave. It has no more capability, no more inherent energy, no more strength or capacity for action than a stone. It will by itself never rise. In this respect the seed corn analogy is just slightly dangerous. The seed contains the germ; the dead body does not contain the germ of life. How then will it rise? It will rise by the power of God. He has said to us, 'I will do it, as surely as I made this world, as I made this body in the first place, I will one day raise the dead.' Each of the three Persons of the Godhead is described in various places as the author of the resurrection. Jesus speaks of the Father raising the dead (John 5:21) and of the Son of Man calling all those in their graves to life again (John 5:28-29). Paul says that 'he who raised Christ from the dead will also give life to your mortal bodies through his Spirit' (Romans 8:11). It takes us back to 'the beginning' when the Trinity said to itself, within itself, 'Let us make man in our image' (Genesis 1:26), and to the resurrection when the Trinity will say, 'Let us raise man.' Father, Son and Spirit will be involved in this tremendous act which is 'matchless, Godlike and divine'. God will put all His power, all His wisdom, all His creativity, all His love into our resurrection bodies: they will do Him honour.

A universal resurrection

The third question is: What is the extent of the resurrection? How many are going to rise from the dead? Is the resurrection universal or not? There is logical space for the idea that only believers rise from the dead but the Bible makes it unmistakably plain that the resurrection is absolutely universal. For example, in Daniel 12:2 we are told that 'multitudes who sleep in the dust of the earth will awake: some to everlasting life, others to shame and everlasting contempt.' This verse does not, on the face of things, teach a universal resurrection because, on the face of things, it says not that everybody is going to awake but that multitudes of those who sleep in the dust are going to awake. But the further point is also made that some rise to everlasting contempt. In other words, the resurrection is not confined to the righteous; the wicked are also going to rise; there is to be a universal resurrection.

The same point is made by the Gospel of John: 'All who are in their graves will hear his voice and come out' (John 5:28-29). Acts 24:15 plainly states 'that there will be a resurrection of both the righteous and the wicked'. Revelation 20:12-15 speaks clearly of those whose names are in the book of life and of those who are not: they are all going to live. The resurrection is universal because the judgment is also universal: 'We shall all stand before the judgment seat of Christ' (Romans 14:10; 2 Corinthians 5:10).

It has been agitated that even granted that the whole human race is going to rise, that nevertheless they will not all rise at the same time. As we saw, it is part of pre-millenial thought that the unbelievers rise only after the millennium, just prior to the great judgment, whereas the righteous rise at the beginning of the millennium to reign with the Lord Jesus Christ. I have a certain hesitancy in raising this issue because the doctrine seems so utterly implausible, but it is a doctrine that is held by many Christians in the world today and that is why it is of some importance. We have seen some of the arguments already.

Another argument centres on 1 Corinthians 15:23: 'Each in

his own turn: Christ, the firstfruits; then, when he comes, those who belong to him'. They say there are three different sequences: first, Christ rises; then, at the millennium, the believing dead rise; then, at the end of the millennium, the unbelieving dead rise – 'each in his own turn'. The one point I shall make in response to that is, that in this passage there are not three orders, there are two: there is Christ, the firstfruits; and when He comes, those who are Christ's. There is no reference whatever to a resurrection of unbelievers.

The argument is made here that, just as there is at least an interval of 2,000 years between Christ rising and believers rising, so there will be a similar time lapse between believers and unbelievers. Why? Because of the word then (*eita*) in verse 23. They say, How long was that 'then'? That 'then', according to them, was at least 2,000 years. All I can say is, when you use the word 'then' does it mean 2,000 years? 'Then' is completely indefinite: it is as long as a piece of string. It has no precise content whatsoever. So there are the two classes in view: there is Christ and then there are Christ's people and there is no reference whatever to the third class and there is no comment offered as to the actual timing of the resurrection.

Another argument is used on the basis of 1 Thessalonians 4:16: 'The Lord himself will come down from heaven ... and the dead in Christ will rise first.' They say the dead in Christ first and the dead not in Christ at some other time. My view and my response is this: The dead who are not in Christ are nowhere on Paul's mind here. He has in mind those Christians who are still alive when Christ comes and those who have died before Christ comes; and what he means is that when Christ comes the first thing He will do is to raise the Christian dead. Then the believers who are alive will be caught up with them to meet the Lord in the air.

John 6:39 is one of the passages in the New Testament which actually gives a deliverance with regard to the extent of the resurrection. Jesus here speaks of those whom the Father has given Him being raised 'at the last day'. What comes after the last day? There is nothing after the last day. There is no other time left when the unbelieving dead can be raised because the last day is the ultimate. It is the terminus. Beyond it there is nothing. God will raise up both the believing and the unbelieving dead at the consummation of history.

Lastly, there is a very direct connection between Christ and the resurrection. He is, in the first place, the *forensic cause* of the resurrection; the meritorious principle. The kind of resurrection that believers will experience, a resurrection in glory, has been secured by and will be determined by what Christ did on the cross of Calvary. The believer's resurrection body will be as glorious as the obedience of God's own Son deserves.

Secondly, He is the *organic principle* of the resurrection. The germ of life is in the risen Saviour. To His body the believer is linked in life, in death, in resurrection. It was impossible that death could hold Jesus because He was God's Son (Acts 2:24); it is equally impossible for death to hold a member of the body of Christ. It will hold him for a moment, but only for a moment in comparison with eternity. We die as we live, in union with Christ and He, the living, risen Saviour, is the life principle of our resurrection bodies. It is more than intellect and logic can handle.

Christ is also the *pattern* of the resurrection body and we have covered that ground already.

Finally, the great words of 1 Corinthians 15:58: 'Therefore, my beloved brethren, be ye steadfast, unmovable, always abounding in the work of the Lord, forasmuch as ye know that your labour is not in vain in the Lord.' We labour, often with blood, sweat and toil and tears, often frustrated with and angry at this recalcitrant organism that will not do what we know has to be done and what we want to be done; but it is not in vain because one day God will give us bodies like the body of the glory of Jesus.

23

Hell

My starting-point in this lecture is a passage in the prophecy of Daniel: 'Multitudes who sleep in the dust of the earth will awake: some to everlasting life, and some to shame and everlasting contempt' (Dan. 12:2).

These words address a question that has troubled the human spirit ever since man fell: What happens when we die? This text reminds us that man survives death and that man rises from the dead. But it also proclaims that different men rise to different destinies. Some rise to everlasting life: others to shame and everlasting contempt. Not all go to heaven. We have to reckon with the solemn possibility of perdition and the solemn reality of hell.

Now I believe with all my heart that God has sent preachers forth primarily as bearers of Good News. We are charged with delivering God's message about His Son. This is why the Bible has much more to say about heaven than about hell. On the whole, indeed, it has little interest in the reprobate and their destiny. That means that if preachers are faithful to the proportions of Scripture they will speak much more often in the joyful accents of the gospel than in the sober accents of the law. They will appear as messengers of hope rather than as heralds of a lost eternity.

But it is also true that if we are faithful to the proportions of God's Word we will give due emphasis to this darker side of God's revelation.

I want to ask, first of all, what we mean by hell and, secondly, why we believe in it.

What do we mean by hell?

The most comprehensive answer is this: hell is the place where men and women experience the unmitigated and unmixed anger of God. It is not, of course, the only place where we experience that anger. God's anger is a reality even on this side of eternity, within history itself. There is anger when God chastens His own children. There is anger when God rebukes His church. There is anger when God gives men over to a reprobate mind (Romans 1:28), abandoning whole civilizations to promiscuity and debauchery. And there is anger when, in the collapse of great empires, God judges imperious, arrogant and rapacious men.

But such anger is always mitigated: mixed with the blessings of God and modified by his forbearance. 'The wrath of God,' wrote Jonathan Edwards, 'is like great waters that are dammed for the present.'[1] In hell, by contrast, the anger is unrelieved and undiluted.

We need to focus on three great facts.

First, God never sends men to hell out of malice. He does it only out of equity. It's not something from which He derives pleasure. He doesn't gloat over human misery or find fulfilment in revenge. He doesn't want anyone to perish. He wants all men to be saved. He looks at the lost and says, How shall I give you over? (Hosea 11:8). The prospect of men going to their doom sets His heart into convulsions and arouses all his compassion.

In fact, the terrible thing about hell is that it puts God in an impossible position: 'Why do you make me do this?' He does it only because it is what sin deserves. And when that dreadful moment comes, God will listen carefully to every plea you can offer in mitigation. He will not condemn unless He absolutely has to. If we can honestly say that we had no chance or that it was done in ignorance or that we were led astray or that we never knew His law and never heard His gospel and that none ever told us of Jesus, then God will listen to us with holy patience. I can give you a categorical assurance that if you have a real case to offer in your own defence you have nothing to fear. No innocent man ever went to Hell; and no man was ever sentenced to Hell if the Judge had another option.

The second fact is this: the experience of Christ. You may imagine that God only *inflicts* hell and knows nothing of its awfulness and horror. But in Jesus Christ, His own Son, God, in the words of the Apostles' Creed, 'descended into hell'. He bore what sin deserved and suffered in His own soul what John Calvin called 'the torments of a condemned and a ruined man'.[2] Calvin was thinking especially of that dreadful moment of dereliction when Christ cried, 'My God, My God, why have You forsaken Me?' That was His Hell: to be forsaken by God. That was His Hell: to cry to God and God not to answer; to look for God and God not to be there. He endured the torment of not knowing that God loved him. He suffered the terrible disorientation that cries, 'Why?' He sank into the abyss of a dreadful self-image. He was 'sin'. He knew that that's what He was and that that was how God was seeing Him and that that was how God would deal with Him. That's where God's own Son was: in the Hell of that unanswerable Why?, standing before God as the sin of the world.

As He looked forward in Gethsemane to that dread-full moment it almost unhinged him. No wonder His anguished cry that it might pass! But I wonder whether any of us faces the possibility of a similar dreadful descent into Hell. And if so, are we stronger and better-resourced than Jesus? Are we better able to bear it? Or ought we, too, to be overwhelmed and amazed and afraid. Ought we, too, to be asking that the cup might pass?

We mustn't trifle. God didn't spare even his own Son. If ever God might have shrunk from the demands of equity, surely it was here. If ever His resolution might have weakened it was here! Christ is the proof that God will not spare. Christ is the demonstration of what Hell involves. And Christ is the paradigm of how you and I ought to feel in the face of such a prospect.

Thirdly, hell is a place of outer darkness. What powerful imagery that is! Hell is *outside-ness*. The picture I have is this: on the one side, there is the *cosmos,* a world of order, beauty and law. On the other, there is *Outside.* Hell is not part of the cosmos. It is not part of the realm of law and beauty. It is absolutely outside.

And it is outside most appropriately, because sin is *anomia*. It is lawlessness: the very negation of law. That's why it must be placed *outside*, where there is no law or order or beauty. Lawlessness is banished to Outer Darkness and Disorder.

Hell is a Black Hole, to which and in which no law applies. No light can escape from it. No light can penetrate it. Sin has caused pain in God, and that is ultimate disorder. Sin is impossible. It is impossible that man should sin. It is impossible that God should feel pain. It is impossible that God's Son should have to become incarnate and die. Yet in the Fall the impossible happened. Sin is the impossible that happened. And when sin happened the even more fundamentally impossible happened: God felt pain. There is no law to any of this. There is no law to sin. There is no law to God's pain. There is no law to hell. Both sin and hell are outside the sphere of the possible. Hell is the cess-pool of lawlessness; because it is lawlessness, it is darkness. There is no light, and hence no possibility of joy or meaning or purity. Above all, there is no love. There cannot be love where there is lawlessness, because love is the fulfilling of the law. Hell is an eternity of hate: of my hating with perfect hatred and of my being hated with perfect hatred. It is the assignation of the human soul to the irredeemably demonic: to the darkness of lovelessness.

I trust I speak God's word and that He will take it and make His own impression with it. We sinners have put God in the impossible position that He has no option but to condemn us. That is a dreadful thing!

Why do I believe in it?

First of all, because the sense of justice is engraved on every human heart. We all believe in justice and equity. That's what makes us moral creatures. When we see sin and wickedness and crime we instinctively condemn it and call for punishment. Nor is this a matter merely of individual reaction. Society itself has erected massive judicial structures. We have legislatures, laws, judicatories, judges and penal establishments, and these all reflect a profound and indelible sense of the ultimate validity of corporate justice. But unless God is just (unless there is ultimate and absolute justice) then our human judicial structures have no validity. No human being has the right to send another to prison in his own name or by his own authority or even by the authority of the state. These things are right only as they are executions of the anger of God. The distribution of judicial institutions throughout human society reflects our ineradicable belief that evil deserves condemnation and punishment. But our limited human systems are totally invalid unless they are reflections of the final justice of God himself. If God has no right to hold his Grand Assize no human judge has a right to hold his. If Hell is immoral, every prison, penitentiary and detention centre in the world is an outrage.

Secondly, I believe in hell because of the witness of Jesus. He is not the only figure in the Bible who speaks of hell. We find the Apostle Paul referring frequently to the anger and judgment of God, we find the Apostle Peter speaking of the possibility of being reserved in chains till the judgment of the Great Day (2 Peter 2:4), and we find the Apostle John in his Revelation speaking most solemnly of the smoke of our torment ascending forever and ever (14:11). But the astonishing thing is that nobody spoke more of Hell than Jesus. In the Parable of the Rich Man and Lazarus, the rich man opens his eyes in Hell (Luke 16:23). In the Parable of the Sheep and the Goats the goats are condemned to the place prepared for the devil and his angels (Matthew 25:41). In the Parable of the Wedding Garment, the man without wedding clothes is thrown 'outside, into the darkness, where there will be weeping and gnashing of teeth' (Matthew 22:13). It is a singularly impressive fact that God's own Son, the 'gentle Jesus meek and mild' should of all others feel this burden and refer to it so frequently.

For me, being a Christian means that my intellect is captive to the mind of Christ. I believe what He believed. There was a time when nineteenth century liberal scholars thought of Jesus of Nazareth as a typical European gentleman, a son of the Enlightenment, with a programme no more disturbing than the bourgeois values of Vienna and Berlin. But then, at the turn of the century, out of these same German universities came the news that in fact Christ was an apocalyptist who believed in resurrection, judgment, Armageddon, heaven and hell.

I cannot be a Christian without believing as he believed. But Jesus is the answer, too, to the common objection that if we really believed in hell and in the possibility of our friends and associates suffering this dreadful experience we wouldn't live as complacently as we do. We all know our guilt in the matter. But Jesus Christ manifestly knew about hell and manifestly believed in it and in His case it prompted Him to the most decisive and most costly action imaginable. He came so that men would not perish. He believed in Hell, and because He believed in it He came to seek and to save those who were lost. Had He believed in universalism or had He believed that Hell was only a figment of preachers' imaginations He would never have come. He came and He acted because he believed it.

Why should we go to Hell?

But surely the most important fact about Hell is that none of us need ever experience it. All the persons of the Trinity are seeking your salvation.

Let me make it as personal as I can. They are seeking *your* salvation. God the Father gave His own Son. God the Son laid down His life. God the Holy Spirit loves us. How then can we go to Hell? Not when there is such love in God! Not when there is such salvation in Christ! Not when all the persons of the Trinity are seeking your salvation! That will be the most terrible thing of all: the moment when God calmly asks, 'Did you hear of My love? Did anyone ever tell you that I sought your salvation? Did anyone ever tell you that My Son and My Spirit also sought your salvation? Did anyone ever tell you that I gave you My Son to be your Saviour? Did anyone ever tell you how it would pain and grieve Me to condemn you. Did no one warn you not to put Me to that grief and pain?'

What will your answer be?

Its place in preaching

I want to raise one final matter: the place of this doctrine in our
overall witness and preaching. There is one simple answer to
that: preach it in biblical proportion and balance. Give it the
prominence it has in the word of God. Preach it with the
frequency with which the Bible itself proclaims it.

But never forget two things. Never forget, first of all, that
Christians are first and foremost bearers of good news. They are
evangelists. 'Go,' said Jesus, 'preach the gospel to every creature'
(Mark 16:15). Tell every man, 'I have good news for you.' His
conscience tells Everyman that he's guilty. His conscience tells
him of the wrath of God, of the imminence of judgment and of
the possibility of perdition. You will reinforce the voice of
conscience, of course. But above all you will tell him, 'Look, I
have good news for you. You don't need to go to hell.'

Rabbi Duncan once said a wonderful thing: 'Sir, you have no
right to go to hell.'[3] He invoked a comparison with a wounded
soldier who, so long as he is wounded, is useless to his general.
Such a soldier might refuse treatment so that he could stay in the
hospital rather than return to the battlefield. But he has no right
to refuse treatment. He is enlisted. 'The gospel is not a mere offer,
it is an imperative offer .... The fellow must get his knee cured,
that he may not have to be discharged, but get well and serve his
Queen. So the gospel does not say, "There is a Saviour, if you
wish to be saved" but "Sir, you have no right to go to hell – you
can't go there without trampling on the Son of God." '

I dare say there may be somebody here who has such a poor
self-image that he says, 'I deserve to go to hell. That's all I
deserve and I'm reconciled to it.' I'm saying to such a man, 'No
human being has a right to go to hell.' He has no right because
God has a right to your love and a right to your faith and a right
to your service and to your obedience. You have no right to opt
for the Black Hole. You have no right to de-commission yourself
or to put yourself out of the action.

Let's remember this, too (and if we remembered it our
churches would be mightily different): remember the priority of

the cross. We preach Christ crucified. 'May I never boast except in the cross of our Lord Jesus Christ,' said St. Paul (Galatians 6:14). We have no right to make psychological calculations and say, 'Ah! Hell! That will terrify them. We'll drive them to God by fear.' Don't let God catch you saying, 'God forbid that I should glory save in the doctrine of Hell.' It is by preaching Christ crucified that we save souls from Hell. Tell them they need to be saved. Tell them about the Hell from which they need to be saved. Tell them Christ experienced Hell for them: that He experienced being with the demons, experienced being outside and experienced the darkness. Show them that Christ was crucified so that they wouldn't go to Hell.

Maybe for the moment the doctrine of Hell is so under threat that it needs to be defended by overstatement. But our churches must never move from Christ-centredness. The Lord knows there is nothing to humble us like the sight of the Crucified One. There are men who can look Hell in the face defiantly, but there are few who can look defiantly at a bleeding Saviour.

Yes, I want us to retain and maintain the doctrine and give it all the emphasis the Bible warrants. But I don't want us to move from the great commission God gave us: 'Preach Jesus Christ and Him crucified.'

References
1. See *The Works of Jonathan Edwards*, London, 1839, vol. II, p. 9.
2. See Calvin's *Institutes*, Book II, Ch. XVI, 10.
3. John Duncan, *In the Pulpit and at the Communion Table* (Edinburgh, 1874), p. 63.

24

Heaven

The Bible speaks often and eloquently of heaven; much more often than it does of hell. The reason is simple. The Bible's main concern is with God's people and their life and destiny. References to the impenitent are little more than incidental.

The teaching on heaven can be organised around three questions: Where is heaven? What goes on there? and, Who are to be there?

Where is heaven?

The Bible points us first of all towards what it calls 'a new heaven and a new earth' (2 Peter 3:13). People sometimes ask, Is heaven to be on this earth? In a manner of speaking, Yes! Not on this earth as we know it today, however, but in a *new* heaven and a *new* earth. One day God will recreate the whole universe. There will be a great moment of regeneration, a moment of new birth for the cosmos itself, when the God who made the world will pull it apart. In its place He will call into being a new universe: one which is a continuation of the old world but yet is radically and splendidly different. Just as the resurrection body is continuous with our current mortal body and the 'new man' is continuous with the old, pre-conversion human being, so there is continuity and yet discontinuity between this present universe and the new world God will one day create.

We don't know in detail what the differences will be. We do know that the world to come will be a world free from the curse (Genesis 3:17) introduced by sin: free from all vanity, all futility, all competition between man and his environment and all competition between man and other creatures.

It's possible, too, that the great forces we are now familiar with will be added to, or made to behave in different ways. The forces of gravity, nuclear power and electromagnetism may be modified. Even the speed of light may be modified. All that is speculative. What the Bible makes absolutely clear is that not only man's soul and body but eventually his whole environment will be transformed and revert to its Edenic condition: even, probably, to a condition more splendid than the original Paradise.

That is the Christian vision: a new soul in a new body in a new universe, each in perfect harmony with the others, and man able at last to live out his full potential to the glory of God.

Secondly, heaven is the place where God's people are. We will be with the Lord *together*, said Saint Paul (1 Thessalonians 4:17). It is not the main thing about heaven. The main thing about heaven is the proximity and fellowship of Christ Himself. Yet it is not an unimportant thing that it is the place where the whole church is gathered: all those who have gone before us; all to whom we were bound in this life by ties of friendship, affection and love and from whom we are now separated by death.

God has promised us to bring us together again. We feel so acutely the frustration of death and bereavement. Sometimes we wrestle with time itself, wishing we could go back into another era where we could find our brother, our father, our mother or our friend. But we know it's not possible. We cannot move out of this present moment back to some past, lost moment in time. We cannot live the same day twice. We cannot traverse the space between ourselves and the dead. We cannot talk with them, or share, however much we might wish to. To know love is to know pain because over all love there stands written, 'Until death do us part.' But God promises reunion. We shall be 'together'. They will not come to us, but we shall go to them (2 Samuel 12:23).

It is, of course, true that in the world to come all such relationships are transformed. But that doesn't mean there is less love. There is more love. 'Shall we know each other in heaven?' we ask. The real theological question is, Shall we be *ourselves* in heaven? Of course we shall! I shall know myself as myself, and others will know me as myself, and this very fact of the survival of our identity means the survival of acquaintance, recognition and love. It remains one of the great if commonplace elements of the Christian hope that death separates believers only temporarily. The Paraphrase (53) is no cliche, but a monumental truth:

A few short years of evil past,
We reach the happy shore,
Where death-divided friends at last
Shall meet, to part no more.

The more the years go by, and the more those we know are taken from us, the more important it becomes that God saves personalities and promises us a church of triumphant immortals, who will know unending fellowship, co-operation and communion.

Thirdly, heaven is where Jesus is. To be absent from the body is to be present with the Lord (2 Corinthians 5:8): to be with Christ, which is far better (Philippians 1:23). The Bible's teaching on this is quite remarkable because it depicts us as sharing so fully and unreservedly in the privileges of God's only Son. Jesus Himself prayed, 'Father, I want those You have given Me to be with Me where I am' (John 17:24). He wants us to be where He is. He wants us in that place where we can see His glory (John 17:24): where we can see the glory of God in His face (2 Corinthians 4:6). He wants us to be so close to Him that we can see the joy, the eminence and the splendour the Father has given to Him. Above all, He wants us to see how much the Father loves Him (John 17:24).

But suppose we ask, Where, more precisely, is He? The answer is given in the great prepositions of John's Gospel: prepositions which carry in them some of our most astonishing pictures of heaven. For example, Christ is *beside* the Father (John 17:5); He is *towards* the Father (John 1:1); and He is *in* the Father (John 17:21).

That's where He is now: back in the glory He had beside God and towards God and in God. He insists (John 17:24) that we are to be there with Him, face to face with God: not merely located near Him, inertly and passively, but relating to Him actively and dynamically. Our love will go out towards Him, and His will return to us. We shall live for Him, and He for us. We shall see the love in His eyes.

But heaven is also *to be in God.* The Father is in the Son and the Son is in the Father (John 17:21). God is in Christ; Christ is in God. The glory Christ has is that He is in God the Father. Language is being stretched to its extremest limits to express relationship and intimacy, to articulate the earnestness and energy of this divine affection. It is impossible to achieve this intimacy in human relationships, but in the Godhead there is this remarkable relationship in which each Person encircles the others. They live in and through each other. This is what the early church Fathers called *enperichoresis*. The Father, the Son and the Spirit live wrapped up in each other, distinct, yet one; penetrating each other in a union of incomprehensible intimacy and yet remaining so distinct as to be *beside* and *towards* each other.

Perhaps we think of it too physically. It may be more akin to the idea expressed in 1 Samuel 18:1: 'the soul of Jonathan was knit with the soul of David.' In some such way our souls shall be bonded with God. We shall never be God, or gods. But we shall be gathered up into the life of the Eternal. The life of God is already in our souls, and our souls in the life of God. But here in this life the participation is partial, limited by the weakness of our own faith. Ultimately, it will be raised to the highest conceivable (and even inconceivable) perfection. Remaining fully ourselves, we shall be *in* God, encircled by His love, secure in His embrace and sharing in the blessedness and peace which lie at His own heart. He will hug us close, enfolding us in the embrace of the Father, the Son and the Holy Spirit.

Of course it stretches our credulity! But it becomes even more incredible when He says, 'I have given them the glory which You gave Me' (John 17:22). We share fully in the relation of the Son with the Father. Equally with Jesus we are sons and daughters of

God. We are not eternal sons; we are not begotten sons; but we are adopted sons and we are joint-heirs with Christ. Every believer has the privileges of a first-born.

Of course, there are levels at which we must insist on the uniqueness and the pre-eminence of the Son, but at this level of biblical teaching all the emphasis falls on the similarity and the identity between my relation to God as a son and Christ's relation to God as a Son. We have the same inheritance. We have the same Father. We shall bear the same image. We shall share His blessedness. We shall even share His throne. More stupendously still, we shall share His nature (2 Peter 1:4), so that in our faces, as in His, angels will see the glory of God.

But heaven is also our home. 'In My Father's house are many rooms' (John 14:2). 'I will dwell in the house of the LORD forever' (Psalm 23:6). 'Then are they glad because they have quiet and He brings them to their desired haven' (Psalm 107:30). For the believer, death is a home-going. Surely this biblical perspective challenges our reluctance to die! Surely, too, it challenges the way we cling to this earthly existence! For the believer, this world is a foreign country. We have here no continuing city (Hebrews 13:14). We are strangers and pilgrims (1 Peter 2:11). We are stateless aliens: colonists far from home (Philippians 3:20). We are beset by sin and harassed by the devil and agitated by restlessness and imperfection.

Why should we want to remain here forever? Home is where our Father is and where our Elder Brother is and where, in increasing numbers, our friends and loved ones are. In New Testament perspective, the believer is not simply 'not frightened' of going home or simply 'willing to go'. He *desires* to 'depart and be with Christ, which is better by far' (Philippians 1:23). It wasn't that the Apostle was weary of life. He had learned the secret of being content in any and every situation (Philippians 4:12). But he wasn't neutral as between living and dying, staying and going. For the good of the church, he was willing to stay (Philippians 1:24), but his desire was to depart and to be with Christ.

I sometimes think that God has very strange children: they never want to come home! Is it God-honouring that we should want to stay in this foreign country? Why, when the alternative is to see Jesus? Is the fact that 'the time is short' (1 Corinthians 7:29) not at last a consolation rather than a threat?

> *Here in the body pent*
> *Absent from home I roam*
> *Yet nightly pitch my moving tent*
> *A day's march nearer home.*

It is just here that we see the contrast between the natural man's view of death and the Christian's:

> *Sunset and evening star*
> *And one clear call for me!*
> *And let there be no moaning of the bar*
> *When I put out to sea.*
>
> Tennyson, *Crossing the Bar*

To the non-believer, death means launching out into the deep, into the Great Unknown, a terrifying, uncharted ocean of darkness and uncertainty. To faith, the prospect is entirely different. The chariot is coming 'for to carry me home'. This was exactly how the psalmist saw it:

> *Then are they glad because at rest*
> *and quiet now they be;*
> *So to the haven he them brings,*
> *which they desir'd to see.*

Matthew Henry put it memorably: 'He whose head is in heaven need not fear to put his feet into the grave.'

What goes on there?
Again, there are three answers to that.

First, what the Father does: 'God will wipe away every tear

from their eyes' (Revelation 7:17). The figure is a maternal one: the mother wiping away the tears, every last one, with meticulous tenderness. Why the tears? Because the children have been in the Great Tribulation (Revelation 7:14) and it's almost as if when they get to heaven the tears are still there and God the Father is saying with such tenderness, 'It's all right, it's all over now!' Not only are the pain and sorrow over. God Himself comes so close. We feel his touch upon our souls.

This highlights once again the uniquely Christian concept of God as Servant. It is as if God exists for the children. It's also so maternal: a mother investing so much of herself in her child, prepared even to lay down her life for him. Here is God Himself serving. On earth, Christ washed His disciples' feet. In heaven, God wipes away the tears and tends the bruises. I'm not sure that the memory of all those tears is necessarily eradicated. The Bible speaks of God putting our tears in a bottle (Psalm 56:8). He knows every one of them and for each He has His own comfort and His own recompense.

Secondly, there is what Jesus does. 'The Lamb at the centre of the throne will be their shepherd; He will lead them to springs of living water' (Revelation 7:17). Christ, too, is active in heaven. Here He is, entitled to His own Sabbath, His work done, and yet what is He doing? It's so beautiful! The Authorised Version says that He will *feed* them. The New International Version captures it more precisely: the Lamb will *shepherd* them. Technically, He will be their pastor. The flock is to be shepherded by a Lamb! He knows what being a sheep is like. He has taken our nature. He has been in our situation. He has been in the crushing. He has been in the valley of the shadow of death. He has been at the very storm-centre of death itself. He remembers.

This image reminds us, too, that even in heaven we are not going to be self-sufficient and autonomous. We are still going to need pastoring. We're still going to have needs. Unfallen Adam had needs, and God met those needs. Glorified, heavenly man will have needs and Christ will meet these needs. We will never lack: not because we shall never want or desire, but because every need is instantly met by the Great Shepherd. Heaven doesn't mean being independent, physically, intellectually or spiritually. It means that we shall have all our needs met in Christ. He will lead us to 'springs of living water'. He will lead us to the fountains of the water of life. And where are these fountains? In the midst of the throne! (Revelation 22:1). In this present world God feeds us from the *river* of life. In heaven, we are fed at the source. The Shepherd takes His flock on this marvellous journey into the very heart of Godhead: into the core of His sovereignty and love.

Of course, John's 'midst of the throne' is pure poetry. But what poetry: the flock grazing eternally, under the loving eye of the Shepherd, at the heart of the grace and glory of God! It is no easy thing to put flesh on this. We certainly have no guarantee that we are nearer the truth when we reduce it to theological propositions. Heaven means standing close to the majesty of God. But that is always the majesty of love, which means that the believer's privilege is to stand eternally where it all began. No doubt he will gaze and gaze upon it, but he is not taken to the fountain merely to look. He is taken to drink. We will quite literally *enjoy* God. In a sense we already enjoy his love, even in this present life. But here it comes through the filter of providence, mixed with adversity and sorrow and distorted by the currents of demonic and human hatreds. There, it comes unmixed and undiluted, directly from its source in the very heart of God Himself.

The journey is an endless one. Death is not the end of our pilgrimage. It's only the end of the beginning. Through endless ages the Lamb will be showing us new things about the glory of God. We shall never exhaust the fountain. The feast will never be over. We shall never, never stop travelling. We shall never stop getting to know God: not, any longer, in a book, but beside Him, face to face with Him, in Him, at the very source of Life.

There will be a future in heaven: an infinitely extended prospect as, day by day, the Lamb leads us to new pastures. God is a God of infinite dimensions. His riches are unsearchable

(Ephesians 3:8). His love passes knowledge (Ephesians 3:19). His peace is beyond our understanding (Philippians 4:7). He will always remain a mystery, never bounded, never defined and never controlled. Never shall we reach the point where we say, 'At last! That's it! I know it all! I know Him through and through. I know all the wonders of His grace.' On the contrary,

When we've been there ten thousand years,
Bright shining as the sun,
We've no less days to sing God's praise
Than when we'd first begun.

What do we do there?

First, *work*. The re-creation of the universe will involve a re-publication of the creation mandates to subdue and replenish the earth (Genesis 1:28). The First Adam reneged on these mandates, but the Last Adam resumes and fulfils them (Hebrews 2:8). The final state of the believer is not going to be a purely spiritual one. Nor will heaven reflect the kind of Puritanism which sacrifices every other human instinct and interest to the religious. We shall have resurrection bodies and these will be, by definition, physical. We shall live in a physical environment and we shall engage in physical, as well as spiritual and intellectual activity. If the Garden of Eden required to be kept and tilled there is no reason to think that the new creation will be any different. Paradise was no mere seminary where Adam and Eve whiled way the hours in theological discussion. I'm sure they did that, and that they did it with more relish than any of my students. But Eden offered scope for art, science and technology as well as theology. The same will doubtless be true of the world to come. Bearing the image of the heavenly, we shall explore, colonise, serve, keep and enhance our magnificent environment. Not only the Creator, but the Creation, too, will be an object of wonder. It will challenge our intellects, fire our imaginations and stimulate our industry. The scenario is a thrilling one: brilliant minds in powerful bodies in a transformed universe. With energy, dexterity and athleticism here undreamed of, we shall explore horizons beyond our wildest imaginings.

We will also *worship* there. We will serve Him day and night in His temple (Revelation 7:15). The New Jerusalem as the Apostle John saw it was a perfect cube (Revelation 21:16), reminiscent of the Holy of Holies in Solomon's Temple (1 Kings 6:20). But John saw no temple in the City. It was *all* temple (Revelation 21:22). The presence of God, the Shekinah, was absolutely everywhere. The insignia of his majesty and the reminders of his love were everywhere. Here, in this life, the knowledge of the One we have never seen moves us to 'joy unspeakable and full of glory'. There, we shall see him as he is. We shall see him face to face. Our worship will be a response to that: not something exacted or extorted, but 'the spontaneous overflow of powerful feelings'. The vision before us (the majesty of God unveiled in the transfigured humanity of Christ) will forbid silence. It will invoke, irresistibly, wonder, love and praise; and these will find expression not only in the voices of individuals, but in the symphony of all the redeemed. They will come from north and south and east and west. They will include black and white, rich and poor, learned and unlearned, the weak and the powerful, introverts and extroverts. Each will sing her own song. But it will be no cacophony. It will be a great harmony, a symphony of grace, awe-inspiring in volume and yet euphonious and melodious as the harp (Revelation 14:1-3): the response of humanity to the wonderful works of God.

And heaven is *rest*. Maybe *rest* above all. Here, in this life, responsibilities, pain and temptation. Here, harassment by the demonic, persecution by the world and disappointment in friends. Here, relentless, remorseless pressure, requiring us to live at the limit of our resources and at the very edge of endurance. But there, rest: 'the battle's o'er, the victory won'. The toil is behind us and the danger past. No more the burden of unfinished work or the frustration of in-built limitations. No sin to mortify. No flesh to crucify. No pain to face. No malice to fear.

But it's not all negative. It's not simply rest *from*. It means sharing in God's Sabbath. And what is that? It is God's delight (Isaiah 58:13) in His own creation; and God's delight in the magnificence of His Son and in the glory of His work. We shall share that, looking at our Saviour and saying, 'Less would not satisfy and more could not be desired.'

Heaven means sharing in the blessedness of God so that in the very depths of our being there is divine contentment, joy and fulfilment. There is total *shalom*: a sense of sheer well-being. Every need is met. Every longing is fulfilled. Every goal is achieved. Every sense is satisfied. We see him. We are with him. He holds us and hugs us and whispers, 'This is for ever.'

Who will be there?
Who are going to be there? They are pictured for us in Revelation 7:9-17. Three things stand out.

First, they have been in the Great Tribulation. They have been crushed. It seems unavoidable. They have been martyrs for Christ. They've been persecuted by the secular and religious powers. They've been pursued by Satan and plotted against by the Parliament of Hell. They've been in the depths. They've sat under juniper trees and prayed to die. They've been depressed beyond measure and sometimes despaired of their very lives. Time and again they wrote themselves off as worthless. But now, there they are, standing before the Throne.

Secondly, they've washed their robes and made them white in the blood of the Lamb. How splendid it is! They've been in the crucible of pain and in the laver of affliction, but they didn't wash their robes there. They washed them in the blood of the Lamb. They hungered and thirsted after righteousness and they found it in Christ. Now they see God (Matthew 5:8). Human, and erstwhile sinners, yet they threaten heaven with no defilement. They are as righteous as Christ and as spotless as the Lamb. They are pure as God is pure.

And they are, finally, a multitude too great to number. Burns caricatured grace, 'sending ane to heaven and ten to hell, a' for thy glory'. On the contrary, where sin was abundant grace was even more abundant (Romans 5:20). How many stars are there in the sky? How many grains of sand are there on the shore? Not half as many as the number saved by grace. And the whole of mankind is represented: every language, every nation, every culture, every type of personality and every level of wealth and ability.

The gospel excludes none. Let none exclude herself. Heaven, in traditional Scottish terminology, is for 'sinners of mankind lost'. It's for the vilest sinner and for the chief of sinners. It's for the man or woman with the lowest self-esteem in the world. It's for the greatest hypocrite and the worst Christ-hater who ever lived.

There is work to do. Go! Gather God's elect. We're not looking for one in a million or even one in a thousand. We're looking for a multitude too great to number.

SCRIPTURE INDEX

PERSONS' INDEX

SUBJECT INDEX

Christian Focus Publications publishes biblically-accurate books for adults and children. The books in the adult range are published in three imprints.

Christian Heritage contains classic writings from the past.

Christian Focus contains popular works including biographies, commentaries, doctrine, and Christian living.

Mentor focuses on books written at a level suitable for Bible College and seminary students, pastors, and others; the imprint includes commentaries, doctrinal studies, examination of current issues, and church history.

For a free catalogue of all our titles, please write to
Christian Focus Publications,
Geanies House, Fearn,
Ross-shire, IV20 1TW, Great Britain

For details of our titles visit us on our web site
http://www.christianfocus.com

Books by Donald Bridge

JESUS - THE MAN AND HIS MESSAGE

What impact did Jesus make on the circumstances and culture of his time? What is it about him that identifies him both as a unique Saviour and the greatest example of gospel communication?

Donald Bridge challenges the way we view Jesus, and our portrayal of him to the world around us. He argues that walking with Jesus today means reading his words, welcoming the impact of his personality, embracing the provision he makes for us, and sharing his good news with others.

Donald Bridge combines a lifetime of study of the Gospels with an intimate knowledge of the land where Jesus lived and taught. He has been both an evangelist and a pastor, as well as working for several years in the Garden Tomb, Jerusalem.

176 PAGES   B FORMAT
ISBN 1 85792 117 8

SPIRITUAL GIFTS AND THE CHURCH
Donald Bridge and David Phypers

First published in the 1970s, when the Charismatic Movement became prominent in British church life, this classic study of gifts, the individual and the church has been revised and expanded in light of developments since then. The authors, Donald Bridge and David Phypers, give a balanced view of a difficult and controversial issue.

The baptism of the Spirit, with its associated gifts, is a subject which has perplexed and fascinated Christians. It is unfortunately one which also divides Christians who disagree over the extent to which gifts should appear in the Church.

Donald Bridge is an evangelist and church consultant and David Phypers is a Church of England pastor.

192 PAGES   B FORMAT
ISBN 1 85792 141 0

Reformed Theological Writings
R. A. Finlayson

This volume contains a selection of doctrinal studies, divided into three sections:

General theology
The God of Israel; God In Three Persons; God the Father; The Person of Christ; The Love of the Spirit in Man's Redemption; The Holy Spirit in the Life of Christ; The Messianic Psalms; The Terminology of the Atonement; The Ascension; The Holy Spirit in the Life of the Christian; The Assurance of Faith; The Holy Spirit in the Life of the Church; The Church – The Body of Christ; The Authority of the Church; The Church in Augustine; Disruption Principles; The Reformed Doctrine of the Sacraments; The Theology of the Lord's Day, The Christian Sabbath; The Last Things.

Issues Facing Evangelicals
Christianity and Humanism; How Liberal Theology Infected Scotland; Neo-Orthodoxy; Neo-Liberalism and Neo-Fundamentalism; The Ecumenical Movement; Modern Theology and the Christian Message.

The Westminster Confession of Faith
The Significance of the Westminster Confession; The Doctrine of Scripture in the Westminster Confession of Faith; The Doctrine of God in the Westminster Confession of Faith; Particular Redemption in the Westminster Confession of Faith; Efficacious Grace in the Westminster Confession of Faith; Predestination in the Westminster Confession of Faith; The Doctrine of Man in the Westminster Confession of Faith.

R. A. Finlayson was for many years the leading theologian of the Free Church of Scotland and one of the most effective preachers and speakers of his time; those who were students in the 1950s deeply appreciated his visits to Christian Unions and IVF conferences. This volume contains posthumously edited theological lectures which illustrate his brilliant gift for simple, logical and yet warm-hearted presentation of Christian doctrine (I Howard Marshall).

272 pages   ISBN 1 85792 259 X   large format

MENTOR TITLES

Creation and Change by Douglas Kelly (large format, 272 pages)
A scholarly defence of the literal seven-day account of the creation of all things as detailed in Genesis 1. The author is Professor of Systematic Theology in Reformed Theological Seminary in Charlotte, North Carolina, USA.

The Healing Promise by Richard Mayhue (large format, 288 pages)
A clear biblical examination of the claims of Health and Wealth preachers. The author is Dean of The Master's Seminary, Los Angeles, California.

Puritan Profiles by William Barker (hardback, 320 pages)
The author is Professor of Church History at Westminster Theological Seminary, Philadelphia, USA. In this book he gives biographical profiles of 54 leading Puritans, most of whom were involved in the framing of the Westminster Confession of Faith.

Creeds, Councils and Christ by Gerald Bray (large format, 224 pages)
The author, who teaches at Samford University, Birmingham, Alabama, explains the historical circumstances and doctrinal differences that caused the early church to frame its creeds. He argues that a proper appreciation of the creeds will help the confused church of today.

MENTOR COMMENTARIES

1 and 2 Chronicles by Richard Pratt (hardback, 512 pages)
The author is professor of Old Testament at Reformed Theological Seminary, Orlando, USA. In this commentary he gives attention to the structure of Chronicles as well as the Chronicler's reasons for his different emphases from that of 1 and 2 Kings.

Psalms by Alan Harman (hardback, 456 pages)
The author, now retired from his position as a professor of Old Testament, lives in Australia. His commentary includes a comprehensive introduction to the psalms as well as a commentary on each psalm.

Amos by Gray Smith (hardback, 400 pages)
Gary Smith, a professor of Old Testament in Bethel Seminary, Minneapolis, USA, exegetes the text of Amos by considering issues of textual criticism, structure, historical and literary background, and the theological significance of the book.

Focus on the Bible Commentaries

Exodus – John L. Mackay*
Deuteronomy – Alan Harman
Judges and Ruth – Stephen Dray
1 and 2 Samuel – David Searle*
1 and 2 Kings – Robert Fyall*
Proverbs – Eric Lane (late 1998)
Daniel – Robert Fyall (1998)
Hosea – Michael Eaton
Amos – O Palmer Robertson*
Jonah-Zephaniah – John L. Mackay
Haggai-Malachi – John L. Mackay
Matthew – Charles Price (1998)
Mark – Geoffrey Grogan
John – Steve Motyer (1999)
Romans – R. C. Sproul
2 Corinthians – Geoffrey Grogan
Galatians – Joseph Pipa*
Ephesians – R. C. Sproul
Philippians – Hywel Jones
1 and 2 Thessalonians – Richard Mayhue (1999)
The Pastoral Epistles – Douglas Milne
Hebrews – Walter Riggans (1998)
James – Derek Prime
1 Peter – Derek Cleave
2 Peter – Paul Gardner (1998)
Jude – Paul Gardner

Journey Through the Old Testament – Bill Cotton
How To Interpret the Bible – Richard Mayhue

Those marked with an * are currently being written.

Also published by Christian Focus and WEC

You Can Learn to Lead
Stewart Dinnen

ISBN 1 85792 2824   *B format 176 pages*

A practical manual for missionaries, church leaders, or anyone in a position of leadership. The author was International Secretary of WEC and therefore had plenty of hands-on experience.

Patrick Johnstone says of this book: 'It was my privilege to serve under Stewart's incisive and courageous leadership. I commend this book as a means for equipping others with like vision.'

And Brother Andrew comments: 'Stewart, your book is a gem! Diamonds! I wish I had written it.'

Rescue Shop Within a Yard of Hell
Stewart Dinnen

ISBN 1 85792 1224   *pocket paperback 272 pages*

The remarkable story of evangelism by Betel among the drug addicts and AIDs sufferers in Spain. In addition to the strategies of the workers being explained, there are testimonies from converted addicts, some of whom became leaders in the church.

Faith on Fire
Norman Grubb and the building of WEC
Stewart Dinnen

ISBN 185792 3219   *large format 240 pages*

Norman Grubb 'inherited' the leadership of WEC from his father-in-law, C. T. Studd. Leslie Brierley said of Grubb, 'To experience his dynamic leadership ... was my unforgettable experience.'

Territorial Spirits and World Evangelization
Chuck Lowe

ISBN 1 85792 399 5   *192 pages*   *large format*

Over the last decade, a new theory of spiritual warfare, associated primarily with the teaching of Peter Wagner, has become popular around the world. This teaching concerns the role of 'territorial spirits', who are said to rule over specific geographical areas. Along with this theory has come a new practice of spiritual warfare: ruling spirits are named, their territories identified, and they are then bound or cursed. evangelism and mission are then said to proceed rapidly with dramatic results. Chuck Lowe, who teaches at Singapore Bible College, examines the full range of biblical, intertestamental and historical evidence cited in support of this new teaching. He affirms the need to be involved in spiritual warfare, but proposes a more biblical model.

'This is a methodologically-clear, admirably lucid, and mission-hearted challenge; a challenge not merely to our theories about Strategic-Level Spiritual Warfare, but to our evangelical technocratic quest for successful 'method'. Lowe argues that the floodtide of confidence in this 'method' has swept away exegetical, historical and empirical caution, and that it has unwittingly produced a synthesis uncomfortably closer to *The Testament of Solomon* and to animism than to any *biblical* understanding of demonology and spiritual warfare. In place of this questionable construction, with its quick-and-easy answers, Lowe points to the grittier, more robust example provided by James O Fraser, a CIM missionary to the Lisu in China. A great read!'

Max Turner
Vice Principal and Senior Lecturer in New Testament,
London Bible College

'So easily do many accept the new and the novel! To all who care deeply about world mission, Chuck Lowe's evaluation of strategic-level spiritual warfare is a needed clarion call; a call to reject what is built on a foundation of anecdote, speculation and animism, and to walk in the established paths of biblical truth and practice.

'Lowe has set himself up as a target for those who follow the SLSW theology. It will be interesting to see how they respond to this book.'

George Martin
Southern Baptist Theological Seminary
Louisville, Kentucky

'I am pleased to commend this careful examination of a controversial subject. The new interest in demons and the demonic, lately fanned by Peretti's novels, obliges Christians to reflect carefully on the biblical basis of all contemporary thought and practice. Not every reader will agree with the conclusions, which are sharply critical of Peter Wagner and others. But you do not have to go along with their theology to take seriously the devil and his minions.'

Nigel M. de S. Cameron
Distinguished Professor of Theology and Culture,
Trinity Evangelical Divinity School, Deerfield, Illinois

'The evangelical community at large owes Chuck Lowe a huge debt of gratitude. With his incisive, biblical analysis of strategic-level spiritual warfare, he shows clarity and sanity. He thoughtfully analyses the biblical, historical and theological tenets of our times with regard to spiritual warfare, showing them to be the re-emergence of the inter-testamental period and the medieval age. He makes a complex subject readable and concise, while remaining charitably irenic toward other Christians with whom he takes issue.

'The greatest strength of this book is the author's dogged insistence that, whatever one's approach to SLSW, one must not build doctrine on vague texts, assumptions, analogies or inferences, but on clear, solid, biblical evidence alone. I fully endorse the contents of this exceptional work.'

Richard Mayhue
Senior Vice President and Dean,
The Master's Seminary, Sun Valley, California

'The Bible makes it very clear that the forces of evil are strong, and that the followers of Jesus are engaged in an unrelenting battle against them. But little attention is given to this struggle in a good deal of modern writing, so Dr. Lowe's study of spiritual warfare is important. He is concerned with modern approaches that do not do justice to what the Bible teaches about the forces of evil. Specifically he deals with those who advocate strategic-level spiritual warfare. His book clarifies many issues, and encourages readers in their task of opposing evil.'

Leon Morris
Ridley College,
Australia

THE CHRIST OF THE BIBLE
AND THE CHURCH's FAITH

Geoffrey Grogan

This book is a theological study
In the main, the odd-numbered chapters are theological. The first
five of these set out the biblical evidence for our understanding of
Jesus, while chapters 11 and 13 reflect on this theologically at a
somewhat deeper level.

It is an apologetic study
This is the function of the even-numbered chapters. They deal with
the main difficulties that have been and still are raised by those
who are interested in Jesus but are not yet committed to him. It is
to be hoped that they will also be of help to the committed. Each
of these chapters follows the theological chapter most closely related to it.

The book will be useful to ministers and theological students. It
has however been written in such a way that many Christians without theological training may be able to benefit from it, plus other
readers who have not yet come to personal faith in Christ but are
interested enough to read a serious book about him.

304 pages   ISBN 1 857 92 266 2   demy

In this wide-ranging and well-written study, Geoffrey Grogan
provides a clear, scholarly and reliable account of the identity of
Jesus of Nazareth. The fruit of prolonged thought about the New
Testament's teaching, *The Christ of the Bible and of the Church's
Faith* is marked on every page by clarity of exposition and reliability
of judgment. Here we have a careful and thoughtful sifting of
evidence and a steady pursuit of conclusions which are in harmony
with it.

While familiar with trends in New Testament studies during
the past two centuries, and grateful for the work of fellow schol-

ars, Geoffrey Grogan has listened first and foremost to the witness of the apostles. He concludes that there is only one answer to the ancient question which Jesus himself asked them, 'Who do you say that I am?'

The result is this sturdy volume. Theological students, Christian ministers and leaders will find it invaluable, but any serious reader to whom Jesus of Nazareth remains an elusive figure will also come to the conclusion that this is a book well worth reading.

Sinclair 'B. Ferguson
Westminster Theological Seminary
Philadelphia, Pennsylvania, USA

This is an apologetic and theological study aimed at preachers, theological students, thinking Christians and interested agnostics. It succeeds in its aims admirably.

Donald Macleod
Free Church College
Edinburgh, Scotland

This beautifully-written book is a feast of scriptural analysis and argument about our Lord Jesus Christ. With profound learning but with lightness of touch, Geoffrey Grogan discusses all the main lines of the presentation of Jesus in the Bible, and then skilfully relates these to the questions that trouble people today about him. So the book is an attractive combination of Christology and apology – explaining Jesus in a way that answers modern doubts and puzzles, cleverly arranged in alternating chapters. Hearts will be warmed and heads cleared by this book – and doubt and unbelief will be turned into confidence and faith.

Steve Motyer
London Bible College

Other Christian Focus titles
by
Donald Macleod

Behold Your God

A major work on the doctrine of God, covering his power, anger, righteousness, name and being. This book will educate and stimulate deeper thinking and worship.

ISBN 1 876 676 509 *paperback* 256 pages

Rome and Canterbury

This book assesses the attempts for unity between the Anglican and Roman Catholic churches, examining the argument of history, the place of Scripture, and the obstacle of the ordination of women.

ISBN 0 906 731 887 *paperback* *64 pages*

The Spirit of Promise

This book gives advice on discovering our spiritual role in the local church, the Spirit's work in guidance, and discusses various interpretations of the baptism of the Spirit.

ISBN 0 906 731 448 *paperback* *112 pages*

Shared Life

The author examines what the Bible teaches concerning the Trinity, then explores various historical and theological interpretations regarding the Trinity, before indicating where some of the modern cults err in their views of the Trinity.

ISBN 1-85792-128-3 *paperback* *128 pages*